Skepticism, Individuality, and Freedom

Skepticism, Individuality, and Freedom

The Reluctant Liberalism of Richard Flathman

Bonnie Honig and David R. Mapel, Editors

University of Minnesota Press
Minneapolis
London

Copyright 2002 by the Regents of the University of Minnesota

All rights reserved. No part of this publication may be reproduced, stored in a retrieval system, or transmitted, in any form or by any means, electronic, mechanical, photocopying, recording, or otherwise, without the prior written permission of the publisher.

Published by the University of Minnesota Press
111 Third Avenue South, Suite 290
Minneapolis, MN 55401-2520
http://www.upress.umn.edu

Library of Congress Cataloging-in-Publication Data

Skepticism, individuality, and freedom : the reluctant liberalism of Richard Flathman / Bonnie Honig and David R. Mapel, editors.
    p.   cm.
   Includes bibliographical references and index.
   ISBN 978-0-8166-3969-4 (HC : alk. paper) — ISBN 978-0-8166-3970-0 (PB : alk. paper)
   1. Flathman, Richard E.—Contributions in political science.
   2. Flathman, Richard E.—Contributions in liberalism.   I. Honig, Bonnie.
II. Mapel, David, 1952–
JC251.F53 S54 2002
320.51'092—dc21   2002002829

The University of Minnesota is an equal-opportunity educator and employer.

Contents

Acknowledgments   vii

Introduction   ix
Bonnie Honig and David R. Mapel

ONE
The Voice of Richard Flathman in the Conversation of Liberalism   1
Patrick Neal

TWO
The Skepticism of Willful Liberalism   33
Linda Zerilli

THREE
Breaking into the Prison of Practice:
Flathman and Oakeshott on Theorizing and Doing   56
Peter Digeser

FOUR
Individuality and Egotism   86
George Kateb

FIVE
The Fetish of Individuality:
Richard Flathman's Willfully Liberal Politics   111
Ronald Beiner

SIX
Freedom, Flathman, and Feminism   127
Nancy J. Hirschmann

SEVEN
Liberty Conceived as the Opposite of Slavery   155
Richard Friedman

EIGHT
Hobbes and the Principle of Publicity   180
Jeremy J. Waldron

NINE
Flathman's Hobbes   212
Richard Tuck

TEN
Liberalism's Leap of Faith   231
Anne Norton

ELEVEN
Mouths, Bodies, and the State   244
Jane Bennett and William E. Connolly

Annotated Bibliography of Works by Richard Flathman   265

Contributors   271

Index   275

Acknowledgments

The project of assembling a volume of essays occasioned by the work of Richard Flathman has been rewarding and pleasurable. We would like first and foremost to thank the contributors to this volume, who wrote thought-provoking essays and delivered them to us almost on time. Second, we would like to thank Carrie Mullen of the University of Minnesota Press, who took an early interest in this project and supported it throughout. We are grateful to Renee Brown, for preparing the manuscript, turning an unruly collection of essays composed in numerous and sometimes incompatible word-processing packages into a uniform, rule-following, and legible manuscript. Torrey Shanks prepared the annotated bibliography of Flathman's work that appears at the end of the volume. Ella Myers did a heroic job proofreading the manuscript and also provided valuable research assistance in the final stages of production. Our final thanks go to Richard Flathman, whose own individual style in political theory has earned him a loyal following among those—liberals, democrats, feminists, poststructuralists—who admire individuality and seek to promote it.

Introduction
Bonnie Honig and David R. Mapel

Liberalism may have been born partly of a fear of zealotry, but this has not stopped many of today's liberals from embracing liberal principles with a passion approaching that which Thomas Hobbes thought dangerous to civil peace. Contemporary liberal theorists are often happy to argue among themselves about such issues as whether and under what circumstances groups are good or bad for liberal politics. But those same liberal theorists avoid challenges from outside their camp to think about the ways in which they have become implicated in a politics of governance that has drifted substantially from liberalism's central commitments to individuality and freedom. Richard Flathman has for years been resisting liberalism's drift into an ideology of governance, all the while also contesting liberalism's corresponding tendency to justify itself on moral and rational grounds rather than on the basis of what Flathman would prefer to see as its extra-moral, independent commitments to individuality and freedom. As one of liberal theory's few minority voices, Flathman has pressed his case in a series of books and articles that spans forty years.

Flathman's distinct voice has become more audible and more noticed in recent years. Why? In the past ten years, liberal theorists have adopted a big-tent philosophy, now including many of those in contrast to whom they used to define themselves. Suddenly, such former adversaries of Anglo-American liberal theory as Charles Taylor and Jürgen Habermas have been invited in and are seen as parties to internecine disagreements about the future of liberal democracy. These new inclusions mark the collapse of liberal theory's cold wars of the '70s and '80s: The liberal-communitarian debate is transmuted into a domestic squabble about what role cultural and ethnic groups should play in politics. The Anglo-American versus Continental divide is now bridged by shared concerns about constitutionalism's future in the face of such common challenges as globalization and immigration. It may be that the neutralization of challenges from the outside has now made room for internal challenges to be heard.

Flathman's peculiar brand of anarchic liberalism stands in opposition to the new consensus among many communitarian, Continental, and liberal theorists that what counts most are reasoned justification in politics and transparency in communication. From Hobbesian liberal premises, but not on libertarian grounds, Flathman arrives at conclusions that are attractive to readers schooled in the works of Friedrich Nietzsche and Michel Foucault, Ralph Waldo Emerson and Walt Whitman. He embraces mutual opacity as a safeguard to individuality and worries that the practice of reason-based justification operates as a homogenizing and normalizing force, while not being understood in that way at all. Contemporary liberal emphases on rationality, transparency, and consent have illiberal effects, according to Flathman. They demand internal conformity, not just obedience to the law. Rarely will contemporary liberal theorists admit that the policies they favor have an impositional quality. The good reasons on which they base their arguments for certain policies are said to guarantee their voluntary adoption—by all who are reasonable, in any case. Resistance and sheer ornery recalcitrance are thus scripted as unreasonableness, and demands for compliance are not seen as coercive. Politics becomes a site of interest or identity formation and negotiation, and the state becomes an important institution of governance about which liberals are not fundamentally skeptical. Instead, they believe the state simply needs to be better informed by liberal theory's guidance.

Flathman develops his position carefully, avoiding the temptations of a simple libertarianism by relying on Ludwig Wittgenstein and Michael Oakeshott, among others, to outline the situated character of human freedom while championing the almost lost anarchic tradition (if one may call it that) of liberalism. This care and the complexity of his position have earned Flathman the loyal readership he deserves, which is to say, a set of readers prone to admiring but cantankerous disagreement.

Perhaps Flathman's greatest contribution to contemporary political theory comes from his repeated turns to thinkers not commonly thought of as liberal or even as political theorists. Like one of his heroes, Isaiah Berlin, Flathman tries to enrich liberal theory by expanding its canon, drawing on an unlikely bunch. Flathman moves from William of Ockham to William James, from Friedrich Nietzsche to Erving Goffman, from Michael Oakeshott to Ludwig Wittgenstein. The result is an airing of philosophical issues too often foreclosed or elided by contemporary liberal theory.

The main elements of Flathman's theory of "willful" liberalism can be sketched as follows: a Wittgensteinian view of language as rule-governed yet indeterminate, enabling individuals to achieve deeply shared meanings but also enabling them to develop highly idiosyncratic and even mutually unintelligible or "opaque" experiences of the world; an understanding of individuals as willful, creative agents, capable of "self-making" through the personal excellences or "*virtùs*" of self-discipline, moderation, magnanimity, and civility; a celebration of individual diversity, mutual opacity, and even conflict; a Nietzschean hostility to any ideal that is promoted as being "for everyone"; an understanding of the public sphere as a necessary but never sufficient (and sometimes dangerous) condition for the achievement of individuality; and a wariness about anything other than largely formal or "adverbial" public constraints on the exercise of agency.

Some of the chapters in this volume take Flathman's willful liberalism as their focus; others take it as their point of departure. All cluster in one group or another around one of the three concepts that are centrally important to his distinctive brand of liberalism and that, together, form the title of this collection: *Skepticism, Individuality, and Freedom*. Writing from different perspectives, liberal and postfoundationalist, respectively, Patrick Neal in chapter 1 and Linda Zerilli in chapter 2 both appreciate the openings Flathman provides to liberal theory by grounding it in a skeptical disposition rather than in discursive democracy or natural law. But both also wonder (along with several other contributors, such as Anne Norton, Jane Bennett, and William Connolly) whether the features emphasized by Flathman, mutual opacity and willfulness, themselves warrant the ideals—mutual respect and liberality—to which his valorization of opacity and willfulness leads him.

Neal and Zerilli argue that liberalism cannot be grounded in skepticism, despite the latter's attractiveness as a substitute for the will to knowledge that often governs liberal politics to illiberal ends. Zerilli, working through Wittgenstein, goes so far as to suggest that Flathman's skepticism about the possibility of transparent mutual understanding remains in thrall to a knowledge project that he, like a range of other skeptics, would like to escape. She goes on to conclude that "the willful liberal's cognitive claim that one human being cannot know (what is best for) the other displaces the ethical work that is entailed in the quotidian practice of acknowledging the singularity of the other." It is this daily ethical practice of acknowledgment, a practice "which has no epistemic guarantee, be it mutual opacity or mutual transparency," that ought to be seen as the sine qua non of a "more magnanimous liberalism."

In chapter 3, Peter Digeser also looks at the problem of skepticism, but, unlike Zerilli, he does not focus on the mutual opacity of intersubjective relations. Instead, he looks at the problematic relation of theory to practice. Flathman has long been a sympathetic critic of Oakeshott's view that theory cannot guide practice, but according to Digeser, Flathman's willful liberalism marks a movement away from this Oakeshottian stance. Even though Flathman's position remains much closer to the nondogmatic skepticism of Oakeshott and Berlin than to the rationalism of contemporaries such as Jürgen Habermas, John Rawls, and Ronald Dworkin, Flathman is not as skeptical as Digeser thinks he ought be about the ability of philosophy to guide politics. Only with an even deeper skepticism than Flathman's can we avoid the risk that willful liberalism might be misunderstood as a substantive ideal for everyone. Despite such criticisms, Digeser, along with Neal and Zerilli, generally approves of Flathman's complex view of the relationship between theory and practice. Other contributors take a much dimmer view of Flathman's epistemological commitments. Ronald Beiner, for example, in chapter 5 worries that Flathman's skepticism may "pull the rug out from under his own activity as a reason-seeking political philosopher."

Can a skeptic like Flathman defend individuality without lapsing into forms of solipsism or egotism that may threaten efforts to sustain social order? The passion that moves willful liberalism is its love of individuality, together with a fierce determination to protect it. Yet love can be blind, and in their very different ways, Zerilli in chapter 2 and George

Kateb in chapter 4 worry that liberalism must founder unless it gives proper due to the imperatives to know oneself and to acknowledge others. In particular, Kateb believes that Flathman's willful liberalism can too easily justify stubbornness and blindness. He argues that we had better turn to an ideal of "democratic individuality" lest we fall—along with Flathman—into egotism. Kateb believes (along with Beiner, Bennett, Connolly, and others in this volume) that an intensified democratic culture is necessary to promote both individuality and solidarity. In chapter 5, Ronald Beiner expresses similar suspicions of Flathman's admiration for the Oakeshottian idea of "self-enactment," as well as for the Nietzschean idea of "self-overcoming." According to Beiner, this "rhetoric of self-making...reinscribe[s] the idea that individuals can make a life for themselves in abstraction from social relations and larger political realities."

Nancy Hirschmann extends this line of criticism still further in chapter 6, where she assesses what Flathman's philosophy of freedom might have to offer to certain versions of feminism and democratic politics. A sophisticated champion of the idea of "negative freedom," Flathman argues that a free individual must always be considered the final agent or arbiter among his or her own conflicting, "situated," or socially influenced desires. But Hirschmann, herself influenced by theories of "positive freedom," argues that Flathman needs to pay even greater attention to the social construction of the self. From a perspective that takes such social processes and powers seriously, she argues, we can see the need for more just distributions of the necessary conditions of individuality (concerns also voiced by Bennett and Connolly).

As Hirschmann's chapter shows, the debate over positive freedom versus negative freedom is a useful way of probing differences about freedom and agency. But the structure of that debate may also limit our thinking. Seeking to surmount those limits, while also casting the debate about freedom in terms that differ from Flathman's own, Richard Friedman in chapter 7 tries to recover a conception of liberty outside the dichotomy between positive and negative liberties. He finds one such conception in Stoic natural law. According to Friedman, the Stoics were not concerned with the universal ethical content of law so much as with its universal scope as the only appropriate way of ruling human beings understood as free agents. Friedman's chapter is the first of the volume's three chapters in the history of political thought. He is followed by Jeremy Waldron (chapter 8) and Richard Tuck (chapter 9), both of whom take Flathman's interpretation of Hobbes as their point of departure. Flathman sees in Hobbes a figure who shares his own deep concerns about the connections between skepticism and individuality, negative liberty and law. But Waldron uses Hobbes to show that there are continuities between Flathman's liberalism and the versions of liberalism offered by those whom Flathman takes to be his adversaries. According to Waldron, Hobbes and Flathman are in basic agreement with such contemporary liberals as Rawls in respecting the ability of ordinary individuals to think for themselves and thus in accepting a "publicity principle" with respect to the grounds of authority. But there is one important difference, according to Waldron, between Hobbes and Flathman: Hobbes could respect the independent thinking of others and still require (as Hobbes indeed did) that the public be instructed in the grounds of proper reasoning. For example, Hobbes favored the idea of teaching the public the second-order skeptical truth that there are no first-order moral truths because he knew that his own skeptical doctrine of political absolutism was so counterintuitive that it would have to be taught in order to gain sufficient support. Flathman, however, would shy away from such a program for his own views: He does not want the liberal state to teach even a nondogmatic skepticism.

Tuck agrees with Waldron's statement that what really horrifies Flathman and Hobbes is the idea that individuals might be required "simply to submit passively to conclusions reached as a result of the reasoning of another," for example, the sovereign. According to Tuck, Flathman and Hobbes also share a particular horror of deliberative democracy's tendency to seek a kind of sameness among citizens, who are supposed to agree upon the merits of the law they must obey. Yet Tuck argues that Hobbes was a somewhat better friend to plebiscitary democracy and a somewhat worse friend to willful opacity than Flathman envisions. Nevertheless, Tuck is persuaded by Flathman's "remarkable insight": that the reputedly illiberal Hobbes was actually deeply interested in protecting individuality.

Are Flathman's carefully qualified but nevertheless very strong charges against government too fearfully conscious of the state? Is his antistatist liberalism too state-centered in its identification of state institutions as the primary enemies of individuality? Neal, Kateb, Tuck, and Norton (in chapter 10) admire this dimension of Flathman's distinctive liberalism and find his great wariness of political authority salutary. Norton reminds us that liberalism has historically been a force that destroys and unmakes political institutions. In short, for Norton, Flathman rightly takes liberalism back to its original spirit. On the other hand, Beiner, Hirschmann, Bennett, and Connolly find Flathman's hostility to the state too reactive. Whereas Neal admires Flathman for having escaped the contemporary liberal idolatry of the state, Beiner sees Flathman as driven by a fear of the state so exaggerated that politics and even citizenship become suspect. Beiner argues (as do Bennett, Connolly, and Zerilli) that Flathman's wariness of the state is less effective in protecting individuality than is engagement in the very political processes and ethical practices that offend Flathman's individualist sensibility. In place of Flathman's recommendations that one maintain one's distance from the state and citizenship, we are told by various contributors to this volume to look to larger political realities (Beiner, Hirschmann) or to some form of specifically democratic culture (Kateb, Norton) or to ethics (Bennett, Connolly) in order to sustain individuality. In particular, Bennett and Connolly argue in chapter 11 that the liberal state is far too implicated in and indispensable to the practices of civility, plurality, and individuality to be merely "grudgingly accepted," as Flathman recommends. They urge a more complicated attitude in which withdrawal is not always privileged as the best option of the willful individualist. Better, they say, to offset the tendency to withdraw with "necessary bouts of political enthusiasm."

Flathman's willful liberalism may not be the real, authentic liberalism—our contributors differ about that—but all the volume's contributors agree that his is an important voice because it reminds contemporary liberals and their critics about what should be at stake. In *Willful Liberalism*, Flathman argues that

> public life at its best cannot create or sustain individuality... it can [however] "hinder" the coarsest of "hindrances" to free-spiritedness. Accordingly, there may be circumstances under which measures characteristic of socialist and welfare states will be appropriate. But it is a blatant misunderstanding and betrayal of that ideal to equate it with the benefits that public life in such polities sometimes provides. (211)

Flathman is out to remind contemporary liberals that it is individuality—not neutrality, not equality, not social justice, not community, not democracy—that is at the heart of liberalism. When liberals pursue these other goods and values, they trade off the good of individuality. There may be good reasons for doing so, in particular cases. Nevertheless, liberals need to recognize these trade-offs for what they are, strive to minimize them, and work to protect the almost forgotten mission of a properly willful liberalism.

CHAPTER ONE

The Voice of Richard Flathman in the Conversation of Liberalism

Patrick Neal

In the introduction to *Willful Liberalism,* Richard Flathman notes that he has "embraced positions more definite and substantial than those" (1) he had defended in earlier work (especially *Toward a Liberalism*). Coupled with the fact that throughout *Willful Liberalism,* Flathman is sharply critical of both communitarian and rationalist liberal theorists, this statement suggests that willful liberalism is intended to take a place as a competitor in the contemporary debate over how best to formulate, articulate, and defend the liberal idea. In a certain sense this is true, for in some ways willful liberalism stands as a sort of third alternative to the two predominant discourses of communitarian and rationalist liberalism. But not in all ways, and perhaps not in the most important ones. I want to suggest that Flathman's willful liberalism is not a full-fledged competitor to these other discourses, owing in an interesting way to its ultimately self-undermining character. I hope to show the senses in which willful liberalism is self-undermining through an examination of various aspects of Flathman's articulation of it. Such an exercise would ordinarily be understood as a critical one, and indeed, quite a destructively critical one insofar as it should prove to be accurate. Who, after all, would wish to be described as having invented a thing that gnaws at itself and threatens to collapse of its own weight? Yet the fact is that I have come more to praise Flathman than to bury him. And so I shall try and explain herein why I think the provocative and distinctive voice of Flathman's self-undermining willful liberalism is a genuine manifestation of the spirit of liberalism and an important addition to the conversation dominated by its apparently more successful contemporary rivals. I can only hope, of course, that Flathman himself would acknowledge the label of "self-undermining" I have placed upon his theoretical construction with the same degree of sympathy with which I have attempted to endow it.

In the section "Locutions and Illocutions," I examine various theoretical locutions Flathman articulates and illocutions he performs as a means of bringing to light the particular character of willful liberalism. In the section "Tensions," I discuss a number of tensions and strains that emerge within that theoretical voice. In the conclusion, I attempt to summarily describe the tenor and tone of that voice following from the analyses in earlier sections, and I also try to explain why I think Flathman's theoretical voice is not heeded by his fellow liberals to the degree it ought to be.

Locutions and Illocutions

Will and Reason

"Rather than Reason, [willful liberalism's] chief emblem is Will construed as largely or at least finally mysterious" (Flathman, *Reflections of a Would-Be Anarchist* [hereafter *Reflections*], 13). I take this passage to contain, in condensed form, the key themes that make up Flathman's idea of willful liberalism. The importance of the will as a concept of understanding and the will's ultimately mysterious character (as well as the consequences of that mystery) are the two obvious markers. But there is a third as well, contained in the opening phrase, "Rather than Reason," announcing what willful liberalism is not as a beginning to trying to say what it is. I want to concentrate on that marker for the moment. As Flathman says when discussing William James, "will and willfulness contrast with and hence implicate reason, reasonableness, and like notions" (Flathman, *Willful Liberalism*, 6). That willful liberalism is a thing that exists essentially in contrast to something else is important to understanding both its particular substantive characteristics and its more general, self-undermining, character. Flathman signals this character consistently throughout his writing, but in a dynamic way, articulating the theme indirectly in the course of making other points. My analysis here is, as it were, static. I want to take the theme out of these other contexts, within which it repeatedly and "naturally" occurs, and isolate it for purposes of observation.

What is the thing that willful liberalism is not but that is nevertheless necessary to saying what it is, or is trying to be? I will call it "mainstream liberalism" for the moment and describe its two primary manifestations. (My choice of descriptive labels differs from those recently chosen by Flathman to describe the landscape of contemporary liberal theories, but I do not think my labels distort the ideas Flathman advances under those different categories of "virtue" and "agency" liberalisms.) One is what I will call rationalist liberalism, the liberalism of John Rawls, Ronald Dworkin, Bruce Ackerman, and Robert Nozick. The other is communitarian liberalism, the liberalism of Charles Taylor, Michael Walzer, Michael Sandel, and possibly the later Rawls, if one emphasizes the conventionalist foundations of his theory. To speak of these as two types of liberalism is to depart from the perhaps more common notion that communitarianism and liberalism are antithetical discourses in contemporary political theory, but it is in line with Flathman's sketch of the landscape of contemporary theory. Flathman objects to both rationalist and communitarian liberalisms, and his objection is aimed at a feature they share in spite of their many differences and variations. That feature is the emphasis both place upon what we as citizens can be said to share and the ensuing project of constructing authoritative principles of political behavior upon that foundation of shared characteristics. Whether the appealed-to consensus is understood to be one of reason (allegedly manifest in various principles, rules, or goods) or history (allegedly manifest in shared values, meanings, or understandings), whether it is understood to be universal or particular, necessary or contingent, the emphasis is upon the common. Against this orthodoxy (though ultimately in the service of the liberalism it represents), Flathman champions the idiosyncratic. The driving rhetorical structure of his exposition is that the orthodox have neglected and forgotten, perhaps repressed and denied, and thus possibly betrayed the animating spirit of their own professed faith (*Willful Liberalism*, 223). Attending excessively to the common, liberals are said to have forgotten that "the most heartening feature of liberalism is its commitment to that extreme but inspiring form of pluralism that is the cultivation and celebration of individuality" (*Reflections*, 41).

Flathman has learned too much from Ludwig Wittgenstein to say that in slighting individuality, mainstream liberalism betrays the "true" or "essential" heart of liberalism rightly understood. I agree with his non-essentialism in this respect, but I note here a difficulty it creates for the project he pursues through the articulation of willful liberalism. On the one hand, Flathman wishes to avail himself of the tropes and themes associated with a rhetoric of betrayal as a means of awakening his primary audience of dormant liberals to the errors of their misguided ways. In *Willful Liberalism,* Flathman summons an array of "strong voluntarists" to speak in an attempt to get his fellow liberals to recognize how their thinking is serving to "diminish both the security and the vigor of liberalism's commitment to individuality and other sources of diversity" (5). He provocatively claims that this diminution is a consequence of the very theoretical developments in which mainstream liberals often take pride:

> But in arguing for a wider and more secure set of rights and for an expanded and deepened social justice, for greater cooperation and social unity, enhanced welfare and the like, they place their emphasis on commonalities not differences among individuals, on the conceptions and understandings, beliefs and values that have already achieved wide acceptance, the hopes and fears, desires and interests that are most generally recognized. Above all they stress the human capacities for rationality, reasonableness, and mutual understanding that they take to be the most secure basis for such unity as we have thus far achieved and for the augmented and intensified unity they seek. (4)

On the other hand, Flathman cannot fully avail himself of the rhetoric of betrayal because that rhetoric functions effectively only when the object of betrayal is defined in terms of some posited essence that is "true" and "deep" enough (perhaps "deeply shared" between the unwitting betrayer and the prophet who would accuse him) to underwrite the sense of outrage, violation, and perhaps even desecration that the act of betrayal elicits. Flathman wants to wake liberals up, but he cannot claim, at least fully and explicitly, that in sleeping they are selling their souls, because without a notion of a definitive essence, it is not clear what they are selling or how dear the price is. What are liberals doing, then? Because by Flathman's own more or less pragmatic description, liberalism is a "many splendored thing," a set of family resemblances known by its history and practices rather than by its essence or telos, the mainstream liberals may alternatively be described as "merely" opting for one array of theoretical concerns and conceptual possibilities instead of another, including Flathman's preferred array. How can Flathman gain a foothold for the critical jolt he wishes to deliver without denying this easygoing and laissez-faire portrait of the self-understanding of liberal theory? On the other hand, how could he make such a denial without affirming some more essentialist notion of liberalism? How are we to know if the "most heartening feature" of liberalism is the heart of liberalism?

Flathman thus must rhetorically negotiate a difficult border between two types of discourse aimed at liberal minds. This is the borderland between *reminding* liberals of something they have forgotten, and hence possibly betrayed, and *showing* them something foreign and different from which they could benefit if they were to attend to it. The "reminding" discourse is oriented inward, aimed at the depths of the liberal spirit, seeking to recover or bring back. The "showing" discourse is oriented outward, aimed at incorporating what is conceived to lay beyond the boundaries of the already known and accepted. The two discourses are intertwined throughout *Willful Liberalism,* and the mixture creates the rhetorical structure of the text. Speaking in the showing mode, Flathman worries that (liberal) readers will ignore the teachings of the strong voluntarists who fall outside, or at best on the margins of, what is understood to be the liberal tradition. And so he gently implores his reader not to prematurely abandon attending to these somewhat unfamiliar voices. But they are only somewhat unfamiliar, and the more they are allowed to speak, the more Flathman draws and points out the connections between their concerns and ideas to those of thinkers ("agency liberals" or "weak voluntarists") who are at least posited as being more firmly entrenched inside the boundaries constituting the liberal tradition. In this vein, the discourse gradually shifts to the reminding mode, as the ideas of the strong voluntarists are shown to now implicate the central concerns of the tradition itself. The "agency liberals" and "weak voluntarists" function as the crucial bridge uniting the two discourses and making it possible to move back and forth between them.

My purpose in contrasting the types of discourse is not to prepare the way for accusing Flathman of mixing his modes (something I am sure he would take as a compliment anyway!). It is rather to point to one of the real sources of the strength and individuality of his voice considered within the context of contemporary liberal voices. The mixing of the modes of discourse and the willingness to speak unabashedly in defense of willfulness instead of sweet reason and pacific consensus mark his voice as unique. But granted its uniqueness, is it beneficial and worth listening to?

One reason for answering yes to that question is that Flathman's defense of willfulness is a great aid in preventing mainstream rationalist liberals from more successfully colonizing and assimilating the conceptual territory of willful individuality than they already have. To explain what I mean, let me sketch the conceptual landscape of contemporary liberal theory: Since communitarianism is conventionally understood to be at odds with individualism, at least in some sense, and since rationalist liberalism is conventionally understood to be the main competitor with communitarianism in contemporary theoretical debates, then "will," "consent," "contract," and similar terms drawn from the lexicon of individualism are, as it were, automatically ceded to the domain of rationalist liberalism. This prepares the way for the appropriation of these terms into the language of rationalism ("consent" becomes "hypothetical consent," "agency" becomes "rational agency," the "chaotic diversity and babel of human modes of experiencing life" becomes the "plurality of reasonable conceptions of the good"). There is both a positive and a negative aspect of this from the point of view of rationalist liberalism.

On the positive side, rationalist liberalism attains access to a set of concepts with a very powerful hold on our imaginations owing to their embeddedness not only in our traditions of thought but also in long-standing social practices bound up with those traditions. This is true even if we deny that the elements and concepts highlighted by willful liberalism can be said to constitute the essence of the liberal tradition. There can be little doubt that they are a significant component of that tradition, even if not the essence. Rationalist liberalism is thus in a position to avail itself of the persuasive resources yielded up by this powerful language.

However, on the negative side, this language must be washed and ironed before it can be made safely serviceable to the ends pursued by means of rationalist liberalism. Left in its unadorned and unrefined state, the language raises the specter, as Flathman constantly notes, of antinomianism and anarchism. Rationalist liberalism thus needs to tame and subdue the potentially explosive content of the lexicon of willful individualism if it is to extract from it the legitimating power of its tropes. It can then deploy those tropes to support some set of reasonable rules and principles of authoritative political order that can demarcate the acceptable from the unacceptable.

There are (at least) two aspects of this process. One is the actual articulation of theories and doctrines that perform this laundering operation. The other is having the good fortune to have an audience that will not ask too many unsettling and potentially embarrassing questions about just exactly what got washed out of these notions in the laundering process. This is where Flathman's voice is especially relevant and beneficial, because his strident advocacy of voluntarism, individuality, and willful liberalism can be understood as one long, incessant refusal to keep quiet about what came out in the wash. The fact that mainstream liberals are not likely to appreciate his irritating performance in this respect is no proof that they would not benefit from heeding his voice.

Here are a few examples of what I think of as liberal laundering operations and Flathman's sensible refusal to accept them at face value: One is the practice of qualifying the nouns specifying the activities by which individuals engage in political activity in order to demarcate the activity into acceptable and unacceptable types. Rawls's distinction between "pluralism" and "reasonable pluralism" is a characteristic example. Political liberalism is concerned to accommodate the reasonable pluralism of competing conceptions of the good that accept the basic terms of liberal justice itself. Those ways of thinking and being that lie outside the parameters of what liberals are willing to consider reasonable are placed into a different category. They are said to give rise to a problem of "containment" rather than recognition. Flathman notes that in the theorizing of Rawls and other "virtue liberals" (he names T. H. Green, L. T. Hobhouse, and Dworkin), "equality, respect or recognition are deeply conditional. I am entitled to standing and respect as an agent only if my desires, goals and purposes meet the criteria of justice, of reason, or of like standards" (*Reflections*, 26). The same tendency is evident in the various formulations of hypothetical consent theory that are so prevalent in contemporary liberal theorizing. Thomas Scanlon's proposal of the principle of political legitimacy whereby one is bound to obey principles that one could not reasonably reject is perhaps the best known of such proposals. It is very close to Rawls's own notion of the "liberal principle of political legitimacy," which is "that our exercise of political power is proper and hence justifiable only when it is exercised in accordance with a constitution the essentials of which all citizens may reasonably be expected to endorse in the light of principles and ideals acceptable to them as reasonable and rational" (Rawls 1993, 217). Flathman complains that such views amount to abandoning the more appropriate liberal emphasis on will and individuality in favor of "moralistic, and indeed moraline, formulations" (*Reflections,* 11). The same is true, in my opinion, of the recent liberal turn to notions of public reason and public justification. These doctrines function in such a way as to make the political world safe for liberalism, at least in theory. They do so by relegating illiberal and nonliberal notions to the netherworld of sectarian comprehensive doctrines, incommensurable private perspectives, and the like. This is a place in the liberal imagination populated by various and sundry types who can nevertheless be lumped together according to one overriding and dominant characteristic: They are fanatics who would commit the original sin of liberalism, which is to impose one's own values on others. On this model of thought, liberals are those who exclude nothing except exclusion, and, in my opinion, it is through this framework of thought that the altogether respectable language of toleration has come to be used (or abused) as an excuse for not listening to people. (In this regard see Rooney 1989.)

It may be objected at this point that there is a great deal to be said in support of rationalist accounts of political order, in support of the virtues of attaining political consensus around reasonable values, and against the vices of, say, romanticizing irrationality and existential willfulness. I think Flathman would be willing to contest those who would make such objections, but within the context of his advocacy of willful liberalism I believe he is saying something a bit different. The issue he forces upon the table is not so much whether there are things to be said in support of such views (obviously there are), but rather, whether self-described liberals ought to be the ones saying them. After all, one might suppose that defenders of natural law or perfectionist theories would generally be perfectly willing and able to speak, as they traditionally have done so well, in defense of such a perspective. (An excellent contemporary example is George 1993.) I take Flathman to be implying that perhaps liberals would be better off leaving this territory to its traditional defenders and that they should instead turn and defend, as he attempts to, the claims of the individual and his or her will and indeed willfulness against the disciplinary force of such rationalisms.

Flathman sees mainstream liberalism as having become contaminated with the mania for consensus and the complacent rationalism that he takes to characterize communitarianism and rationalist liberalism, respectively. In fending off the communitarian challenge, liberals have been concerned to demonstrate their own respectable awareness of and due regard for the forms of consensus approved by communitarianism. It is as if Flathman expects a "we're all communitarians now" capitulation from numerous liberals who, as he sees it, ought to know better. Liberals have also been faced with powerful rhetorical challenges from conservative thinkers since the 1980s, and part of a successful response has involved demonstrating that liberalism is not, as many conservative critics claim or imply, premised upon philosophical skepticism or, heaven forbid, "relativism." Seeking to demonstrate (to confess?) their commitment to rationality and truth and to prove that they are not (as their conservative critics say they are) first cousins to such dreaded species as postmodernists or nihilists, mainstream liberals have tended to play down the elements of willful individuality, skepticism, and voluntarism that Flathman insists upon emphasizing; instead, they emphasize their faith in reason, truth, and objectivity.

Of course, mainstream liberals may well see Flathman's affirmation of a skeptical theoretical temperament along with strong voluntarism and its themes of idiosyncrasy, singularity, and divergence as an overreaction to the communitarian and conservative challenges. Even if they were right, his voice would still serve the useful purpose of keeping them honest when it comes to the point of remembering what liberalism is for.

Opacity

One of Flathman's most interesting concepts is that of opacity. At one point, he speaks of his task as trying to "assemble reminders" of "meaninglessness and other forms of indeterminacy" in order to try to enhance "receptivity to the idea that quite radical diversities, incommensurabilities, and so forth, including those strongly protected by limited mutual intelligibility, are to be welcomed, not feared" (*Willful Liberalism*, 216–17). His repeated emphasis on the opacity of ourselves to others is a feature of this program.

At one level, opacity would seem to function primarily as a protective concept. To the degree that we and our intentions are inaccessible to one another, then the ability of some to discipline others in the name of what we share or hold in common is limited and restrained. Speaking of the fact that a number of the thinkers (William James, Søren Kierkegaard,

Jean-Paul Sartre) he refers to (sympathetically) as strong voluntarists do not regret "the various ways in which our claims to mutual intelligibility are delusive, if not vain, conceits," Flathman remarks that

> [l]urking and sometimes explicit in these several views are variants of the idea that I initially drew out of some of Wittgenstein's observations, namely, that *opacity creates spaces protective of individuality and plurality*, makes it difficult and sometimes impossible for those who are other to individuals and groups to know or understand them well enough to diminish their distinctiveness by acting with or against them. (*Willful Liberalism*, 112–13)

Thus, to acknowledge opacity is to call into question, and thus potentially to chasten and limit, the disciplining and homogenizing political power that would exercise and legitimate itself in the name of the consensual and common, whether rational or historical. To the degree this actually happens, opacity would have served to secure and protect, and possibly even to extend, freedom and the individuality it makes possible.

The value of opacity as a mode of self-understanding is not, however, exhausted through its protective aspects. There is a more positive use for it. Speaking of the theological voluntarists who root the concept of opacity in man's inability to understand God, Flathman remarks that

> [i]n insisting, endlessly, that human beings cannot and should not try to understand God, the theological voluntarists make evident their own powerful desire to do just that. Nor is this mere weakness, failure, or self-betrayal on their part. They call on themselves and are called on by others to act; whatever else it involves, action requires beliefs and judgments, intentions and purposes; these require considering; considering requires considerations that are more than episodic, more than transient. By adopting the belief that they cannot understand God, that their attempts to do so are futile and counterproductive, the theological voluntarists create within themselves, as it were, beliefs and desires countervailing to the desire to understand God and hence also countervailing to the desires that make them unreceptive or unresponsive to God's will. The insisting on what from one perspective can be viewed as metalevel questions (the question whether we can understand, as distinct from the question whether this or that understanding is plausible, cogent, warranted) can be viewed as a way of sustaining these countervailing beliefs and desires and hence of sustaining their responsiveness to God's will because it is God's will. (*Willful Liberalism*, 218)

This penetrating passage is at once a statement of the positive aspect of what superficially appears to be an entirely negative idea and an allusion to Flathman's own relation to the community of liberal thinkers. Let us consider these matters in turn.

Viewed from the perspective of the legislator (whether actual or vicarious, as in the form of G. W. F. Hegel's philosophers intent on "giving instruction as to what the world ought to be" [1952, 12]), the notion of opacity appears wholly negative. The legislative temperament seeks the expression of positive rules or principles capable of serving politically as behavioral guides or philosophically as standards of judgment (Bauman 1987). To meet what is understood from this perspective to be this urgent practical purpose, the legislative temperament seeks the consensual ground that might function to structure and ground the principles expressed. In this framework, which is too often treated as if it were more or less definitive of the practice called political or sociopolitical philosophy (or at least "serious" or "responsible" political or sociopolitical philosophy), talk of the mystery of the will and the opacity of persons to one another (let alone of the person to him or herself, or worse yet, to God!) is worthless, or at best an irritant that stands in the way of rational and humane progress.

Flathman's insight, drawn from the strong voluntarists, is to see that the acknowledgment of opacity is, or at least can be, the vehicle that actually serves the ends sought by the legislative temperament, though in a complex way. Of course, the understanding of those ends themselves is changed (in this case, "chastened") through the recognition that their direct pursuit—that is, by means of a program or schedule—is self-defeating, or at least counterproductive. In theological terms, openness to the word of God is sustained through the refusal to idolize any speech about the word of God while at the same time refusing to cease attentively seeking a hearing. In political terms, fidelity to sustaining the possibility of the individuality that is at the heart of Flathman's liberalism enjoins resistance to the self-understanding of liberalism that is presupposed by the legislative imperative of mainstream liberalism in its rationalist and communitarian forms. Still, as in the religious context, this resistance (it can be argued) is self-reflective and mature only insofar as it refuses the temptation to flee into the fantasy of a critical subjectivity detached from the roots of that which it resists. This difference, we might say, is the difference between faithless criticism and faithful resistance, and it is resistance that Flathman both recommends and seeks to enact by recommending. The resistance is intended to be faithful to what mainstream liberalism understands itself to be faithful to and yet perhaps betrays. Flathman enters the conversation of liberalism not to destroy, deconstruct, or deny, but to invigorate, inspire, and enliven. From this perspective, the notion of opacity turns out to be a key positive aspect of the attempt to serve the end of living together in a humane and decent way. The denial of the inflated conception of the shared, rational, and common elements of our being is thus seen to be ultimately in the service of a chastened but appropriate conception of such elements.

Nevertheless, to leave it at this would be to flatten out Flathman's thinking in an inaccurate way. The chastened ends of politics are not ends unto themselves; rather, they are also means to the possibility of enacting individuality. Flathman does not mourn, indeed he revels in, the fact that opacity limits the possibilities of a stable political order. His discourse does not simply skeptically inform mainstream liberals that they cannot have as much rationality, consensus, and order as they might want; it also delights in this fact in the name of the individuality it celebrates. "In a willful liberalism, in liberalism at its most engaging, the variability that has been much remarked in liberal theory and practice is due not to lack of resolution or any other form of weakness but to an appreciation for the splendor of these ideas and ideals" (*Willful Liberalism*, 224). We shall have occasion later to consider how easily these skeptical and celebratory moments of his theorizing sit with one another. But for the moment, I hope to have made clear the notion of opacity as it functions in Flathman's theorizing.

Idolatry

If, as I have suggested, mainstream liberals are in effect accused by Flathman of idolatry, what is it they idolize? Most of Flathman's overt indictments name rationality and consensus as the objects of which liberals are said to be overly fond. It is "reason, reasonableness, and like notions" that are "implicated" by the idea of will. There is a related sense, though, in which it makes sense to see the object of Flathman's charge of liberal idolatry as the political state itself. To see this, it will be useful to examine another of the well-known taxonomies of liberalism as it appears within Flathman's perspective.

This taxonomy stems from Rawls and turns on the contrast between "merely" political forms of liberalism and "comprehensive" types of liberalism. Rawls, speaking in defense of political liberalism, says that the salient characteristic of political liberalism in relation to comprehensive liberalism is its modesty. Pursuing the method of avoidance, Rawls understands the political liberal to have disciplined himself against the temptation to use the practices of political democracy in order to impose (or attempt to impose) his particular conception of the good on everyone else. From this perspective, the comprehensive or perfectionist liberal is at one with various stripes of illiberal fanatics insofar as she would place the pursuit of the good (or in liberal parlance, her particular conception of the good) above the duty of respect owed to one's equals (the duty of respect necessitates the subordination of the good to the right). From this perspective, the political liberal is understood, conversely, as one willing to take seriously the autonomy and equality of the other, as is exemplified in his willingness to consider the rights of others as equal to his own rights before embarking upon any particular project. His ethical superiority to the liberal (or illiberal) perfectionist is manifest in the act of refusing to engage in any particular pursuit of some idea of the good unless it can first be reasonably established that such pursuit will not violate the duty he owes to others of equal respect. Viewed from this angle, the contrast is then between the political liberal who manifests civility through self-restraint and the inconsiderate and selfish perfectionist who, rather like a bull in the moral china shop, overrides the differences of others through her headlong pursuit of her own ends and ideals.

Of course, this flattering perspective on political liberalism comes from within the perspective of political liberalism itself. Alternative perspectives paint the portrait very differently. The milder critical perspective derives from liberal perfectionism, which chastises the political liberal for being unnecessarily reticent in affirming the substantive account of value ("the idea of the good"), which, perfectionism says, does in fact constitute the heart of liberalism. The perfectionist liberal is understood here as willing to affirm the particular account of value that constitutes liberalism as one among a number of possible alternative accounts of political morality. The somewhat naive political liberal, by contrast, harbors the (vain, as it is seen) ideal of showing liberalism to be not simply one among a number of competing views operating at the same epistemic level but a uniquely privileged view that operates at an epistemic level whereby other accounts of political morality are themselves properly ordered and placed (and subdued). Perfectionist liberalism is a type of comprehensive liberalism because it unabashedly affirms liberalism as a doctrine of value applying to the whole of life, not "only" to the political sphere. Political liberals seek consensus (under conditions of pluralism) partly by means of trying to separate the liberal principles appropriate to the political realm from those appropriate to the realm (private, social, or civil) of character development and the formation of identity. Comprehensive liberals (or perfectionists generally) see the political not as a realm or space apart from other realms and spaces, each with its own morality, but as one site upon which the single and general morality is manifested.

The more sharply critical portrayal of political liberalism comes from those who understand themselves to be outside the boundaries of the ideology altogether; hence, they are critics of liberalism rather than inside competitors in the contest over how best to interpret and understand it. On this (the radical, critical, or postmodernist) view, the political liberal's attempt to respect difference by disciplining his pursuits in light of a more mutually encompassing governing framework (of reasonableness or shared value or social consensus) is understood as an attempt to pass the particular off as the universal, and thereby to at once hide (under the cloak of impartiality or universality) and sanctify (in the name of impartiality or universality) the particular end or ideal being pursued. This passing off is understood to be either unintentional (in which case, the political liberal is portrayed as naive) or intentional (in which case, he is portrayed as a deceitful and willful oppressor).

I take it these ready-for-polemical-battle sketches are recognizable to anyone familiar with the literature of contemporary political theory. I think that one interesting consequence of Flathman's theorizing is that it casts these familiar positions in a different and therefore illuminating light, a light that also serves to reveal the sense in which mainstream liberalism might be said to idolize the political state.

An unintended consequence of limiting liberalism to the political sphere is to incline it toward making itself into a state-centered ideology. The primary task of political theory comes to be understood as the criticism or justification of the state and its policies, and this understanding is insulated from challenge insofar as discourse from outside the realm of the political state, its structures and policies, and their justifications is understood as being in the realm either of ethics (i.e., it is discourse about the "good") or of the personal, that is, external to the sphere of politics proper. In this sense, the attempt to practice "modesty" in regard to the claims of political theory pushes that theory in the direction of serving the state. This may seem an overly harsh judgment, since such theory understands itself to focus on the *criticism* of the state, requiring the actual state to be measured by, and hence insisting that it measure up to, the standards of right, justice, or goodness that are discerned by theorizing. It would seem, then, that far from idolizing the state, such a conception of theory would produce just the opposite: a criticism of the actual and historical state (its practices and principles) in light of the rational and true state (its practices and principles).

I think this self-conception is deceptive. The crucial fact is not that the actual is criticized in the name of the rational but that the state is criticized in the name of the state. This is the source of the idolatry I am trying to specify. What the actual state cannot be criticized in terms of, due to the emphasis upon the "merely" political character of theory, is what I will call the "ideal that is not of the state." Perhaps this ideal is one of individual character, or perhaps of some form of collective life. It might be a manifestation of what Robert Cover memorably described as a "paideic community" in tension with the imperial ethos of the modern state (Cover 1983, 15–16). In any case, such an ideal is necessarily prevented from challenging the state and its ideal form *on the state's own ground,* because by definition the ground of the state stands apart from and above the conceptual territory occupied by such ideals. The state is the comprehensive form of association that consists of the practices (and underlying principles) by which all so-called particular ideals are ordered and arranged. In contrast to such particulars (which are diverse, various, and plural), there is the general, which is the concept of the state itself. On the self-conception of theory I am now seeking to make clear, the general cannot be contested by the particular; the only possible contest is between the ideal general and the historical general. Whatever the result of the contest, "the general" is safe and secure from the first moment; indeed, "the general" is buttressed and strengthened no matter what the result of the contest between the actual and the ideal general, because either way "the general" wins. Except that it does not really "win," because it was never contested. It is buttressed or reinforced because it frames the contest rather than being a part of it. Such a mode of thinking cannot be a genuine challenge to the state, regardless of how much it understands itself to be engaged in critical thinking about the justification of the state.

Suppose that the arguable and certainly not obviously true view just advanced is correct. Is it proper to speak of this mode of theorizing that I have criticized as constituting *idolatry* of the state? I think this depends on the degree to which one does or does not understand oneself to be authoritatively claimed and bound by some ideal that is not of the state. I say "authoritatively claimed and bound by" to distinguish from the case of someone who understands him- or herself to believe in or practice such ideals, but who understands such belief and practice to be subject to the prior and overriding requirement that the general rules of the state (or its underlying principles) take precedence over the ideals. Such persons will not, of course, agree with the view that their perspective amounts to idolizing the state. But their "respect" for general principles may look like obsequiousness to those principles from the perspective of those who believe in an ideal that is not of the state in the strong sense that they assess states (and their attendant general principles) in terms of those ideals, not ideals in terms of states. The difference in perspective is, it seems to me, as sharp as it is obvious: One side's humility is the other's obsequiousness, and one side's dedication is the other's fanaticism. From the point of view of a strong believer in an ideal that is not of the state (among whom I include Flathman, with his commitment to individuality and self-enactment), it is a form of idolatry of the state to conceive it in such a manner that its foundational claim to sovereign authority (a jealous and exclusive authority) is rendered beyond the realm of challenges that issue from sources other than itself. It is in this sense that I submit that mainstream liberalism can be understood as a form of idolatry with regard to the state.

This is one reason I share Flathman's regret at the rise to prominence in contemporary liberal conversation of doctrines of public reasonableness and public justification. If it is true, as Stephen Macedo has suggested, that the project of public justification is "the moral core of liberalism" (Macedo 1990, 262), then I think that liberalism will have become less a moral challenger to the modern state than the state's bureaucratic servant, producing legitimations of state sovereignty by means of criticism of its practices, unable to grasp its own servility as a consequence of being so busy at the task of criticism.

Individuality and Nondogmatic Skepticism

Flathman's challenge to mainstream liberalism is advanced from two different perspectives, one negative and the other positive. The negative is the position that he calls "nondogmatic skepticism," a view he derives from the strong voluntarists and agency liberals whom he admires. He says that

> liberal thinkers of this orientation manifest a certain skepticism. Although not dogmatic or programmatic skeptics in any technical epistemological sense, they doubt the power of reason or mind to arrive at general truths, especially general truths concerning morals and politics. At the same time, they fear the effects of attempts to subjugate thought and action to a rigorous rule of reason. (*Reflections*, 4)

Flathman mentions names like Michael Oakeshott, Benjamin Constant, and Isaiah Berlin in the context of this passage, though, like many of Flathman's passages, it also calls to mind the voices of reformed Protestant theology. One might wonder at the insistence on the point that the skepticism Flathman admires in these thinkers be understood as nondogmatic or nonprogrammatic. Flathman does not elaborate the point, but I take it to derive from the sense that a programmatic, or positive doctrine, of skepticism is in a way self-contradictory. To formulate skepticism as a doctrine is to adopt a nonskeptical attitude about the issue to which the skeptical doctrine is proposed as an answer or solution. Flathman's skepticism is intended to be more an adverb than a noun, more an attitude than a doctrine. On the other hand, the price of such a formulation is that it is almost impossible to get a handle on what the practical implications of its adoption might be. The ambiguity is expressed in Flathman's final sentence. We are told that such skeptics will "fear the effects of attempts to subjugate thought and action to a rigorous rule of reason," but it is not clear what this fear might lead to, and the qualifier "rigorous" leaves one unsure as to how such skepticism understands itself to relate to "rules of reason" generally, including, presumably, flexible, generous, and otherwise nonrigorous ones.

Nondogmatic skepticism may provide a podium from which one might say no to rationalist liberalisms, but it does not provide a podium from which one might say yes to some alternative, including that of willful liberalism. It is the idea of individuality, understood as self-enactment, that serves this purpose in Flathman's discourse. That idea is closely linked in his thinking to the notions of pluralism and diversity, but it is ultimately individuality that is primary. The notions of plurality and diversity may apply to many different objects. In line with his skepticism, Flathman is at one with Berlin in recognizing and enjoying the plurality of incommensurable values that can be said to characterize human being. But he is decidedly less congenial to lines of thinking that stress the plurality of modes of group life, for although such plurality contributes to diversity at one level, it does not necessarily serve, and indeed may well hamper, the individuality and singularity that Flathman prizes. Indeed, although Flathman does not hide his frustration with rationalist liberals who, as he sees it, are lately worrying too much about the justification of order, the most-stinging irritants to his theoretical sensibility are clearly the communitarians, some of whom happily acknowledge the notions of plurality and diversity when applied to the object of collective practices. On this count, Flathman is at one with rationalist liberals in complaining that communitarians fail to sufficiently appreciate the value of individuality; he goes so far at one point as to (hyperbolically?) suggest that it is a shame Alasdair MacIntyre's dire description of our society as an individualist wasteland is not closer to the descriptive truth (*Reflections*, 42).

Here again, Flathman can be understood as seeking to redescribe the conceptual landscape of contemporary debate in such a way as to prevent rationalist liberals from co-opting and taming the lexicon of individuality for use in their contests with communitarians. The individuality Flathman defends and wishes to see injected into the clogged arteries of liberalism is more than a notion of an agent who eschews (communitarian) conformity to received tradition in favor of obedience to general and reasonable rules that he or she affirms insofar as he or she is reasonable. It extends to those who are skeptical of either or both the existence and the desirability of heeding such safeguards (against what?) in the expression of life, and who would act without respect to or regard for them. In some ways, such an individuality is the madwoman in the attic for contemporary rationalist liberalism as it does battle with communitarians and conservatives. Flathman is at the door to the attic, loudly demanding that liberalism recognize its own.

Tensions

Criticizing Reason

Flathman's attempt to provoke and enlighten by criticizing the liberal emphasis upon reason and reasonableness puts him in a difficult performative situation. The rhetorical difficulty is to figure out how to criticize what one sees as an overly rigid and narrow conception of reason or reasonableness without falling into what I will label "the Trap." The Trap can be understood as a response from the criticized rationalist: Do you not appeal to the very reason you would criticize in order to articulate that criticism? Is this not self-defeating?

There are two ways to respond to such questions. One, linked to the fear of being labeled nihilistic or irrationalist, is to grant that "of course" one wishes both to utilize and endorse something called "reason"; one only wishes to protect the (good) reasonableness from being mistaken for the (bad) particular, and overly rigid, conception said to be at work in the theorizing of the criticized. So here it turns out that the disagreement between critic and criticized is, so to speak, relatively shallow. Both affirm the general virtue of rationality and reasonableness and now understand themselves to be quibbling over the details of how best to express the common thing they share. This I will label the "entirely respectable" strategy for dealing with the accusation that one has contradicted oneself in thinking oneself to have criticized reason.

The fact that this strategy *is* so entirely respectable is what is gnawingly unsatisfying about it. One realizes that one's criticism has not so much been registered as it has been digested and rendered so innocuous that it simply is not criticism at all. One had thought oneself to be launching an attack on the pretensions of reason, but lo and behold, one finds oneself on bended knee confessing one's faith (after all) in what (now "rightly understood," to be sure) turns out to be unassailable.

So we might consider the other strategy of response, which can be labeled the "utterly disrespectful" one. This is to refuse to allow oneself to be brought into the fold, choosing instead to remain outside and to at least try to speak in defense of simple willfulness, haphazard idiosyncrasy, and pure, obstinate, will. This strategy has the virtue of satisfying the perhaps perverse (but surely all-too-human) desire to avoid confession (not to say apology) before one's inquisitors, and it also maintains the possibility of agitating the criticized, or at least the observers of the contest, into recognizing the dangers to which one is pointing. But it cannot do much more than "maintain" this possibility, and the truth of the matter is that in most cases that will not amount to very much, for in the eyes of the criticized, the only thing demonstrated by a continued attack on reason is the attacker's unreasonableness, which just also happens to be what the criticized considers righteous justification for refusing to listen anymore. So, damned if you do, damned if you don't. This is the structural reality of being in a subordinate position of power with regard to rhetorical possibilities.

Flathman moves back and forth between the strategies in an attempt to keep the issues alive, and as far as I can see that is about the best that can be done. The playing off of one theme against its counterpoint occurs in various contexts, as Flathman attempts to criticize and instruct his liberal audience without going so far as to alienate it. Thus, for example, after a sustained period of criticizing rationalist and communitarian liberals (and thus raising suspicions that he is an ideological foe rather than a concerned friend), he will remind the reader that he rejects the anarchist rejection of political authority and is aware of his debt to the "inheritance" of support for individuality provided by liberalism (*Reflections*, xvi, 6, 79–80, 128, 161). After objecting to the weak and relatively tame accounts of "plurality" defended by "weak voluntarist" liberals in their attack on the "unicity" of communitarians and championing instead the "singularity" that reveals the weakness of "plurality," he will remind the reader (perhaps reassuring the reader who fears he is heading for some solipsistic atomism) that he has not forgotten that the idea of individuality is intelligible to us only because it is *not* entirely opaque and idiosyncratic but is, rather, linked to social practices based on what Wittgenstein called "agreements in judgment" (15). Or, finally, having spoken in defense of voluntarism and the will to the point of proposing Nietzsche as the tutor for wayward liberals, he stresses that strong voluntarism is not to be mistaken for romanticism (13–14). Indeed, he claims that "strong voluntarists view romanticism as a form of 'letting go,' as a lack or want of discipline" (14). "Strong voluntarism" is detached from any unsavory connection to romanticism by stressing its commitment to "self-discipline" and "self-overcoming." I have no criticism to make of such estimable notions, but I wonder if they are not more likely to be associated with John Calvin and Immanuel Kant than with Friedrich Nietzsche.

It is impossible to make any general assessment of Flathman's success at employing this strategy of discourse; what can one say beyond acknowledging that each reader will have his or her own reaction to the message he imparts? I find his advocacy of voluntarism persuasive in many respects, but then again I was predisposed toward such a position to begin with. My guess is that many mainstream liberals will react more in the way Flathman himself alludes to in remarking that "I must be prepared for the possibility that some will regard this book—in my view mistakenly—as moving away from, not further toward, a liberalism, as illiberal and therefore anti-liberal" (*Willful Liberalism*, 1).

Lingering Formalism?

One of the perplexing features of Flathman's account of willful liberalism is the possible existence of what I will call a "lingering formalism" in his articulation of the ideals of willful liberalism. I have to say "possible" existence, because there are ambiguities in the formulation of Flathman's position that make it difficult to say for sure whether the position is open to the objection I am about to raise or not. I will discuss these ambiguities later in this section, but for the moment I will proceed without these qualifications so that the problem can be laid out as clearly as possible.

Flathman is critical of the strain of liberal theory that attempts to portray itself as neutral regarding the question of the good and as keeping itself aloof from the state and its power by supporting, not only "preventively" but also "productively," the ideals making up (what is posited as) the good. Liberalism, he is fond of saying, must be a "something," not an "anything" or a "nothing," and it must consist of more than "a series of denials" (*Reflections*, 18, 128, 131; *Willful Liberalism*, 208). This line of criticism may be seen clearly in the following passage discussing mainstream liberalism:

> Virtue liberalisms (numerous protestations to the contrary notwithstanding) feature more or less encompassing and substantive conceptions of what is good for human beings generally or good for the members of this or that culture or society. Confident that anyone who rejects these conceptions can be shown to be in error (philosophical or rational) or in

the grip of some form of misapprehension (cultural or historical), virtue liberalisms assert that if policing is an effective way to correct mistaken thinking and acting, there is no reason to hold back from it. And if policing is the only way to make those corrections, then it becomes wrong not to police. (*Reflections*, 131–32)

Flathman goes on to say that his preferred conception of "agency-oriented," "willful," or "strong voluntarist" liberalism is also an idealism and hence also advances substantive, and hence arguable, "conceptions of good and harm." This idealism is constituted by the commitment to "individuality, distinctiveness and singularity" (132). All of this would seem to indicate that Flathman is willing to let willful liberalism stand on the same theoretical ground as mainstream liberalism, and indeed, as any concept of political morality, whether liberal or not. The contest, it would seem, is one of substance, a contest of the plural and competing and not fully commensurable conceptions of value by means of which human beings make manifest their free nature. Conversely, what would seem to be ruled out by this characterization is the notion that liberalism occupies a different and higher-order theoretical space (the "meta-moral high ground," we might call it) based on which other moral claims (of substance) might be placed and ordered (formally or procedurally).

Yet Flathman seems to me to appeal to just the sort of formalism he has discredited when he chooses to describe the attractions of willful liberalism in terms taken largely from Oakeshott's contrast between civil and enterprise associations. Thus, he says that the ideals he supports are "more formal than substantive. We distinguish individuality from numerous other things—from conformism, slavish imitation or submission, herd and mob behavior, and so on—but there are as many forms of individuality as there are individuals who bring off some degree of self-enactment" (*Reflections*, 132). Or, in another formulation, he says that "liberalism as I envision it is committed to the ideal of individuality and hence self-enactment as a formal but not substantive end and to the widest possible freedom of action as a necessary but not sufficient condition of effective pursuit of this ideal" (31). In another formulation, he says, "[Voluntarists] have promoted 'adverbial' (Oakeshott) *virtùs* such as civility, courage and magnanimity. These *virtùs* speak to the manner or style in which one does whatever one chooses to do, leaving questions of ends and purposes, aspirations and ideals to be decided by groups and more especially by individuals" (44). Finally, he says, "a strongly voluntarist liberalism would be the most open and accommodating, the least censorious and restrictive, of any theory" short of anarchism (*Willful Liberalism*, 208).

These formulations seem to me to be in tension with themselves, for they speak *about* the ideals of willful liberalism as substantive but choose to emphasize their formality and limited character when actually *defining* them. The passages seek to persuade the reader through an appeal to spatial characteristics of the ideal ("widest possible," "leaving open," "whatever one chooses") rather than through a substantive statement of what constitutes the ideal as particular and controversial—which would include naming what is excluded (including the valuables that are excluded) by the ideal. To that extent, I think they resemble too closely the (objectionable) neutralist form of liberal discourse, which rhetorically sells itself by suggesting that it prohibits "less" where other programs prohibit "more." Such forms of spatial or quantitative appeal (and self-understanding) are probably endemic to any political view, such as liberalism, that acknowledges and accepts the plurality of conceptions of value and projects built upon them. Coupled with any considerable degree of skepticism about the ability of any one such conception to prove, demonstrate, or otherwise reveal itself unambiguously to be truer to human nature than the others, the temptation to repair to a spatial and quantitative, rather than substantive, lexicon of persuasion is considerable. Still, my view is that clarity of understanding is served by resisting it. When the temptation is indulged, liberalism defends itself (spatially) by denying itself (substantively) and hence at the cost of knowing itself for what it is and is not, what it creates and what it destroys. On spatial understandings, liberalism excludes or destroys nothing of genuinely valuable substance; it excludes only what would itself exclude, or what would destroy freedom, or what would uselessly and senselessly and irrationally prohibit more when it is possible to prohibit less (as liberalism is thus thought to do). Thus, understood spatially, liberalism excludes only other, irrational, forms of spatiality. This is potent as legitimating ideology, but I do not believe it provides us with a true account of who we are and what we do, for better or worse, as liberals. When Flathman pauses to mention the things from which he distinguishes individuality, that is, "conformism, slavish imitation or submission, herd and mob behavior," one can see the price of the formalism. The contrast is too loaded, and what is lost is the sense, otherwise emphasized and indeed illuminated by Flathman (following Berlin), of the deep plurality, limited commensurability, and hence tragic conflicts between the valuable (that is, genuinely valuable, not simply "subjectively held to be valuable") ideals and projects characteristic of humanity.

To be fair, I should point out again that what I am criticizing here is a moment of Flathman's articulation of liberalism, not the whole of it. His texts manifest constant reminders, as already illustrated, of the folly of understanding liberalism as other than a set of ideals that not only inform the constitution of but also wash over and under and in the cracks of distinctions between the public and private or between the political and nonpolitical. However, it is just these features of his thinking that make perplexing, to my mind, his avowal of the merely formal and adverbial nature of the ideals he champions.

This tendency is also manifested in certain of the formulations he chooses to articulate the ideal of willful liberalism as a political theory. It is also in these formulations that one can see what I described earlier as the self-undermining character of that ideal.

For example, at one telling point, Flathman remarks that "if there is or could be such a thing as willful liberalism it is or would be an accentuation and intensification of agency liberalism" (*Reflections,* 13). This comes just after descriptions of virtue and agency liberalisms, characterized as mainstream forms from which willful liberalism is a deviation. But it is difficult to make a statement of what something is not into a statement of what it is. In fleshing out the conception, Flathman goes on to say that "willful liberals place yet greater emphasis (greater than, for example, agency liberals such as Mill and Berlin) on the irreducible diversity of divergent, incommensurable, and perhaps interpersonally or intersubjectively inexplicable goods, ends, and especially ideals" (13). This "greater emphasis" can be understood relative to agency liberalism in a very general way ("greater"), but it still leaves a great deal of ambiguity around the notion of willful liberalism. Now, admittedly, Flathman acknowledges this, and indeed at times he counts it as a virtue of willful liberalism that it cannot be more clearly delineated in positive terms of content:

> Liberalism thus conceived differs profoundly from the collectivist and rationalist ideologies to which the terms *idealism* and *utopianism* are most commonly applied.... It of course follows that liberal ideals are

always and necessarily underdetermined, can never be reduced to
formulae or rules. But this is at once their beauty and their strength,
their inspiring but also their realistic character. (*Reflections*, 45)

As in the formulations cited earlier, what is noticeable here is the elusive and essentially negative character of the articulation of a positive definition.

Again, my point is descriptive rather than critical. I do not meant to criticize Flathman for failing to articulate willful liberalism in terms of principles and policies and standards, for the critique of such notions is at the heart of his idea itself. But that means that the idea cannot be a full-fledged competitor to the rivals it criticizes, because it aims at criticizing those rivals for playing the wrong game in the first place. Given that criticism, a successful positive definition of willful liberalism would destroy it, constituting a cure worse than the disease of ambiguity and being defined relative to something else. Willful liberalism is pushed to define itself positively by the need to make itself heard in the court of mainstream liberalism, but it is also pushed to resist that process because of its substantive elements (skepticism and voluntarism, which militate against positivity). It is a difficult set of poles within which to maintain one's balance.

The negative form of definition, where the emphasis is placed upon critical awareness, does create dangers. The greatest, I think, is a tendency sometimes manifest in forms of radical social critique: It is the tendency to define the difference between the critic's view and the view of the criticized as being constituted by the critic's greater awareness of and sensitivity to the difficulties and ambiguities of judgment; the critic may object not to the substance of the criticized's decision but to the criticized's posited lack of awareness of the difficulty, even agony, of the decision. This is to enter into the dangerous terrain of judgments about who "really" cares or takes seriously the plurality of perspectives and difficulties of judgment when engaging in practical decision making. I call it dangerous because it can easily devolve into attacks on the character of the other position in the scenario, attacks that can hardly be based on anything like intimate knowledge of the other. I have expressed my general sympathy for Flathman's opposition to rationalist liberalism, but I admit that the sort of critique I am describing often occurs in the context of attacks on those who are held to be in the grip of too easygoing and casual a belief in the powers of reason to generate truth and authority.

This rhetorical dynamic can lead not only to a regrettable impugning of the character of those who disagree with one's own views but also to an inflated sense of one's own ethical superiority based upon one's (alleged) greater sensitivity to the ambiguities of the world. I hasten to add that Flathman avoids such unfortunate scenarios even though he practices the negative form of definition (and even though he obeys no general prohibition against saying what he thinks). This is at least partially linked to his decision to remain a faithful, though perhaps heretical, liberal rather than to leave the fold altogether.

Liberality and Nobility in Liberal Character

Flathman is fond of José Ortega y Gasset's characterization of liberalism: "Liberalism . . . is the supreme form of generosity; it is the right by which the majority concedes to minorities and hence it is the noblest cry that has ever resounded in this planet" (quoted in *Willful Liberalism* at 103 and in *Reflections* at 41–42; Ortega y Gasset 1932, 83–84). I am interested in this passage not so much as it might be taken as being about the political structure of a liberal polity but as it illustrates the ideal of character that Flathman admires and points toward through the use of terms like "individuality" and "self-enactment." The ideal is, I think, both deeply attractive and yet ultimately objectionable, and for much the same reason. Flathman brings out the attractive aspect throughout his writings, and I do not mean to deny it; but I do want to remark upon what seems to me to be its potentially darker side.

To do so, I want to call up two passages from Shakespeare that speak to the same ideal, passages that Walter Kaufmann identified as expressive of the great humanist ideal of individuality embodied in Shakespeare's work (Kaufmann 1960).

> O, it is excellent
> To have a giant's strength; but it is tyrannous
> To use it like a giant.
> *(Measure for Measure,* 2.2. 107–9)

> They that have the power to hurt and will do none,
> That do not do the thing they most do show,
> Who, moving others, are themselves as stone,
> Unmoved, cold, and to temptation slow:

They rightly do inherit heaven's graces
And husband nature's riches from expense,
They are the lords and owners of their faces
Others, but stewards of their excellence.

(Sonnet 94. 1–8)

What I take to be common to all three passages is that all note the necessity of power to the successful performance of powerlessness as a feature of the ideal exemplified. It may be that I do an injustice to Flathman's understanding of the ideal of individuality in seeing this as a crucial aspect of it and in linking it to the ideal expressed by Shakespeare. I am tempted to partially blame this on Flathman, for not saying more about the character of his ideal. But the nobler path is surely to accept responsibility for the attribution and connections myself, leaving the chips to fall where they may—so I will, proceeding on the assumption that my connections are accurate.

Flathman likes Ortega y Gasset because even if he "can't quite bring himself to celebrate deviance, at least his liberalism eschews the claim to a reason, to a truth, or to any privileged standpoint on the basis of which to condemn or to regret instances of deviance" (*Reflections,* 22). I, too, find this renunciation of what amounts to foundationalism attractive, but it distracts attention from the further fact that what is not renounced, but indeed is rather presupposed, is the vantage point of power from which such noble acts of liberality through self-restraint might proceed. Only the giant can manifest the excellence of renouncing the tyrannical possibilities of gianthood; perhaps it is true that this renunciation is necessary to making him, as we democrats would now probably say, truly a giant in the deepest sense, but it is still a virtue of the high and mighty, not of the ordinary and plebian, and it requires a field of inequality for its conception and execution.

But is this necessarily a bad thing? I think it depends upon what might be posed as alternatives. It is not some version of an egalitarian alternative that I wish to offer up here as a contrast but, rather, the possibility of a renunciation more thorough than what is displayed by the noble giant. As Niccolò Machiavelli mischievously pointed out when discussing the virtue of liberality in the sixteenth chapter of *The Prince,* the liberal prince needs money, preferably someone else's, to spend, and so the exercise of the so-called virtue seems to rest upon the practices of so-called vices, such as theft and stinginess. A prince who is truly liberal will quickly go broke and become despised for his stinginess. Thus it is, that many things that appear to be virtues are not. Machiavelli "ventures to say" that "when you have them [virtues conventionally understood] and exercise them all the time, they are harmful to you; when you just seem to have them, they are useful" (Machiavelli 1977, 50). A similar dynamic characterizes the noble man of power in our example. His concession is to tolerate what he could destroy, but he needs the power to destroy to effect the concession in its noble form. He needs power in order to renounce it, and thus is at odds with himself. But what if he renounced the power by abandoning it? What if he decided not to tolerate the weak, nor even to go further and manifest equal concern and respect for them, but decided instead to serve them, according to their need and their expression of their need, leaving power behind? I believe this possibility calls into question the ideal expressed in Ortega y Gasset's formulation, by radicalizing its element of renunciation. But I claim no more than that, knowing that such an ideal of life is preached more than it is practiced, if indeed it ever is.

Conclusion

> A self-esteeming and cheerful, certainly a buoyant if only intermittently optimistic man, Hobbes was not one to regret what might be regarded as the insouciance or even malice of God, the fact that the "Author of Nature" had written human beings into largely unfriendly circumstances and left them to cope as best they could by their own inventings and devisings.... Hobbes did not stint in detailing the difficult, troubled character of human affairs. He nevertheless believed that there are a number of respects in which human beings have done quite well in and with their makings, yet other respects in which by his time they were positioned to do markedly better for themselves than their predecessors had managed. (Flathman, *Thomas Hobbes*, 3–4)

I do not know Richard Flathman well enough to say whether in thus engagingly describing the character of Thomas Hobbes he is describing himself. I am rather more confident, having read Flathman's writings, in saying that in describing Hobbes he is describing significant elements of the character to which he would aspire. And I know that he is describing a character that I think admirable.

The theorizing that occurs in Flathman's texts is both in and out of harmony with the predominant mode of discourse in political theory. It is in harmony insofar as the object of its attention is nothing other than that mode of discourse itself. This remains true even allowing for the fact that Flathman wishes to invite into that conversation some guests whose liberal credentials are questionable at the least (his "strong voluntarists": William James, William of Ockham, Hobbes, and especially Nietzsche). For if these are guests rarely invited to the liberal conversation, it nevertheless remains true that Flathman wishes to bring them into that conversation, not to follow them elsewhere. *Willful Liberalism* is a plea to liberals for a hearing, and a promise that such a hearing will be fruitful.

The sense in which Flathman's theorizing is out of harmony with the dominant mode of liberal discourse is thus not primarily a matter of the voices he would have us entertain. It is, rather, that he has no fully positive program (rules or principles) of his own to put forth as a contestant in the great battle over how to properly articulate the terms of liberal political order, what is allowed and not allowed, what is acceptable and unacceptable, what is to be done and what is to be denied—in short, the terms of how to run the world. The contractarians and the utilitarians, the perfectionists and the neutralists, the deontologists and the teleologists, the libertarians and the paternalists, the republicans and the proceduralists, the advocates of virtue and the advocates of law, the merely political and the fully comprehensive, the foundationalists and the antifoundationalists, and so on and so forth; all stake a claim, put forth a program, take a position on how to properly exercise rule, whether in the sense of actual ruling or of the vicarious ruling that takes the form of arguing about how to properly argue over how to rule and how to argue about it. To participate fully and completely in this contestational dialogue, one must affirm a program of one's own. That program can arise out of the ashes of the alternative programs one has torched, but anyone without a position to propose and defend is not fully in the game.

"Willful liberalism" is Flathman's proposal in this context, but I do not believe his heart is fully in it. It is, as he himself admits in passing, a view that "leaves open most of the issues of public policy" (and he does not go on to say what falls outside that "most") (*Willful Liberalism*, 13). Now, to be sure, Flathman reminds us (and himself?) that "liberal political theory need not...restrict itself to the question of what the state should and should not do" (*Reflections,* 44). But he is swimming against the tide in saying so, and the strain of that exercise characterizes his articulation of the willful type of liberalism. Flathman at times speaks of himself as "haunted" by anarchism, and the importance of that haunting to his thinking is revealed by the fact that he goes so far at times as to say that liberals generally ought to be haunted by it; a generalization of attitude that he usually resists and indeed criticizes, often referring to Nietzsche's willful refusal to will that his ideal should be generalized to everyone: "'This is what *I* am; this is what *I* want:—*you* can go to hell!'" (quoted in *Willful Liberalism*, 177, 190; and in *Reflections*, 167 n. 9, 168 n. 3; Nietzsche 1967, para. 349, p. 191). Anarchism, understood for the moment simply as the refusal to participate in the enterprise of political ruling, haunts Flathman because he takes it so seriously, to the point that (as I read him) he thinks his ultimate refusal to affirm anarchism, choosing instead to "countenance...notions such as the state, authority and rule" (*Willful Liberalism*, 208) may be a failure or inability on his part rather than a sound judgment. I indulge this hypothesis on the observation that although Flathman chooses at a number of points to declare that he does not affirm anarchism, he chooses never to engage in any criticism of it. (For example, see *Reflections*, 79–80.) And he is not ordinarily reticent about stating what he thinks is wrong with a position he thinks is wrong.

Mainstream liberalism, however, shows little sign of being haunted by the thought that anarchism may be the better part of its conscience. Devoted to the business of specifying the appropriate terms of rule, whether in the form of general principles of justice and order or justifications of particular policies, discourses like Flathman's appear from its purview to be indulgences that fail to engage truly serious concerns. The theme is repeated in many of the reviews of *Willful Liberalism*. Raymond Belliotti speculates that political theorists "may tire of the author's lengthy discussion of voluntarism, will, and mutual intelligibility, and instead yearn for a clearer exposition of the practical implications of Flathman's refined liberalism" (Belliotti 1993, 612). In a generally positive review, Don Herzog nevertheless complains that "Flathman does not take up the constructive task of even sketching what our new and improved liberalism will look like in any serious detail" (Herzog 1993, 475). And even Richard Rorty, not ordinarily known as a proponent of the constructive tasks of political philosophy, complains that "it is hard to figure out what problem Flathman is addressing and what he has contributed to its solution" (Rorty 1994, 190).

These criticisms presuppose a conception of what a political theory should be doing, and my contention has been that Flathman's theorizing is best understood, despite appearances, not as a contributor to that activity on its own terms but as an attempt to call those terms into question through partial participation within them. The "lengthy discussion[s] of voluntarism, will, and mutual intelligibility" are not preludes to the serious business of laying out authoritative rules but attempts to remind us of what the purpose of having such rules is and of the price that must be paid for them. I think that a better description of the aim of theory as realized in Flathman's efforts is indirectly given in one of his remarks aimed at explicating Oakeshott's idea of the rule of law. Flathman says there that the "distinguishing features of this vision... are not its institutions or practices in what we might call their material, rule-governed form but rather the understandings its *personae* have of themselves, of their relationships with one another, and of the arrangements to which they mutually subscribe" (*Reflections*, 72).

The discourse of willful liberalism as I read it aims at invigorating and deepening the self-understanding of the reflective consciousness of the liberal mind. There is no direct payoff of such an enterprise in terms of problems solved or decisions made. Whether such an enterprise is nevertheless to be judged to be useful is one of the oldest questions in political life. The horses tend to doubt it, and the gadflies claim otherwise.

References

Bauman, Zygmunt. 1987. *Legislators and Interpreters*. Cambridge: Polity Press.
Belliotti, Raymond. 1993. "Review of Willful Liberalism." *Review of Metaphysics* 46, no. 3 (March 1993): 611–12.
Cover, Robert. 1983. "Nomos and Narrative." *Harvard Law Review* 97, no. 1 (November 1983): 4–68.
Flathman, Richard E. 1989. *Toward a Liberalism*. Ithaca, N.Y.: Cornell University Press.
———. 1992. *Willful Liberalism: Voluntarism and Individuality in Political Theory and Practice*. Ithaca, N.Y.: Cornell University Press.
———. 1993. *Thomas Hobbes: Skepticism, Individuality, and Chastened Politics*. Newbury Park, Calif.: Sage Publications.
———. 1998. *Reflections of a Would-Be Anarchist: Ideals and Institutions of Liberalism*. Minneapolis: University of Minnesota Press.
George, Robert P. 1993. *Making Men Moral: Civil Liberties and Public Morality*. Oxford: Clarendon Press.
Hegel, G. W. F. 1952. *Philosophy of Right*. Trans. T. M. Knox. Oxford: Clarendon Press.

Herzog, Don. 1993. "Review of Willful Liberalism." *American Political Science Review* 87, no. 2. (June 1993): 474–75.
Kaufmann, Walter. 1960. *From Shakespeare to Existentialism.* Garden City, N. Y.: Anchor Books.
Macedo, Stephen. 1990. *Liberal Virtues: Citizenship, Virtue, and Community in Liberal Constitutionalism.* Oxford: Oxford University Press.
Machiavelli, Niccolò. [1537] 1977. *The Prince.* Trans. Robert Adams. New York: W. W. Norton.
Nietzsche, Friedrich. [1901] 1967. *Will to Power.* Trans. Walter Kaufmann and R. J. Hollingdale. New York: Vintage Books.
Ortega y Gasset, José. 1932. *The Revolt of the Masses.* New York: W. W. Norton.
Rawls, John. 1993. *Political Liberalism.* New York: Columbia University Press.
Rooney, Ellen. 1989. *Seductive Reasoning: Pluralism as the Problematic of Contemporary Literary Theory.* Ithaca, N.Y.: Cornell University Press.
Rorty, Richard. 1994. "Review of Willful Liberalism." *Political Theory* 10, no. 1 (February 1994): 191–94.

CHAPTER TWO

The Skepticism of Willful Liberalism

Linda Zerilli

> The life of skepticism with respect to (other) minds...require[s] a history of its imagined overcomings, particularly of its idea that to know or be known by another is to penetrate or be penetrated by another.
>
> —STANLEY CAVELL, *The Claim of Reason*

Reading a recent essay by Richard Flathman, "Liberality, Idiosyncracies, Idiolects," I came across the following parenthetical remark: "Most of the liberal theorists mentioned above [e.g., John Rawls, David Truman, Amy Gutmann, T. H. Green, Ronald Dworkin] write as if skeptics from Sextus to Cicero to Montaigne to Pascal to Hume and up to the emotivists and deconstructionists never put pen to paper."[1] Notwithstanding its syntactic placement as an observational aside, the remark is telling because it marks the difference between Flathman and the liberal tradition that he writes both with and against. Flathman's debt to skepticism marks the difference between him and other liberals, a difference that is expressed in his desire to move "beyond toleration and respect for rights to liberality and magnanimity toward idiolects" (*Reflections,* 27). Indeed, in contrast to liberals who avoid the skeptical tradition (such as Rawls) or who are deeply wary about what they take to be the political consequences of skeptical views (such as Richard Rorty), Flathman embraces the skeptic's objections to any claim to commonalities, especially those grounded in "the operations of shared reason" (*Reflections,* 26).

The skeptical tradition provides Flathman with an alternative genealogy from which to rethink "liberal settlements" (*Reflections,* 27), to question epistemic conceptions of social and political community, and to articulate what he calls "willful liberalism" or "the notion of liberality treated as an individuating *virtù*" (*Reflections*, 17). The liberal notion of shared rationality and reasonableness as the basis for community, he argues, is not sustainable in the face of skeptical critiques of knowledge and belief. What is valuable for the willful liberal is the skeptic's stance toward every attempt to justify beliefs. If competing beliefs cannot be justified, as the skeptic maintains, then we are compelled to suspend judgment, and if we suspend judgment, says Flathman, we can avoid the social violence generated by a conviction of the truth of one's own views and the falsity of another's; we can practice not just tolerance but magnanimity—the distinguishing trait of a willful liberal.

"Rejecting the view that we hold our beliefs because of something apart from us and in principle accessible to all of us," Flathman's willful liberal, then, looks to skepticism to contest what he sees as the unwarranted intrusions, sometimes tolerated or justified by liberals themselves, into the lives of those with whom one disagrees. There are at least two dimensions of the skeptical outlook that Flathman finds useful for cultivating magnanimity among theorists and practitioners of willful liberalism: (1) The "skeptical outlook largely deprives others of the possibility of refuting my beliefs and hence of the *justifications* for actions vis-à-vis me that may be provided by evidence or argumentation showing that my beliefs are false." According to the skeptic and famously argued by David Hume, *all* belief is unjustified. (2) "On the extension of skepticism just outlined, you are also unable or little able to understand why I hold my beliefs, how I came to hold them. It follows that the *possibility* of your acting skillfully and efficaciously to alter my beliefs is diminished, if not eliminated."[2]

Citing Ludwig Wittgenstein's remark that "one human being can be a complete enigma to another" (quoted in *Willful Liberalism*, 100), Flathman affirms that "our claims to mutual intelligibility are delusive, if not vain, conceits" (112), for which a healthy dose of skepticism is the antidote. "Opacity creates spaces protective of individuality and plurality," he writes, "[making] it difficult and sometimes impossible for those who are other to individuals or groups to know or to understand them well enough to diminish their distinctiveness by acting with or against them" (112). I take this claim to mean two things: (1) that individuality consists in some way in unknowability, and (2) that opacity sets limits to legitimate intrusions into the lives of individuals on the part of the majority, society, or the state. Consequently, two sets of questions arise for me: (1) Why should we assume that mutual opacity is a condition of human singularity? Why should one person's distinctiveness depend on his or her remaining an enigma to others? (2) Why should a phenomenological fact about our mutual opacity—assuming that we are in fact mutually opaque—generate a normative idea of individuality as something to be protected? Why should what one person cannot know about another lead beyond toleration to a generous (personal and political) acknowledgment of others' singularity?

Flathman recognizes that in certain circumstances, mutual opacity can generate not liberality but indifference and even violence toward others (*Willful Liberalism*, 115, 116, 118). He also recognizes that if "pressed very hard, the view that there is not (or should not be) *any* mutual intelligibility" leads him to "the brink of absurdities" and cannot in fact be sustained (113). In light of these and similar qualifications to his claim that mutual opacity protects individuality, I am led to rethink that claim as an attempt to make visible the antiliberal elements in those liberal political theories that begin with the premise that transparency obtains or ought to obtain in human affairs. Flathman wants to question the "shared but seldom examined assumption" that "self- and mutual understanding" (92) is fundamental to all social and political interaction, that is, that we know what we are agreeing or disagreeing about. He is trying to complicate the debate over "the relationship between individuality and other forms of plurality" (7) by defending "the thesis of complementarism": the idea "that robust and widely distributed individualities are productive of group and associational life, and that the latter support and stimulate the former" (8). Although Flathman takes issue with theorists like William James and Friedrich Nietzsche, for whom groups almost always spell the death of individuals, his real target is the body of recent liberal political thought that seems to have forgotten that "an emphasis on individuality is rooted in the liberal tradition" (9).

Flathman's valorization of "indeterminacy, opacity, and incomprehensibility" (*Willful Liberalism*, 119), then, should be read as an attempt to reveal how liberalism comes to be at odds with its own best ideals precisely to the extent that it valorizes determinacy, transparency, and comprehensibility. This is an important and difficult insight. Opening himself to the absurdities mentioned above, Flathman allows us to see how liberalism, when it emphasizes the legibility of social subjects and the communicability of their differences, is driven in the direction of its opponents: "group theories... and communitarian theories that insist on deeply situated and harmonized selves" (119). He also allows us both to imagine alternatives to political theories that compromise, finally, the very thing they want to protect—individuality—and to rethink the normative project of making people transparent to each other that undergirds large elements of the liberal tradition.

I am strongly sympathetic to Flathman's critical project, especially as it concerns the development and appreciation of human singularity, but I am not convinced by his intellectual strategy. To oppose the drive for transparency in human affairs with the valorization of opacity, as Flathman generally does, is to remain entangled in the classical epistemological model of knowledge (of others), a model that raises serious problems for Flathman's efforts to renew liberalism. Notwithstanding Flathman's creative, and to my mind unique, attempts to bring liberalism into dialogue with Wittgenstein, who radically questions the classical model, willful liberalism is haunted by the ghost of privacy as it is described by Stanley Cavell in the epigraph to this chapter. This notion of privacy as a boundary or line that separates subjects from each other, and whose crossing constitutes a violation or transgression, is central to the liberal tradition, both as it emerged and as it is still, tethered to the legacy of René Descartes and the modern skeptical tradition. It is based on a concept of the self as fundamentally private, as something that is hidden from others. According to the classical model, one's relation to one's own private states is a relation of knowledge; this knowledge is immediate and incorrigible, and it presents the definitive model of what knowing a mind is. It therefore follows that one can never know another as one knows oneself. One can be certain about one's own subjective states, but at best, one can only infer those of others.

It is not quite right to say, as I did above, that what distinguishes Flathman from other liberals is his engagement of the skeptical tradition.[3] And it is not quite right to say, as Flathman does, that liberals write as if skeptics never put pen to paper. On the contrary, both the willful and all the other liberals write within the frame of the skeptical problematic; the difference is that the former does it, shall we say, willfully, and the latter, reactively. Flathman consciously draws on skepticism in order to raise questions about the very solutions (e.g., rationalism, foundationalism, empiricism) that liberalism has adopted to combat the effects of skepticism. He rightly rejects liberalism's various attempts to solve the fundamental problems that skepticism raises for politics, namely, solipsism and worldlessness, inasmuch as those solutions drive liberalism toward communitarianism. But what Flathman does not see clearly enough is that the willful liberal's principle of mutual opacity is not the answer to, but merely the flip side of, the communitarian liberal's ideal of mutual transparency, and that both are structured by the problem of other minds as it arises within the classical model of knowledge. To counter transparency with opacity is to sustain the fundamental concept of the unknowableness of the other, of the self as private, and thus to sustain the distinction between the inner and the outer.

As I discuss in detail below, Flathman is concerned not to substitute the principle of opacity in human relations for that of transparency but to find a balance that would accord with his thesis of complementarism. My quarrel with Flathman is not that he places too much emphasis on the theme of opacity; that emphasis makes sense in light of the counteremphasis on transparency and the entire epistemic structure of the liberal arguments that he is criticizing. Rather, my point is that he does not question—at least, not clearly or deeply enough—that epistemic structure itself. I find intriguing Flathman's unwitting concession to the classical model, not least because he is a careful and appreciative reader of Wittgenstein. In what follows, I want to read Wittgenstein with and against Flathman to locate the places where Flathman's interpretation of Wittgenstein differs from mine, and where the problems I have indicated arise.

We have seen that Flathman cites Wittgenstein's remark that one human being can be a complete enigma to another as support for the idea that human affairs are in important respects characterized not by transparency but by opacity. However, if we read that remark in the context of Wittgenstein's critical account of epistemic privacy, for which the classical opposition transparency/opacity is fundamental, we can see where Flathman's interpretation remains tied to the very epistemic model that Wittgenstein questions. The remark, which I now want to cite in full and set in context, occurs in part II, section xi of the *Philosophical Investiga-*

tions. It is part of a broader discussion of the notion of privacy, or the idea, as Wittgenstein puts it here, that what is *internal* is hidden from us:

> If I see someone writhing in pain with evident cause I do not think: all the same, his feelings are hidden from me.
>
> We also say of some people that they are transparent to us. It is, however, important as regards this observation that one human being can be a complete enigma to another. We learn this when we come into a strange country with entirely strange traditions; and, what is more, even given a mastery of the country's language. We do not *understand* the people. (And not because of not knowing what they are saying to themselves.) We cannot find our feet with them.
>
> "I cannot know what is going on in him" is above all a *picture.* It is the convincing expression of a conviction. It does not give the reasons for the conviction. *They* are not readily accessible.
>
> If a lion could talk, we could not understand him.[4]

In *Willful Liberalism,* Flathman invokes the second paragraph cited above in his argument with the transparency liberals, that is, those who emphasize a system of "shared beliefs, rules, and conventions." In such a setting, writes Flathman,

> we sometimes even "say of some people that they are transparent to us." The very features of language-games that enable such relationships and interactions, however, also diminish or disable these possibilities between or across the boundaries of the games. "It is, however, important as regards this observation [of transparency] that one human being can be a complete enigma to another." (*Willful Liberalism,* 100)

Flathman invokes Wittgenstein here, first, to concede a point about mutual transparency, and second, to contest it. We are thus left with the impression that Wittgenstein would have us appreciate the *experience* of mutual transparency but also limit it with that of mutual opacity. (We saw above that this is the very position that Flathman himself adopts in the conclusion to chapter three of *Willful Liberalism.*) If my account of Flathman's reading of this passage from *Philosophical Investigations* is correct, his interpretation of Wittgenstein on the question of other minds is problematic. Wittgenstein is not trying to balance one account (mutual transparency) with another (mutual opacity), as Flathman would have us read him; he is questioning the very structure of this opposition itself.

Wittgenstein begins with a commonplace: "[W]hat is *internal* is hidden from us."[5] He does so in order to show us the other commonplaces that sustain it, the first of which is none other than the claim "We ... say of some people that they are transparent to us." That some people are transparent to us is something *we say*, not something that either is or is not in a metaphysical or ontological sense. The notion of transparency belongs to a language-game of other minds, of what it means to know another human being. We may imagine and articulate our relationship to others in terms of transparency—or its opposite: "It is, however, *important as regards this observation* that one human being can be a complete enigma to another." I have italicized part of this sentence to call attention to the relationship that Wittgenstein draws here between one observation (some people are transparent to us) and another observation (some people are not transparent, they are enigmas). This relationship between two mutually constitutive perspectives on knowing the other is clearer in the original German: "Wir sagen auch von einem Menschen, er sei uns durchsichtig. Aber es ist für diese Betrachtung wichtig, daß ein Mensch für einen andern ein völliges Rätsel sein kann." [We also say of someone that he is transparent to us. It is, however, important for this observation that one human being can be a complete enigma to another.] When translated this way, we can see that, according to Wittgenstein, it is important to consider what we also say about opacity, but not because it is an alternative to the experience of transparency, as if we needed to take both experiences into account. Rather it is important *for* the observation that one person is transparent to another—for what we say—*that* we make the opposite observation, namely, that one person is opaque to another, an enigma, and vice versa.[6]

The problem here is not our ordinary language. Wittgenstein is not making a general statement, as philosophy does and as Flathman tends to do, about the opacity or transparency of other people. It is significant in this context that the German is written in the singular ("*von einem Menschen*" [of someone]) and not the plural ("of some people"). We can and often do say of *someone* that *he* is transparent to us. We can and often do say of *someone* that *he* is an enigma to us. The problem that Wittgenstein is elaborating in these sentences is not our ordinary use of such terms—which concerns judgments about particulars—but the tendency to move from the particular to an abstract generalization about the status of other minds.[7] This is the very tendency that leads Flathman to read these passages from *Philosophical Investigations* as if they were a commentary on our general experience of other people, whereas they are at best a commentary made by *someone* about *someone*. That a particular statement (we say of someone that he is an enigma to us) comes to be formulated as a universal statement (human beings are enigmas to each other) is the very problem that Wittgenstein associates with traditional philosophy and its highly abstract interpretation of—that is, flight from—ordinary language.

When Wittgenstein, in the very next passage, writes, "'I cannot know what is going on in him' is above all a *picture*. It is the convincing expression of a conviction. It does not give the reasons for the conviction. *They* are not readily accessible," he calls our attention once again to something *we say* and to the invisible frame of reference in which we say it and within which it has meaning. That Wittgenstein should call what we say about (not) knowing the other a "picture" is consistent with his critical use of the term as one that expresses our human disappointment with the reach of human knowledge.[8] This picture image follows beautifully from his comment "Aber es ist für diese Betrachtung wichtig." Although Anscombe translates *Betrachtung* as "observation" (which is actually *Beobachtung* in German), *Betrachtung* indicates an act of looking in the sense of "contemplation" *(das Betrachten)* or way of looking at things *(die Betrachtungsweise)*. The English notion of observation suggests, to my mind at least, a more empirical point of view, such as the dual experience of transparency and opacity that corresponds to Flathman's interpretation of these passages. The notion of contemplation or way of looking at things suggests, in contrast, an attitude and thus the rather different point that I have been trying to draw out of Wittgenstein's remarks on what we say: We are caught in a picture of other minds.

Whereas Flathman reads Wittgenstein as calling our attention to "the experiences of opacity, occlusion, and even stark incomprehensibility [of others]" (*Willful Liberalism*, 100), I read him as trying to clarify those experiences as part of a language-game of other minds, a game that remains within the classical model of knowledge. Wittgenstein's remarks on opacity and transparency are less observations on what we experience than investigations of what we say about our experience (of ourselves and of others) and about how what counts as that experience is shaped by what we say. This is an important distinction. If one reads Wittgenstein as a theorist of experience, as I believe Flathman does, one misses or misconstrues his fundamental contribution to the debate on epistemic privacy, namely, that our language of experience has meaning only insofar as there exist public criteria for its correct use (hence, there cannot be, on Wittgenstein's account, a completely private language). My sense is that Flathman both recognizes and resists this crucial insight. In what follows I will try to explain why this is the case.

In many respects, Flathman appreciates Wittgenstein's public conception of language and critique of epistemic privacy, employing it to criticize the tendency toward solipsism in thinkers whom he otherwise admires, such as William James (*Willful Liberalism*, 73). But if we pause for a moment and turn to Flathman's reading of James (which is, not coincidentally, sandwiched between two readings of Wittgenstein), we can perhaps see if and to what extent Flathman clings to the very notion of privacy that he also understands Wittgenstein to have rendered incoherent. What Flathman finds appealing in James's radical empiricism is his idea of mutual opacity, an idea that emerges clearly in his *Principles of Psychology*, in which the mind is described in the skeptical terms of "absolute isolation." So radically private are thoughts, wrote James, that "neither contemporaneity, nor proximity in space, nor similarity of quality and content are able to fuse thoughts together which are sundered by this barrier of belonging to personal minds" (quoted in *Willful Liberalism*, 72).

Turning to the late Wittgenstein and his critique of the idea of a private language, Flathman recognizes the incoherence in James's "near, if not actual, solipsism" (*Willful Liberalism*, 73). Wittgenstein teaches us, he writes, that "meaning or intelligibility is exclusively a public or social or group phenomenon in that it requires a minimum of two persons who share standards or criteria the satisfaction of which makes perceptions, thoughts, and feelings, *this* perception, *this* thought as opposed to any other or none" (73). The solipsist lacks the criteria with which to make such distinctions and therefore cannot even have any thoughts at all, let alone strictly private ones.

Having agreed with this critique, Flathman goes on to wonder: "If we accept Wittgenstein's arguments, does it follow that we must do without the 'relish' and the protections for individuality that James found in and hoped for from his privatism and solipsism?" (*Willful Liberalism*, 73). The question itself already indicates that Flathman is inclined to equate the fact of the publicness of language with the "dreary conformity" that he laments throughout *Willful Liberalism* and that he finds either present or latent in all forms of commonality and group association. Accordingly, the common (plurality) demands mutual intelligibility, but individuality demands mutual opacity. But since we cannot talk coherently about individuals without talking about the common, as Wittgenstein shows and Flathman agrees, we are faced with the question of how to concede the latter without destroying the former. Consequently, Flathman's strategy is to redeem the opacity that is problematically associated with James's solipsism but necessary to his individualism by making unintelligibility into the necessary condition of a Wittgensteinian public conception of meaning. This can be seen by turning to Flathman's immediate qualification of his interpretation of Wittgenstein's private-language argument:

> [Wittgenstein's] account of the conditions necessary to meaning or intelligibility is also and equally an account of the conditions of meaninglessness or unintelligibility.
> ... That is, identifications of instances of meaninglessness are always and necessarily parasitic on identified (to our satisfaction) instances of the meaningful, but instances of the latter enable identifications and valorizations of the former. To adapt a familiar... metaphor, standing on the deck of the ship... of meaning that we have built and thus far managed to keep intact, we can locate and welcome or regret unmeaning in and about us. Understood in this way, Wittgenstein has nothing to jeopardize the "meaninglessness" or the possibility of the special challenge and savor of acting against "it." (*Willful Liberalism*, 74)

If I understand this account of the relationship between meaning and unmeaning in Wittgenstein, it appears to assume that we do not have to sacrifice, in Flathman's parlance, mutual unintelligibility (the condition of individuality) for mutual intelligibility (the condition of plurality and the common) because the one is the condition of the other. There is something correct in this interpretation, namely, that according to Wittgenstein, an instance of meaning is not a self-identical form that is absolutely distinguished from an instance of nonmeaning; we can never attain a position of pure meaning from which all instances of nonmeaning would be barred. And yet there is also something wrong here. Consider the sentence that immediately follows the passage just quoted: "Never *entirely* meaningful (whatever that might mean), our thinking and acting are distributed along a host of continua that move from (for example) the fluently articulated and readily grasped to the uncertain, the confusing, and the bewildering" (74). This does not seem quite right to me. To say that our thinking and acting are indeterminate, as Wittgenstein does, is not to say that they are never entirely meaningful. Rather, our thinking and acting are meaningful despite being indeterminate. That insight is at the core of Wittgenstein's devastating critique of the classical conception of rule-following.

The point here is not to rule out genuine instances either of nonmeaning (moments when we speak nonsense) or of varying degrees of unintelligibility (moments when we do not quite understand what someone is saying or thinking or feeling) but, rather, to argue with the idea that what is mutually intelligible and therefore common is defined somehow by a dreary uniformity that can only be undone by what is mutually unintelligible and therefore individual. Following Wittgenstein, one can valorize individuality, by turning not to instances of unintelligibility and nonmeaning (as Flathman does) but to instances of meaning, that is, cases in which we do follow a rule correctly, in which our speaking and acting are, therefore, intelligible to others. That is because, as Flathman surely knows, to follow a rule—say, to speak meaningfully—is in Wittgenstein's sense, a social practice carried on in a wide array of circumstances by a wide variety of people, who will vary from each other in their sense of how to apply a rule. And yet in each of these cases, we can say that they followed the rule. The rule itself is structurally indeterminate. A rule is not an object that governs our activity either from above (in the Platonic sense) or from below (in the communitarian one); a rule does not preexist individual acts of applying it.[9] What we perceive as "dreary conformity" is not an effect of rule-following as such, of the common as such, or of what is mutually intelligible as such.

The assumption that what is individual cannot be common, as Wittgenstein explains, is rooted in the skeptical conception of the mind as a private theater in which various objects—thoughts, sensations, and the like—are presented to the mind's eye. Each of us "lives out his mental life in a phenomenal bubble," as David Pears summarizes the solipsist's position.[10] The skeptic or solipsist claims that we cannot know how things stand with another person because we cannot have, literally, that person's feelings or thoughts. I cannot have your pain, to take Wittgenstein's famous example, and you cannot have mine. I *know* that I am in pain; you can only infer that I am in pain based on my behavior, which you interpret according to how you act when you are in pain:

that is, by analogy with yourself. Consequently you can never know my pain as I know it. Wittgenstein's account and response to this stance is most dryly expressed in paragraph 253 of the *Philosophical Investigations:*

> I have seen a person in a discussion on this subject [the ownership of pain] strike himself on the breast and say: "But surely another person cannot have THIS pain!"—The answer to this is that one does not define a criterion of identity by emphatic stressing of the word "this." Rather, what the emphasis does is to suggest the case in which we are conversant with such a criterion of identity, but have to be reminded of it.

Interpreting this passage, Cavell asks, "Why is this *the* answer, or any answer, since obviously it refuses to see what was meant, I mean to see what the breast-striker had in mind." Surely he did not mean to offer a criterion of identity. But that is just the point, says Cavell. "That's the humor in Wittgenstein's answer. It's point is that that's all, at best, that you *could* have comprehensibly been doing. You had the impression that you were demonstrating something profound, some metaphysical uniqueness, but you were demonstrating *nothing whatever,* except perhaps some species of emptiness." The "rebuke in Wittgenstein's answer" is directed at the "attempt to make an exception of myself in this way," an attempt that is at odds with what Cavell calls "the moral of the *Investigations* as a whole,"[11] namely, "the fact, and the state, of your (inner) life cannot take its importance from anything special in it. However far you have gone with it, you will find that what is common is there before you are" (*Claim of Reason,* 361).

This idea of the common as that which is there before I am is precisely the teaching of Wittgenstein that Flathman both recognizes and resists.[12] It is to escape some of the consequences of this teaching for a willful liberal's ideal of human singularity, itself shaped by the skeptical notion of privacy, that Flathman imported elements of a theory of meaning that are specific to the epistemic framework within which the solipsist James writes into Wittgenstein's account of the irreducible publicness of language. Although Flathman recognizes the flaw in the solipsist's attempt to cut out from the common world a private world of his own, what he resists, finally, is what appears to be Wittgenstein's trivialization of my inner life and thus of the difference between you and me. As Cavell explains,

> The importance about my sensation [say, pain] is that I have it. The uniqueness in question points not to some necessary difference between

> my sensation and yours (there may be none [i.e., you may well have a pain quite like mine, quite as excruciating]) but to the necessary difference between being you and being me, the fact that we are two. (*Claim of Reason*, 356)

The problem, in other words, is how to articulate the idea and the fact of human separateness.

The genuine insight of the skeptic, as Cavell explains, is to call our attention to human separateness. One person does not know with certainty what another feels or thinks. "But then something happens, and instead of pursuing the significance of these facts, he is emeshed... in questions of whether we can have the same suffering [or thoughts]."[13] Rather than treat the important insight into human separateness as the basis for a different way of relating to the other, the skeptic becomes obsessed with reiterating the impossibility of knowing the other (what Flathman will call mutual opacity). That is why the fantasy of a private language is so central to skepticism. This fantasy, writes Cavell,

> can be understood as an attempt to account for, and protect, our separateness, our unknowingness, our unwillingness or incapacity either to know or to be known. Accordingly, the failure of the fantasy signifies: that there is no assignable end to the depth of us to which language [the common] reaches; that nevertheless there is no end to our separateness. We are endlessly separate, for *no* reason. But then we are answerable for everything that comes between us. (*Claim of Reason*, 369–70)

Is it possible to preserve this fantasy of a private language while conceding that language is irreducibly public?

That is precisely the question that Flathman faces in his attempt to read Marcel Proust as the guardian of mutual opacity. In *Reflections of a Would-Be Anarchist*, Flathman tells us that Proust is able to acknowledge the "respects in which Charlus and Françoise go beyond the distinctive, the deviant, and the idiosyncratic to the unique, the singular, and the idiolectical" (28). The basis for this distinction is Flathman's argument that the first set of qualities (distinctive, deviant, idiosyncratic) "are always by contrast with and under the sign of the normal, the ordinary, the expected" (26). The problem, in other words, is that of individuality versus plurality or the common. Then, inasmuch as the notion of an idiolect raises the specter of a private language, Flathman adds that because their utterances count as language, "their performatives, rather than being private in the deep sense that Wittgenstein argues is a linguistic impossibility, must in principle have meaning for some number of others" (29). Still, what makes their utterances unique and idiolectical rather than distinctive and idiosyncratic (hence common), argues Flathman, is that which is unintelligible, that which the narrator Proust himself cannot understand. This reasoning seems circular to me. Inasmuch as Flathman has framed the problem of the common in terms of a "dreary conformism," whatever is uniquely individual is per definition not common, that is, not mutually intelligible. But if what is individual is really unintelligible (to the speaker as well as to others), then it would be a private language, and that drives Flathman into the absurdities that he, as a careful reader of Wittgenstein, knows all too well. And so we are back to saying that something in an idiolect means something to someone. But that is just another way of saying that it is common without actually saying as much.[14]

What exactly is Flathman's notion of mutual opacity construed to protect? Our separateness and unwillingness to know or to be known? Or is it perhaps a response to something else, namely, the fear of remaining unknown?

As Cavell sees it, the question Do I know of the other's existence? becomes the question Does the other know of my existence? And so it is that "a proof [skepticism] designed to cast doubt on the existence of *other* human beings winds up casting doubt on my own existence" (*Claim of Reason*, 460). And so it is that I am driven to insist on my difference, my existence—*this* pain! Resisting Wittgenstein's teaching, as Cavell writes, "I may be wishing to convey that you just do not know who or what I am. Far, accordingly, from wishing or sensing a need to define criteria with which we would be mutually attuned, I wish, or sense a need, to convey how perfectly, originally, I satisfy the criteria" (462). The perceived need to refine singularity that drives John Stuart Mill to claim that "the only proof of liberty lies in idiosyncracy" (*Claim of Reason*, 462), says Cavell, ends "when we no longer know whether we are idiosyncratic or not, which differences between us count, whether we have others" (*Claim of Reason*, 464). This is nothing other than the "dreary conformism" that Flathman would combat with his valorization of mutual opacity. But what if it turns out that a liberalism that celebrates mutual opacity does not promote individuality but, rather, contributes to our refusal to acknowledge it? What if our openness toward what is singular and unique was not at odds with the common, as Flathman assumes, but depended instead on our willingness to recognize the common, to recognize what is there before us?

Flathman sees that one's recognition of the limits on mutual understanding does not automatically translate into more liberality; the liberality is not given in the recognition of those limits itself but depends on what one does with it (see *Willful Liberalism*, 117–18). According to the argument that we have been considering from *Willful Liberalism*, then, the skeptical teaching of opacity does not guarantee liberality; it is merely its setting. But even if we agree with Flathman (as I do) that the transparency liberals are dead wrong, we are left with the question of whether my skeptical recognition of mutual opacity—the gap that separates you from me, that makes you and your beliefs an enigma to me—can ever serve as the setting for liberality and the enhancement of individuality and plurality. There are differences between Flathman's claim that we are often opaque to each other and the skeptic's claim that we can never know another, but what they share is the assumption that the question of the other is a problem of knowledge. But is it?

"What skepticism threatens is precisely irretrievable outsideness, an uncrossable line," writes Stanley Cavell.[15] Caught in the skeptical picture of other minds, we imagine that our relation to the other is akin to our relation to the speaking lion that Wittgenstein invoked in his comments on the relationship between the transparency and opacity of other human beings. "If a lion could talk, we could not understand him," not because this is the sort of opacity that we experience in relation to some human beings but because sharing a form of life is a condition of mutual intelligibility. But if humans do share a form of life—at a minimal level and in all the variety that Wittgenstein gives to that easily misunderstood phrase—what can it mean to say, except in the ordinary sense, that I do not understand someone, that someone is an enigma to me? The skeptical stance of mutual opacity that Flathman valorizes seems to limit what it means to acknowledge an other to an acknowledgment of the limits of my knowledge of that other, to an acceptance of the limits of my knowledge. But is my ethical or my political relationship to the other one of knowing, or of not knowing?

The lesson Wittgenstein teaches is not that either opacity or transparency defines human relations but that the very demand to know the other is incoherent. I can neither know nor not know the other because that demand is premised on the classical model of knowledge, the very model that is in question. I neither have nor do not have your pain. What is required of me, as Cavell shows us, is that I acknowledge your pain. But to do that, I have first to acknowledge our separateness, and that means that we are separate for no reason. Following Wittgenstein, Cavell shows that our incoherent demand to know the other is entangled with our claim that we do not know the other because something stops us: The other will not let himself be known. We are blind to the possibility that it is not the other who deceives us but, rather, we who deceive ourselves. We already "know" all there is to know about the other, but we have a stake in denying what we know. As Cavell says in his reading of Shakespeare's great tragic figure Othello: "What this man lacked was not certainty. He knew everything [about Desdemona: her love for him, her faithfulness to him], but he could not yield to what he knew, be commanded by it. He found out too much for his mind, not too little."[16]

The tragedy that Othello embodies is not the failure of knowledge. Rather, it is a failure of what Cavell calls acknowledgment. Accordingly, the issue is not whether or not I can know (with certainty) what you feel, but whether I acknowledge it. The issue at stake here is not your so-called legibility—how can I really know what you feel?—but my attitude toward you. Your pain is an expression that I have to be willing to count—to acknowledge—as something. I have to be willing to count that wince as something. "A failure to know might just mean a piece of ignorance, an absence of something, a blank. A failure to acknowledge is the presence of something, a confusion, an indifference, a callousness, an exhaustion, a coldness," writes Cavell (*Claim of Reason*, 264). Or, as Wittgenstein put it, "If I see someone writhing in pain with evident cause I do not think: all the same, his feelings are hidden from me." We can now better appreciate how this sentence from *Philosophical Investigations* relates to the sentences immediately following it, about how someone can either be transparent or an enigma to us. The issue for me when I see someone "writhing in pain" is not my experience of the transparent or the enigmatic character of other minds. The issue is not what I know, but what I will acknowledge.

In his brief references to Cavell on the difference between acknowledgment and knowledge, we can see how Flathman tends to blur the crucial distinction between acknowledging a limit to knowledge of the other and acknowledging the other. In his discussion of Proust, Flathman cites Cavell's notion of acknowledgment and treats acknowledgment as something that requires the failure of knowledge. Thus, we are told, Proust does not himself understand the idiolects of his characters Charlus and Françoise, but he acknowledges them. The problem with this interpretation is that it misses Cavell's whole point, which is not that we fail to know the other and thus must acknowledge him, but, rather, that our failure to acknowledge the other is not a failure of knowledge. We know all we need to know, but we fail to acknowledge it. This is an important difference. Acknowledgment goes beyond knowledge, as Cavell argues, because the other makes a claim on me. Responding (or not) to that claim is what acknowledgment (or its failure) entails.

Holding fast to the idea that acknowledgment entails recognizing the limit of our knowledge of the other, Flathman is driven to agree with and celebrate the very teaching of skepticism that Cavell, following Wittgenstein, questions. "The moral of skepticism," writes Cavell, is that "the human creature's basis in the world as a whole, its relation to the world [and the other] as such, is not that of knowing, anyway not what we think of as knowing" (*Claim of Reason*, 241). As James Conant shows in his reading of this passage, Cavell's point here is not to verify the skeptic's claim that we cannot know the other. Cavell is not saying with the skeptic—and by extension with Flathman—that our relation is one of *not knowing*; he is saying that our relation is not *that* of knowing.[17]

If we continue to construe the relation to the other, in skeptical fashion, as one of knowledge—the relative opacity or transparency of the other—we advance the mistaken view that what we lack is either more knowledge or the recognition of its limits. These two positions may seem opposed, but they are not. They are two interwoven responses to skeptical despair. Shunning opacity, the position advanced by the transparency liberal seeks more and better knowledge of the other, but that knowledge will be based on a series of arguments by analogy, which assume that the other is like the self (and thus knowable). Accepting opacity, the position advanced by the willful liberal respects the limits of that knowledge. The one liberal laments what the other liberal respects (opacity), but both draw the relation to the other in terms of knowledge, and specifically in terms of a boundary or line that, regrettably or happily, cannot be crossed. Once drawn, that line constitutes the surest way into the impasse of skepticism, argues Cavell: It marks the satisfaction of our craving for knowledge as requiring the transgression of a limit, human finitude. That is why the quasi-Kantian solution to the limits of knowledge, which Flathman's Wittgenstein accepts and Cavell's Wittgenstein rejects, is no solution at all but merely an invitation to transgression. I have difficulty seeing how it could serve as the basis for a more magnanimous liberalism.

I can see how Flathman might think that acknowledging the limits to our knowledge of others might generate a more magnanimous liberalism because, after all, so many crimes against others are carried out in the name of knowing (what is best for) them. For a person to recognize that he does not know (what is best for) another, as Flathman sees it, is to recognize that that other is an autonomous being capable of self-discipline and of defining his own ideals. Inasmuch as the claim to knowledge (of others) is often entangled with power (over them), argues Flathman, willful liberals abjure such a claim as well as the notion of shared reason that often accompanies it. They assert not the knowability but the "incomplete intelligibility" (*Willful Liberalism*, 219) of the other's will. Although willful liberals like Flathman do not look to reason to guarantee the common (as transparency liberals do), I argue that they betray their own ideal of strong voluntarism when they turn to (the limits of) cognition to secure that very ideal. Inasmuch as the relationship to the other is not given in shared reason (or beliefs or ideals or whatever) but is something to be constructed and practiced daily, Flathman's broad phenomenal claim about mutual opacity strikes me as an avoidance of that daily work. Not unlike the transparency liberal's claim about shared reason as the basis for ethics, the willful liberal's cognitive claim that one human being cannot know (what is best for) the other displaces the ethical work that is entailed in the quotidian practice of acknowledging the singularity of the other. It is this daily ethical practice, which has no epistemic guarantee, be it mutual opacity or mutual transparency, that I associate with the ideal of a more magnanimous liberalism.

When seen in terms of acknowledgment, the question of others is not one of being mutually opaque or mutually transparent but one of being mutually attuned. This attunement in language does not reduce to concepts of knowing or not knowing (intelligibility or unintelligibility, transparency or opacity); rather, it indicates our prior agreement in judgments—precisely the "ungrounded ground" of our believing that Flathman cites as Wittgenstein's contribution to the notion of self- and mutual opacity.[18] Such attunement by no means assures us that we do in fact know what another thinks or feels because the very concept of attunement itself is characterized by indeterminacy. But this indeterminacy in our attribution of feelings to others, as Michel Ter Hark explains, cannot be eliminated; it is not like a deficiency in skill or knowledge. According to Wittgenstein, he writes, "the pointlessness of sceptical uncertainty does not mean that 'Menschenkenntnis' is knowledge that can be formalized."[19] Indeterminacy in our relations with others is not something that we can overcome; rather, it is the horizon within which acknowledgment is both possible and necessary.

What enables us to acknowledge an other whom we cannot know in the way that skepticism both demands and denies is precisely the Wittgensteinian/Cavellian notion of the common that goes under name of the ordinary. As Flathman himself admits of strong voluntarists like James and Nietzsche, the mystery, the singularity, the mutual inaccessibility that they esteem and promote reside within and among and are inconceivable apart from the manifest, the ordinary, the shared, even the common elements of human experience (*Willful Liberalism*, 218).

Here, on the very last pages of *Willful Liberalism*, we have the insight that would lead Flathman out of the skeptical impasse that his work both reveals and contests. The real challenge for willful liberals, I conclude, is expressed in Flathman's rearticulation of this apparent antinomy: What is singular versus what is common, ordinary. To acknowledge the singular, one must begin with the ordinary. That is the lesson that Cavell draws from Wittgenstein and that is implicit in Flathman's critique of a liberalism based on shared reason.

What is the difference, Cavell asks, between knowledge and acknowledgment? "It isn't as if being in a position to acknowledge something is *weaker* than being in a position to know it. On the contrary: from my acknowledging that I am late it follows that I know I'm late ...; but from my knowing I am late, it does not follow that I acknowledge I'm late.... One could say: Acknowledgment goes beyond knowledge. (Goes beyond not, so to speak, in the order of knowledge, but in its requirement that I *do* something or reveal something on the basis of that knowledge)" (*Claim of Reason*, 256–57). Isn't this akin to what Flathman is suggesting when he concedes that my recognition of the limits on mutual understanding does not automatically translate into more liberality? The liberality is not given in the recognition of the limits to our self- and mutual understandings; rather, it depends on what I do with that recognition (see *Willful Liberalism*, 117–18). Indeed, the very ideal of a liberalism premised on strong voluntarism, on will rather than reason, demands the quotidian and particular work of acknowledgment rather than the abstract and universal guarantee of (failed) cognition. What has to be acknowledged is not the limits to cognition but the other. I have to acknowledge *you*. If Wittgenstein teaches us anything in this context, it is that to do just that, to acknowledge you, I can remain fully agnostic on the question of knowledge. To (not) know you, after all, does not mean to acknowledge you. That is something every willful liberal ought to know—but can he acknowledge it?

Notes

1. Richard Flathman, in *Reflections of a Would-Be Anarchist: Ideals and Institutions of Liberalism* (Minneapolis: University of Minnesota Press, 1998), 26; hereafter *Reflections*.

2. All from Richard Flathman, 1992. *Willful Liberalism: Voluntarism and Individuality in Political Theory and Practice* (Ithaca, N.Y.: Cornell University Press), 111; hereafter *Willful Liberalism*. See also *Willful Liberalism*, 109.

3. Flathman's use of the term "skepticism" seems to pertain to any thinker who questions claims to truth and belief. The sort of doubt he has in mind is not that of a Descartes but a less corrosive skeptical stance of the sort other thinkers have taken toward the morals and prejudices of philosophy, politics, and daily life. Among these thinkers, he includes not only obvious candidates like Hobbes but also Hannah Arendt: "Arendt's skepticism in the domains of metaphysics and epistemology, historiography and social theory is clear from her earliest essays forward . . . but she . . . conquered or concealed her doubts concerning the most distinctive claims of her political theory" (*Willful Liberalism*, 12). As far as I can tell, however, Arendt was not a *failed* skeptic because she never aimed to be a skeptic. Works like *The Human Condition* are powerful engagements of the skeptical problematic and its implications for politics and the common world. Arendt's focus, of course, was not the "gentleman's skepticism" of a Michel Montaigne, to borrow Myles Buryeat's description, but the all-consuming doubt of a Descartes; Myles Buryeat, "The Skeptic in his Time and Place," in *The Original Skeptics: A Controversy*, ed. Myles Buryeat and Michael Fried (Indianapolis: Hackett, 1997), 92–126, 99. Flathman does not engage skepticism at the same level as does Arendt; consequently, the problems (such as worldlessness) that deeply worried her never arise for him.

4. Ludwig Wittgenstein, *Philosophical Investigations,* trans. G. E. M. Anscombe, German-English edition (Oxford: Blackwell Publishers, [1953] 1997), 223; hereafter *Philosophical Investigations*.

5. As Michel Ter Hark explains, Wittgenstein distinguishes between the usual meaning of "hidden" and its metaphysical meaning: "In the usual sense 'hidden' means that one can't find something but that it *can* be found. In the philosophical sense the terms refers to something that is not just hard to find, but cannot be found at all: it is *impossible* to find"; see Hark, *Beyond the Inner and the Outer: Wittgenstein's Philosophy of Psychology,* trans. Anthony P. Runia (Dordrecht: Kluwer Academic Publishers, 1990), 128. The confusion of empirical and logical aspects leads to the idea of what Wittgenstein calls "a metaphysical hiding." One can say that someone hides his feeling from another, but not that they are a priori hidden. Feelings are not essentially hidden. Here as elsewhere in his work, Wittgenstein is not suggesting that we need to reform ordinary language. He is addressing a problem in philosophical thinking, a problem that arises in large part through a flight from the ordinary meaning of such sentences as "He is an enigma to me." Philosophical thinking turns this ordinary observation into a general principle of human relations, that is, that we can *never* know other people, and thus runs into nonsense.

6. "Wir sagen auch von einem Menschen, er sei uns durchsichtig" (*Philosophical Investigations,* para. 223). Translating the passage as "We also say of some people that they are transparent to us," Anscombe wrongly translates the singular ("*von einem Menschen*") as plural ("some people"). This translation makes it seem as if Wittgenstein were making a general statement about the opacity of other minds, whereas, as I argue, he is actually commenting on how a particular person may appear to us (i.e., as opaque). See note 7 below.

7. As Marjorie Perloff explains, "The use of the singular rather than Anscombe's plural is important because, in Wittgenstein's view, it is not *people* but only an individual who can be judged to be 'transparent' (or not transparent)"; Perloff, *Wittgenstein's Ladder: Poetic Language and the Strangeness of the Ordinary* (Chicago: University of Chicago Press, 1996), 75.

8. James Conant makes this point in his reading of Cavell; see Conant, "On Bruns, on Cavell," *Critical Inquiry* 17 (Spring 1991): 616–34. Perhaps the most famous use of the picture metaphor appears in *Philosophical Investigations:* "A picture held us captive. And we could not get outside it, for it lay in our language and language seemed to repeat it to us inexorably" (para. 116).

9. There is a huge debate over Wittgenstein's account of rule-following. Although no one (to my knowledge) argues that Wittgenstein endorses a Platonic notion of rule-following, some critics follow Samuel Kripke's argument that Wittgenstein endorses a communitarian view, largely in order to avoid the putative rule-skepticism opened up by certain sections of the *Philosophical Investigations;* see Kripke, *Wittgenstein: On Rules and Private Language* (Cambridge, Mass.: Harvard University Press, 1982). For a powerful critique of the communitarian view, see Henry Staten, *Wittgenstein and Derrida* (Lincoln and London: University of Nebraska Press, 1984).

10. David Pears, *The False Prison: A Study of Wittgenstein's Philosophy,* vol. 1 (Oxford: Clarendon Press, [1987] 1990), 48.

11. Stanley Cavell, *The Claim of Reason: Wittgenstein, Skepticism, Morality, and Tragedy* (Oxford: Oxford University Press, 1979), 461; hereafter *Claim of Reason.*

12. This sense of the common as an assault on individuality emerges in Flathman's critique of Arendt. Although there is much to admire in Arendt, says Flathman, "by locating the meanings of my 'actions' entirely in the responses of others to

them, in the stories that others tell about what I do," Arendt undercuts her critique of conformity (*Willful Liberalism*, 119, n. 38). Flathman's objection to Arendt is telling. For one thing, it reveals that he places far more importance on self-understanding than his account of opacity appears to allow. For Arendt, in contrast, it is the actor who remains an enigma to himself because he cannot control the meaning and effects of his actions. Arendt's notion of who someone is, in contrast to what he is, is deeply rooted in a public conception of speech and the subject of action.

13. Stanley Cavell, "Knowing and Acknowledging," in *Must We Mean What We Say?* (Cambridge: Cambridge University Press, 1976), 247.

14. Just after these comments on Proust, Flathman cites Wittgenstein's comment that religious notions like transubstantiation and immaculate conception are incomprehensible to him. "More generally he [Wittgenstein] argues that every attempt to articulate an ethic falls into unintelligible nonsense." But, Flathman adds, Wittgenstein maintained a deep admiration for that which "he cannot understand," and that "manifests, or rather embodies, the *virtù* of liberality" (*Reflections*, 30). This does not seem quite right to me. For one thing, Wittgenstein abandoned his earlier idea that religious propositions are in some sense unsayable and unintelligible, which seems to be Flathman's point, and turned instead to an analysis of their grammar. Words like "transubstantiation" come to play a particular role in a language-game and a form of life. When Wittgenstein asserts that he cannot understand these terms, what he means is not that they are unintelligible in the sense that Flathman seems to think, but that they cannot be made sense of if one uses an outside framework, like science. Religious statements are not knowledge claims. The same goes for Wittgenstein's views on ethics. Flathman's appropriation of Wittgenstein, in other words, is beholden to the picture-theory of language that was at the core of one of Wittgenstein's early works, the *Tractatus*, and that he later abandoned in favor of the notion of language-games, for which the "inside/outside" or "sayable/showable" or "intelligible/unintelligible" oppositions do not hold.

15. Stanley Cavell, *Disowning Knowledge in Six Plays by Shakespeare* (Cambridge: Cambridge University Press, 1987), 29. Quoted in Conant, "On Bruns, on Cavell," 633.

16. Cavell, *Disowning Knowledge*, 141. Quoted in Conant, "On Bruns, on Cavell," 631.

17. I am indebted here to James Conant's perceptive critique of Gerald Bruns's (mis)reading of Cavell; "On Bruns, on Cavell," 627.

18. Flathman argues, with Wittgenstein, that we simply cannot be aware of "the full range of assumptions and beliefs that inform our judgements and intentions and hence the actions we take" (*Willful Liberalism*, 94). In thoughtful readings of passages from *On Certainty*, Flathman emphasizes what Wittgenstein calls the "ungrounded grounds" of our thinking, believing, and acting. Once again, however, Flathman chooses to emphasize the "ways in which our languages and practices (along with and in part due to the ways in which they are serviceable for us) are incomplete, indeterminate, opalescent, opaque and occluded, are of the ambiguous, the dissonant, and the incomprehensible in our experiences of ourselves and others" (*Willful Liberalism*, 97). To the extent that this argument is directed at the rationalists and deliberative democrats who seem to think that we can in fact know the grounds of our believing, I am in full agreement with Flathman. Once again, however, the question I want to raise concerns the nature of Flathman's wager, namely,

that once we recognize the groundlessness of our believing, we will be, at the very least, more tolerant and hopefully more magnanimous in our support of genuine cultural diversity. My sense is that Wittgenstein, although he certainly does call our attention to the fact that we cannot have a view from nowhere but must judge from within a form of life, does not articulate this condition of judging in terms of intelligibility and unintelligibility. Rather, he emphasizes the background as the necessary but indeterminate context within which we exercise a skill. The ungrounded ground is where questions about meaning—Why is this color called red?—no longer make sense. This is what I *do*. It is my action that lies at the bottom of the language-game.

19. Hark, *Beyond the Inner and the Outer*, 146.

CHAPTER THREE

Breaking into the Prison of Practice: Flathman and Oakeshott on Theorizing and Doing

Peter Digeser

Sometime around the writing of *Willful Liberalism* (1992), Richard Flathman became a "lumper"—an idiosyncratic lumper, but a lumper nonetheless. Prior to that point, Flathman was a "splitter." In his earlier investigations of political concepts and ideas, Flathman painstakingly parsed distinctions and categories, analyzed all arguments great and small, and by gaining one yard at a time, showed (among other things) the significance of language to the study of politics, the meaning and value of authority, and the conceptual incoherence of positive freedom. In his later investigations, as Flathman has disclosed his own vision of liberalism and individuality, we get lumps of thinkers: John Locke, Immanuel Kant, G. W. F. Hegel, Jean-Jacques Rousseau, John Stuart Mill, T. H. Green, L. T. Hobhouse, John Rawls, Jürgen Habermas in one camp (virtue liberals); Mill (on his better days), Isaiah Berlin, William James, Friedrich Nietzsche, Michael Oakeshott in another camp (willful liberals); and other more idiosyncratic lumps—José Ortega y Gasset, Marcel Proust, and Ludwig Wittgenstein—or lumps of positions: civic, republican, democratic, and vocational forms of education. For the most part, Flathman's lumping has been in the service of moving beyond a set of positions and ideas that are impatient with or unfriendly toward the idiosyncratic, the unique, the individual. But old habits die hard. Whereas a pure lumper would be willing to divide the world into institutionalists and anti-institutionalists, lovers of rules and antinomians, or authoritarians and anarchists, Flathman refuses to endorse such easy distinctions. The complexity of the world requires splitting and complicating such lumps. As the title of his book *Reflections of a Would-Be Anarchist* (1998) suggests, Flathman would be an anarchist—if only his commitment to his perfectionist ideal of individuality did not require the very practices and institutions that constantly threaten and frequently cripple that ideal.

Flathman has also, I believe, remained a splitter on the fundamental question of the division between theory and practice. For pure lumpers, theory is one thing and practice another. In contrast, Flathman believes that theorists and practitioners are never just theorists or just practitioners: Theorizing cannot be entirely disconnected from practice, and practitioners unavoidably engage in a sort of theorizing. Consequently, the relationship between theory and practice is neither unidirectional nor simple. Moreover, Flathman's attentiveness to the complexity of this relationship has been an enduring theme throughout his work. In *Reflections of a Would-Be Anarchist*, however, we get what may be the strongest formulation of theory's role in practical life. Flathman argues that the great, enduring objectives of political theory include critically examining the deeper patterns of practices, institutions, beliefs, rules, and norms that justify and define a way of life as well as envisioning ideals worthy of pursuit (1998, xii–xv). In taking these objectives as his own, Flathman's political theory claims to be able to judge and guide practical life. Not only can it point to what is wrong in the world, but it can also show us what is right.

Yet there is something paradoxical about Flathman's ideal. If he is advocating a very strong sense of individuality, how can theory advance this ideal without violating the ideal itself, without turning the ideal into just another oppressive norm "for everybody"? Flathman's response is that the ideal is formal or adverbial and that consequently, it "not only allow[s], but invit[es] and celebrat[es] a changing diversity of substantive realizations" (1998, xiii). To understand what he means by the adverbial character of his ideal, it is important to highlight its Oakeshottian roots. For Oakeshott, moral rules (as opposed to theories) are adverbial in the sense that they may tell us how to do something, but they cannot tell us specifically what to do. From this perspective, moral rules are much like the rules of etiquette. They may tell us how to hold a soup spoon or how to make an introduction, but they do not tell us precisely what to eat or say. To the extent that Flathman sees political theory as adverbial, it tells practitioners how to do something but not precisely what to do. It cannot lay out specific policy recommendations, but it can tell us that policies should respect, cultivate, and encourage the particular ideal being advanced. In Flathman's case, "the highest ideal of liberalism is individuality understood as self-making or self-enactment" (1998, xvii).

Flathman's use of the term "self-enactment" is also Oakeshottian. For Oakeshott, self-enactment occurs when agents choose what sentiment to adopt in pursuing whatever they are pursuing (in contrast to self-disclosure, which entails choosing and pursuing wished-for ends) (Oakeshott 1975, 76). Oakeshott writes,

> The compunctions of self-enactment are, then, demands an agent makes upon himself in which he requires of himself a *delicatesse* of conduct which cannot be required of him by another, which he may not make a show of requiring of others, but which are not merely his own good opinions about himself: the requirement of thinking about himself as he should while doing what he ought. (1975, 77)

Self-enactment takes place when we impose on ourselves the demand to act with a generous spirit or with the sentiment of good faith. It is, of course, difficult to discern what another's motivations actually are, but that does not mean we cannot demand certain motivations from ourselves. To the extent that Flathman's ideal of individuality is a form of self-enactment, it is an ideal recommending the adoption of a particular motive or set of sentiments. On this reading, individuality is less a matter of pursuing specific, concrete goals and more a matter of adopting a particular motivational stance vis-à-vis the world. For Flathman, the relevant sentiments entail such things as virtuosity, free-spiritedness, civility, fastidiousness, and magnanimity.

Flathman, however, may be using "self-enactment" in a broader fashion to refer not only to our sentiments but also to whatever we wish to pursue. In this case, his notion of self-fashioning may include what Oakeshott calls self-disclosure. On this interpretation, Flathman is concerned with virtuous, civil, magnanimous performances and actions and not just feelings. Even on this broader reading, the ideal is adverbial in the sense of not specifying this or that action. We express our individuality in the way we pursue our interests and not necessarily through a set of substantive performances.

Given that Flathman's action-guiding theory has an adverbial character and that he refuses to advance "recipes, decision procedures, or logarithms for the making of public policy" (1998, 16), his conception of the relationship between theory and practice is very modest, even chastened. His conception of willful liberalism does not seek to advance a set of ideals that are definite, substantive, and for *everyone*. His ideals are not a substitute for the self-understandings of ordinary practitioners unless they choose to adopt them. Finally, his institutional criticisms would be compelling only if one accepts his liberal conception of individuality.

Nevertheless, as formal and adverbial as his theoretical ideal may sound, it is still powerful enough to lay the groundwork for criticizing what he calls institutions and institutionalisms that are incompatible with it. If policing, education, and law (for example) generate patterns of rules and norms that are unfriendly toward his ideal, then, he feels, they need to be reconceived, perhaps even replaced. More strongly, if such institutions and rules regularly disable or undermine our individuality, Flathman would call for their abandonment—if only those institutions were not also necessary for cultivating and maintaining our capacity for self-enactment. However precarious this position may be (and Flathman is well aware of the difficulties in which this position places him), it is clear that he believes that this critical stance is enough to turn political theory into a descriptive-normative enterprise. Theory can describe practice, advance an ideal, and judge our arrangements. Even though theory does not yield a set of policy prescriptions, it is both a positive guide to action and a critical response to institutions.

Despite the limits of the vision of theory that Flathman offers, it would still be far too powerful for Oakeshott or Wittgenstein: two writers who have significantly influenced his approach to political theory. In part, it may be because his own work draws so heavily on these thinkers that Flathman has had to address their claims for a radical detachment of theory from practice.[1] In general, Flathman's response is that this kind of radical skepticism cannot be sustained on its own grounds, that despite Oakeshott's and Wittgenstein's explicit arguments and pronouncements, a significant connection between theory and practice can be rendered consistent with each of their positions. Although Flathman thinks that their warnings about philosophers and theoreticians replacing practical arrangements and ordinary ideas with gimcrack plans and theories should be heeded, he also believes that Wittgenstein and Oakeshott should accept (on their own terms) a modest role for theorizing: that of rendering our practical arrangements more meaningful or coherent.

Leaving to the side Flathman's view of Wittgenstein, it is important for Flathman to defeat decisively the more radical elements of Oakeshott's skepticism. Such a defeat is necessary if his own chastened conception of the relationship between theory and practice is to hold. If he is not successful, then the potential usefulness of his theory dissipates, leaving only a set of ghostly abstractions that are irrelevant to practice. From Oakeshott's perspective, the bloodless, abstract character of theory should never be confused with the vibrancy of practical life. Theory cannot yield principles of conduct from which it would be possible to certify the correctness of performances. Nor should theory replace or displace the understandings of ordinary identities. To the extent that Flathman's critical project is one of certification (or decertification) and to the extent that his ideals of self-making and self-enactment are advanced as being able to replace the self-understandings of those who happen to adopt them, then Flathman's chastened theory of theory is not chastened enough. In its strongest formulation, Oakeshott's skepticism would exclude even these weaker claims of willful liberalism.

Much of this chapter involves setting out an interpretation of Oakeshott's theoretical skepticism. It focuses on the basis and nature of that skepticism and whether Flathman provides an adequate response to it. To some degree, Flathman's internal critique of Oakeshott is correct: Oakeshott is committed to seeing a kind of theorizing (what I call conditional theorizing) as intimately linked to practice. Unfortunately, this connection is not enough to stop the practical utility of a more robust conception of theorizing (or unconditional theorizing) from ultimately bleeding away, particularly when theory is understood as a descriptive-normative enterprise. Consequently, to the extent that Flathman's own work aspires to offer more than a conditional form of theorizing, it does not have the resources to umpire the correctness or improve the coherence of our practical engagements. Although Flathman and many of his readers seek to push his work toward increased political applicability, Oakeshott's skepticism tugs at Flathman's (or anyone else's) unconditional theorizations and points to the possibility of an unbridgeable gap between theorizing and doing.

Overview

Before beginning a discussion of Oakeshott's view of theory and practice, it may be helpful to set out an important assumption about my interpretation. Although a dispute exists over the degree to which Oakeshott's early work (particularly *Experience and Its Modes,* 1933) is consistent with his later work, I believe that his views regarding the relationship between philosophy (and theory) and practice remained essentially unchanged.[2] I will not here defend this interpretive claim; however, I will focus on his later work and make only a few references to his early work, *Experience and Its Modes.* More specifically, his argument against the practical applicability of theory is made in a very compressed form in the first few pages of *On Human Conduct.* Very roughly, the gist of Oakeshott's position is that all understanding rests on a set of assumptions or conditions that cannot themselves be called into question without calling into question the understanding they support. In practice, the acceptability of a set of understandings turns on the role they play in assisting us to achieve whatever wished-for or desired satisfactions we are pursuing. Their acceptability rarely turns on our ability to call those assumptions into question or even to understand them in any deep sense. In contrast, theoretical understanding entails refining and defining an object of inquiry and attempting to understand the conditions or assumptions that identify it as whatever it is. But, obviously, all theoretical understandings must themselves posit and hold in place a set of assumptions in order to support a set of conclusions regarding a given object of inquiry. Consequently, the truths of theory are conditional. In order to render them less conditional, one must investigate their assumptions. But such an investigation has the paradoxical effect of generating another set of assumptions, and these assumptions must be held in place and not explored in order to render a new understanding. In order for theory as theory to possess a warrant to judge or replace practice, it would have to make good on its assumptions—all the way down. The assumption that all understanding is conditional means that no theory can accomplish this task. No theory is unconditionally true. In other words, for practitioners to replace their understanding with the understanding of theory is to be sold a bill of goods.

The inability of theory to certify the correctness of our performances is also connected to the ways an object of inquiry must be transformed and refined in order for its conditions to emerge and be understood. For example, in practice, we already have an understanding of a thunderstorm, a tug-of-war, or an election, even before the theorists come on the scene. For Oakeshott, we conventionally understand these entities through a multifarious set of *characteristics* (in the case of a thunderstorm: the sound, the smell, the lightening, the change in temperature, the way the sky looks, the sudden onset of rain). When the theorist of electromagnetism, mechanics, and rational choice refine, operationalize, and define these entities, they replace the assemblage of *characteristics* (or *features*) with a more precise set of *postulates* (or *assumptions*). The conclusions and forms of understanding that result from the work of theorists are different from and according to Oakeshott, irrelevant to practice. Oakeshott's account of understanding and his distinction between characteristics and postulates, however, does open up the possibility for distinguishing between different kinds of theorizing. What I call *conditional* theorizing, which seeks to map out the characteristics of and relationships between identities, can have practical implications, or so I will argue. In contrast, *unconditional* theorizing, which seeks to understand identities through their postulates, is irrelevant to doing.

Practical Understanding

In order to set out Oakeshott's theoretical skepticism, it may be best to begin with practice. According to Oakeshott, theorists see ordinary practical life as a prison: "Its inhabitants are 'prisoners', not merely because they are wholly ignorant of its conditions but because the level of their understanding excludes even the recognition that it is conditional" (Oakeshott 1975, 27). As mentioned above, it is this recognition of the conditionality of practical understanding that serves as the starting point for theorizing. Before reaching this point, however, it will be helpful to consider the kind of understanding that Oakeshott believes is part and parcel of practical life. For the image of ordinary life as a prison is not an unfamiliar one in philosophy: It goes back to Plato's allegory of the cave. Oakeshott's twist is that the prisoners of ordinary life differ from theorists in that they do not know what they do not know: the conditionality of their understanding. Aside from this ignorance, however, ordinary practitioners are "sagacious and knowledgeable persons" (Oakeshott 1975, 29), whose understanding of the world permits them to act, judge, and diagnose their situation. What they know should not simply be dismissed, and how they act is neither unreflective nor blind. They are, Oakeshott notes, in his rewriting of Plato's allegory, "'like ourselves', only more so than Plato will allow" (27).

The reality of the practical world is not only that it rests upon ignorance, but also that this ignorance does not preclude an understanding of or action in the world. But what is the practical, ordinary understanding of the world? According to Oakeshott, if we are adept practitioners, then we are capable of recognizing and identifying things in the world as well as drawing complex connections, mapping out relationships, and diagnosing situations. In this description, "recognition" and "identification" are theoretical terms that Oakeshott uses to represent the practitioners' level of understanding.[3] When we *recognize* something, according to Oakeshott, we turn to its particular *characteristics*. We know that X is not the same as Y because their shapes, tastes, sounds, movements, colors, and so on are different, even though we may not be able to *identify* X and Y. In *recognition*, we take hold of something in terms of its "casual and marginal resemblances and differences of recognizable characteristics" (Oakeshott 1975, 5). In contrast, *identification* entails understanding X "in terms of an ideal character composed of characteristics" (5). Although Oakeshott never fully sets out the difference between these terms, identification seems to entail bringing a more complex, abstract understanding to whatever it is we are seeking to comprehend. It is by bringing a general category to bear on a particular entity that we can identify something as a concert, a movie, a trout, a waterfall, and so on, despite the difference between individual concerts, movies, trouts, and waterfalls. In the case of identification, what is understood is a "unity of particularity and genericity" (5), for we already possess an understanding of an ideal character (concert, movie, trout), composed of an abstracted set of "marks" or "characteristics"[4] drawn from contingent "goings-on" when we encounter a particular unknown. Identification involves the deployment of an *ideal character* (composed of characteristics) as an instrument for understanding the particular.

It should be emphasized that the level and kind of understanding entailed by recognition and identification is very sophisticated, despite the fact that it yields the familiar world we inhabit. In fact, if we take Oakeshott's general definition of theorizing as the attempt to understand a "going-on," then clearly there is a kind of theorizing from the beginning.[5] And, as we shall see, this kind of theorizing can get very complicated, although at this level of understanding, it will always remain what Oakeshott calls a conditional adventure.

Conditional Theorizing

In addition to recognizing and identifying things of the world, practitioners occupy what Oakeshott calls a "platform of understanding" when the world-as-it-is-understood is understood in terms of the ideal characters composed of characteristics used in identification. This does not mean that we are always able to identify something correctly or that all the unknowns we encounter possess an unambiguous character. Rather, Oakeshott means that we occupy a platform of understanding when every particular thing is understood in terms of some ideal character (Oakeshott 1975, 6–7). This has been achieved in ordinary understanding when we can identify things of the world in terms of their characteristics.[6] Oakeshott calls it a "platform" because it is constituted or supported by a set of conditions that are frequently not attended to or understood by the actors. Before considering what conditionality means, we need first to set out two activities that this platform of understanding now permits.

First, we can explore this platform of understanding by discerning the relationships between ideal characters. By relating, comparing, classifying, and juxtaposing these identities, practitioners can map out their world in imaginative and sophisticated ways. Because this mapmaking is a form of understanding (or theorizing) that rests on a platform of understanding composed of ideal characters identified by their characteristics, we can call this activity "conditional theorizing."

Second, this platform of understanding also permits diagnosis and action. Arriving at a determination that "'this is a case of measles', 'that is a bank robbery', 'guilty but insane', and 'this is combustible' are diagnoses when they are understood to prescribe utterances such as 'isolate the patient', 'sound the alarm', 'detain during Her Majesty's pleasure', 'put it on the fire', or performances which correspond to these utterances" (Oakeshott 1976, 7–8). The upshot is that correctly identifying something may also commit one to further utterances and action. The significance of this claim is that conditional forms of theorizing can lead to action if the understandings that result are also diagnoses. By carefully observing the contours of the language and attending to the relationships between our conventions and beliefs, mapmakers who take on the mantle of political theorist may arrive at the determination that "this is unjust," "that is illegitimate," "this is within my rights," or "that is neither necessary nor proportionate." These determinations are diagnoses when they prescribe such utterances as "Down with the king," "Begin the impeachment proceedings," "I'm taking you to court," or "Change the strategic doctrine." Examples of conditional theorizing can include exploring the characteristics of justice, legitimacy, rights, or proportionality when these entail explicating the shared rules and conventions governing the use of these terms. Conditional theorizing as a kind of cartography can be employed to judge the correctness of performances and the coherence of practices. It is important to note that on this view of theorizing and doing, the standards of correctness are those that have been learned by practitioners while engaging in their activities or those that are implicit in the conventions and rules and elicited by competent mapmakers or conditional theorists. As we shall see below, this question of judging the correctness of performances is central to Oakeshott's argument that (unconditional) theorizing is irrelevant to doing.

At this point, what must be emphasized is the extent to which, as Flathman notes, Oakeshott treats "practice as a form of theorizing" (Flathman 1989, 29).[7] Because all intelligent conduct entails understanding and because all understanding is a kind of theorizing, all conduct rests on conditional theory. This form of theorizing resembles at least one of the ways Flathman himself has used the concept of theory. In his book *The Practice of Rights,* for example, Flathman notes that "*Practice and theory* are very far indeed from being univocal terms" (Flathman 1976, 15–16). In light of the richness of the concept of theory, he sets out three different uses of the word. Of these uses, one of them corresponds very closely to conditional theorizing. Flathman writes,

> The set of shared ideas, values, rules, and concepts by which participants make sense of a practice and their place in it might be viewed as constituting a sort of theory; and their development, application, and interpretation of it might be viewed as a sort of theorizing. (1976, 23)

This form of theorizing, which entails discerning patterns of meaningful conduct within a practice and illuminating those patterns by comparing, juxtaposing, contrasting, and refining other terms, concepts, ideas, and beliefs would seem to be a species of mapmaking par excellence. Given the theory-like quality of practice, theorizing here consists of doing more systematically what practitioners already must do if they are to engage in practical life. For example, Flathman notes that his work on rights is "devoted to identifying and analyzing the theory of the practice of rights in this sense of *theory*" (Flathman 1976, 25). I believe that Flathman also deploys this sense of theory to some degree when he systematically charts and identifies the practices of obligation, authority, and freedom in his other works.

If conditional theorizing is a matter of doing something systematically that practitioners do haphazardly, then perhaps it is possible for the actors and reflective practitioners to develop and chart their concepts "so fully... that there is little for political philosophy to contribute" (Flathman 1976, 26). Indeed, from a Wittgensteinian perspective, this development may be so complete that the most philosophy can do is "'issue reminders' of what human beings as participants already know" (26). This is plausible, however, only if the phrase "already know" includes what participants are implicitly committed to, given their conventions and understandings. Yet we know that there are practitioners who are more proficient, adept, and knowledgeable than others about what it is they are doing and how it relates to other ideal characters. This suggests that there is at least some room for the activity of expert mapmakers and conditional theorists in the practical world. From a certain perspective, however, conditional theorists are nothing more nor less than expert mapmakers.

Flathman finds the Wittgensteinian position implausible for additional reasons, and he is moved to offer a second and third form of theorizing. The second kind of theorizing emerges from the difference between knowing how to do something (which practitioners must know) and being able to give a systematic account of what it is that one is doing (which they need not know). The third kind of theorizing appears when Flathman notes that even those who can give a more systematic account of what they are doing may not be able to give the kind of comprehensive account that theory is able to offer. For example, a legal theorist attempts "to abstract from the details of day-to-day practice and identify higher-order rules and principles under which that detail can be subsumed, comprehended, and viewed in relationship to other aspects of the legal system" (Flathman 1976, 28). For Flathman, this third kind of engagement is theorizing in a "full descriptive-normative" sense (28).

Flathman's additional conceptions of theory move it beyond a conditional adventure. This is certainly the case in the second form of theorizing, where knowing how to give a systematic account of what one is doing entails understanding the conditions, postulates, and assumptions of the engagement. Indeed, this form of theorizing includes the systematic study of the presumptions and propositions that underlie "use of the notion of a practice as an orienting and organizing concept in the study of human affairs" (Flathman 1976, 16). As we shall see below, attempting to understand the conditions of an engagement (including the conditions of studying an engagement) is a necessary starting point for unconditional theorizing.

In the third way of understanding theory, what Flathman means by discerning higher-order rules and principles is not entirely clear. He could merely mean looking at practical life with a more discerning eye, a process that resembles mapmaking. Or this engagement could involve making "additions to the account of the practice provided by practitioners" (Flathman 1976, 28), and this possibility is consistent with the view of theory (offered in his latest work) that seeks to provide an ideal and a component critical of current practice. This vision of theory, as we have seen, is more optimistic about the possibility that theory can make a unique contribution to practice—unique in the sense that it is qualitatively distinct from what practitioners already do and perhaps even transformative in its aim. In other words, Flathman's third conception of theory directly raises the issue being pursued here: Can unconditional theorizing certify or judge the correctness of performances?

Unconditional Theorizing

Once Oakeshott moves beyond his discussion of recognition, identification, and platforms of understanding (which occupies the first eight pages of *On Human Conduct*), his use of the words "theory," "theorist," and "theorizing" are always connected to an *unconditional* engagement. As we shall see, it is toward what I call unconditional theorizing that Oakeshott expresses his deepest skepticism. But what is unconditional theorizing? Theorizing becomes unconditional when a number of further developments occur (beyond identification, recognition, and mapmaking) in our learning to understand. The first development is that we are no longer satisfied with simply using or deploying ideal characters to understand something; rather, we seek a greater understanding of the ideal characters themselves. In this development, we become aware that our understanding is conditional in the sense that ideal characters are normally used but rarely explored. Competent practitioners ably deploy terms such as "time," "justice," or "choice," but rarely do they focus on what these terms mean.

The movement to an unconditional engagement can come to a halt, however, if in exploring an ideal character we are satisfied with a mere list or account of characteristics or if we are satisfied with a more definite formulation of the relationship between that ideal character and the features or occurrences of other ideal characters (Oakeshott 1975, 8–9). As I suggested earlier, if either one of these responses satisfies us, then we are not engaged in unconditional theorizing but, rather, in a more refined form of mapmaking or conditional theorizing.

To make this clearer, I may become concerned with the meanings and connections between the ideal characters of "person" and "fetus" because of an ongoing political dispute over abortion. Despite our ability to use these terms in unproblematic, meaningful ways, they have in recent U.S. politics become contested terms. In this dispute, the question of whether a fetus is a person acquires moral and legal significance, and how we answer it could greatly affect a variety of practices and actions. This being said, it would not be surprising to ask, "What is a 'person,' anyway?" In asking this question, we are no longer using an ideal character (person) as an instrument of understanding; rather, we are trying to understand the instrument itself. This turning is the beginning of unconditional theorizing. On the reading of Oakeshott offered here, this kind of question is the starting point to theorizing in an unconditional fashion, but it is not itself sufficient. For we may turn away from unconditional theorizing either by being satisfied with a list of characteristics of persons (capacity to feel pain, human shape, intelligence, tool user, possesses an identity over time, can formulate goals and interests, and so on) or by drawing connections between this ideal character and others (persons and things, persons and plants, persons and animals, persons and a heap of chemical compounds, persons and fetuses). In addition, we may then further compare and contrast these ideal characters, draw out patterns of usage, explore exceptional meanings, devise ways to illuminate more clearly the shared meanings and understandings. There is, indeed, a great deal of work for actors/practitioners/conditional theorists to do here within the platform of understanding we ordinarily occupy. And the conclusions at which we arrive may be entirely satisfactory or useful. As an engagement of theory, much of this work falls under the first conception of theory mentioned above in Flathman's work. Or to put it another way, conditional theorizing can correspond very closely to the beginnings of unconditional theorizing.

It is possible, however, not to be satisfied with listing characteristics or with mapping out connections between one ideal character and another. The reason for this dissatisfaction is never clearly set out by Oakeshott. Nevertheless, we do know that conditional theorizing has a prison-like quality, given its obliviousness to its own conditionality. An additional source of dissatisfaction, I believe, is connected to the Platonic flavor of Oakeshott's account of understanding. Characteristics, from this perspective, fail to satisfy because their assembly and composition into identities is conditioned by the prevailing conventions and practices, the shared judgments and rules that exist at a given time. These judgments, conventions, and practices are rough and inexact; they can differ from place to place and can change over time (however slowly). They yield an intelligible world and the criteria for correctness, but they are imprecise and mutable. At this level of understanding, conditionality is conventionality (which is the theorist's prison). This realization may drive one to ask what *exactly* is this event called a thunderstorm, this animal called a fish, this concept of justice, or this entity called a person. By refining and trying to discern a stable identity, one is seeking to find what must be the case in order for this to be whatever it is. And the answer to this query cannot be supplied by the rough, but always ready, composition of characteristics. Rather, it requires not only that we refine that identity to remove all ambiguity, but also that we understand it through its postulates.

According to Oakeshott, a theorist who is dissatisfied with the conditional ordinary understanding of something may "tinker with his identities, abstracting them more decisively and specifying them more exactly in order to endow them with characters capable of being investigated; for, only a 'going-on' purged of ambiguity qualifies as an identity waiting to be understood and prescribes an inquiry" (Oakeshott 1975, 8). What does this tinkering and purging mean? Oakeshott is suggesting that instead of focusing on characteristics of an ideal character, we may seek to deploy an explanatory language in order to understand some event or thing. In order to do this, he believes that we must prepare and refine the identity so that it is susceptible to one explanatory idiom or another. Of course, Oakeshott is presupposing that a set of sophisticated modes of explanation are already waiting in the wings. These include what he calls "orders of inquiry" and "idioms of inquiry." The order of inquiry, according to Oakeshott, depends upon whether or not the identity is an exhibition of human intelligence (Is it a wink or blink?). An idiom of inquiry is an unambiguous system of theorems within the two orders of inquiry that can be used as an instrument of understanding. As examples, Oakeshott lists ethics, jurisprudence, and aesthetics as idioms of inquiry falling within the order of human intelligence. In the order ot things that are not exhibitions of human intelligence, he lists physics, chemistry, and psychology as distinct idioms.

Oakeshott, however, is not merely presupposing a set of explanatory frameworks waiting in the wings; he also claims that we must render the ideal character compatible with such explanatory frameworks. Refining an ideal character means that it must be purged of all ambiguity. It must be clear to what order and idiom it applies. In other words, what is explained through any order and idiom of inquiry is not an ideal character composed of a jumble of characteristics, but an extraordinarily refined entity in which the particular identity fades from view. The specific "going-on" that is to be explained becomes, in effect, a creature of the idiom of inquiry (Oakeshott 1975, 17). To use one of Oakeshott's examples, consider trying to understand a game of tug-of-war. The characteristics associated with a particular game of tug-of-war may include two opposing teams pulling on a rope over a boundary of mud at a park on a hot Saturday afternoon in front of family and friends after having a cookout of hamburgers and hot dogs. In other words, we do have an understanding of a game of tug-of-war as an ideal character that turns upon a loose assemblage of characteristics. In order to bring the idiom of inquiry known as mechanics to bear upon this event, many (perhaps all) of these features will be deemed irrelevant. Indeed, in this explanation, the specific game of tug-of-war "has no necessary place and... it is no more than one of an untold number of contingent 'goings-on' from which an identity capable of being understood in the terms of 'mechanics' may be abstracted" (Oakeshott 1975, 10). In contrast, if we were to deploy a sociological explanation, those attributes identified as essential to mechanics would be seen as irrelevant. In making these refinements and purging an identity of its ambiguity, we are no longer interested in some *particular* event, action, or thing; instead, we have constructed a fairly rarefied entity that will fit into the available languages of explanation.[8] It is that abstract entity that we explain by turning to its conditions.

Oakeshott claims that in performing these refinements,

> [the theorist's] exertions will be rewarded when, almost without premonition, he finds himself to have acquired a new employment.
> His enterprise now is to make his identities more intelligible, neither by reidentifying them in a reconsideration of their component characteristics, nor by relating them more decisively to one another in terms of their features and of the circumstances of their occurrence, but by seeking to understand them in terms of their postulates; that is, in terms of their conditions. (Oakeshott 1975, 8–9)

When we seek to understand an ideal character in terms of its conditions, we are asking for something different than we are when we seek to understand it in terms of its characteristics. In the case of conditions, there is a form of explanation taking place that says, "In order for *this* to be whatever it is (an abstracted ideal character called a thunderstorm, a trout, a person, a wrongful act), these further assumptions or postulates must also be given." The theorist attempts to understand ideal characters through what is posited as necessary for their being whatever they are, and it must be kept in mind that what is being explained is a further refinement of the ideal character used to identify a particular entity.

No such refinement or positing occurs when we understand ideal characters through their characteristics. In relying upon the characteristics of a fetus or a person, there is no claim being made that this composition or combination of characteristics encompasses the essential components of this ideal character (unless one is trying to pass off characteristics as postulates). Rather, these ideal characters emerge from usage and are more or less stable depending upon the circumstances. The point of identification is to understand, not to "secure a knock-down conviction at any cost" (Oakeshott 1975, 5).

The aim of unconditional theory is to make an essential claim about conventional entities: This abstract ideal character, which can be approached through these modes of inquiry, can be understood through these postulates or assumptions. Or to put it in another way, theory entails "seeking to understand a familiar identity in terms different from those in which it is already understood" (Oakeshott 1975, 9).[9] The identity is already understood in terms of its characteristics. Theory seeks to understand it in terms of its conditions (postulates or assumptions).

Yet we still have not arrived at a full understanding of what unconditional theorizing entails. As I have suggested, it cannot be the simple realization that our conventional understandings of the world rests upon assumptions held uncritically. Although necessary, this realization is not enough. In addition, it cannot be the attempt to understand identities through their characteristics, for to so understand them is to be trapped in the prison of practice. So at the very least, unconditionality implies that the theorist's understanding of the ideal character is not determined or governed by the shared beliefs of the platform of our current understanding. Instead, unconditional theorizing rests upon postulates or assumptions that are taken as necessary and sometimes sufficient for understanding an abstracted identity. In this respect, the postulates or assumptions used to understand an identity compose yet another and in some sense deeper platform of understanding. Despite its name, even unconditional theorizing will be conditioned by a set of postulates or assumptions. Consequently, what is unconditional about this theorizing is that there is an open invitation to explore the postulates that support this new platform. For example, Oakeshott notes that electromagnetism may be postulated to understand an abstracted ideal identity called a thunderstorm, but we can also theorize electromagnetism. And those theorems will rest upon a set of postulates that can, in turn, be theorized. Postulates, which at one level are instruments of understanding, can now become invitations for exploration. As Oakeshott notes, "The irony of all theorizing is its propensity to generate, not an understanding, but a not-yet-understood" (Oakeshott 1975, 11). Yet he acknowledges that perpetually calling into question the postulates that one wishes to use in order to understand cannot get one anywhere. So in order for theorizing to take place at all, the invitation to explore the postulates of a theorem must be deferred. But a deferral is not a denial of unconditionality.[10]

Nevertheless, it is not clear if the attempt to understand an abstracted ideal character in terms of its postulates is a sufficient account of unconditional theorizing. For Oakeshott also writes that unconditional theorizing is constituted by the "continuous recognition of the conditionality of conditions" (Oakeshott 1975, 11). The words "continuous recognition" suggest that physicists must always have metaphysics in the back of their heads when they theorize. But I do not think this is quite right, for unconditional theorists can be unreflective. They may ignore or refuse to hear the invitation to explore further those postulates. "And for a theorist not to respond to this invitation cannot be on account of his never having received it. It does not reach him from afar and by special messenger; it is implicit in every engagement to understand and is delivered to him whenever he reflects" (Oakeshott 1975, 11). A physicist deploying the laws of physics who is oblivious to metaphysics is still engaged in unconditional theorizing. The point, perhaps, is that she will recognize the unconditionality of her theorizing only to the extent that she understands the conditionality of conditions she has advanced. Oakeshott, of course, believes that any theorist worth her salt will recognize a standing invitation to explore those postulates upon which her theory rests.

Ultimately, the danger of failing to recognize the conditionality of conditions is that the theorist may come to believe that he can certify the correctness of performances because his theory possesses unconditional truth. When this has happened, or when the theorist misunderstands his calling, he runs the risk of becoming what Oakeshott pejoratively labels a "theoretician." In general, the theoretician seeks to direct the actions of practitioners by substituting his understanding for their understanding (that is, replacing an understanding of ideal characters based upon characteristics with an understanding based upon postulates) and to judge the correctness or incorrectness of particular performances. In not realizing or ignoring the conditionality of his understanding, he attempts to bridge the gap between theory and practice. For Oakeshott, the theoretician is a "fraudulent tutor; and the certificates he issues are counterfeit, acceptable only by those who share his belief in the truth of his theorems and share also his delusions about their character" (Oakeshott 1975, 26–27). Understanding the mistakes made by the theoretician will make the basis of Oakeshott's skepticism more evident.

The Errors of the Theoretician

Oakeshott's brief but disparaging comments suggest that there are several possible errors the theoretician may be making. One mistake involves confusing thinking within a practice and thinking about a practice; for example, confusing "theorizing moral conduct with knowing how to subscribe to a moral practice" (Oakeshott 1975, 26). A second mistake is confusing postulates with principles. And although I believe that this second mistake stands on its own, Oakeshott blends this mistake into (what I believe to be for him is) a third: When postulates are taken for principles, the theoretician then mistakenly believes that principles can actually specify what should be done (Oakeshott 1975, 26). A final mistake entails confusing "the postulates of an identity with its features" or "pass[ing] off either for the other." Do these "mistakes" support Oakeshott's argument that unconditional theorizing is irrelevant to practice? Let us look more closely at each of them.

I do not see Oakeshott's skepticism as resting on the possibility of making the first error. Although there is something important in the basic distinction between thinking within and thinking about a practice, this distinction is not enough to render theory irrelevant to practice. In conditional theorizing, it is possible that reflection upon the characteristics of an ideal character could help one judge the correctness of a performance. *A* may accuse *B* of murder after seeing *B* step on a bug. *B*, of course, may respond in any number of ways to *A*'s accusation, but it surely is possible for *B* to point out that the death of bugs is not among the many characteristics of the ideal character of "murder." Reflecting upon an ideal character used in a practice can very easily lead us to judge the correctness of performances, and so thinking about a practice *can* inform what we do within a practice.

The second possible error entails mistaking postulates for principles. In order to understand the character of this mistake, it is necessary to say a few things about Oakeshott's understanding of principles. According to Oakeshott, principles of conduct are elicited from practice; they do not exist in a realm beyond experience and human engagement. More specifically, they emerge from the lore regarding "the likely meanings and outcomes of actions" (Oakeshott 1975, 90). Consequently, these generalizations rest on claims regarding the relationships between characteristics and between identities. They are based not on postulates but on the shifting nature of experience. From this perspective, the conversion of postulates to principles is simply a misunderstanding of principles of conduct. Once this category mistake has been made, however, individuals are then liable to make the additional mistake of believing that principles can be used to specify conduct. To a certain extent, however, it is possible to see these as independent arguments. For the belief that principles are derived from experience is separable from the question of whether those principles (however they may be derived) can specify conduct. In order to make the strong argument that something distinctive called "theory" can guide practice, the theoretician must be able to support both claims; that is, the principles must result from something more than conditional theorizing *and* they must be able to specify performances. In order to attack this strong formulation of the argument, the skeptic need only reject one of these claims—although Oakeshott rejects both.

On what basis does Oakeshott believe that principles should not be confused with postulates? Part of the answer is that unconditional theorizing abstracts from and transforms the entity being theorized. In order to clarify and precisely identify what is being examined, the theorist will, as we have seen, strip away what is seen as irrelevant and highlight what is understood as necessary. That which is taken as necessary if the identity is to be whatever it is will be taken as a postulate of that entity. A principle based on postulates is not a principle regarding concrete reality, but a ghostly abstraction. In order to illustrate how a principle could be confused with a set of postulates, consider Oakeshott's own discussion of the ideal character called "civil association." What Oakeshott calls civil association has been glimpsed "here or there," but it is not a "premeditated design for human conduct" (Oakeshott 1975, 180–81). As a theorist, Oakeshott notes that he is concerned with understanding civil association not in terms of its features (although considering those features may give one an idea of possible postulates) but in terms of its postulates (Oakeshott 1975, 182). One of the postulates of civil association is the idea of association "not in terms of affection, of a choice to be related in the pursuit of a common substantive purpose, or of conscription in such an enterprise, and not that of self-moved bargainers negotiating with one another for the satisfaction of their chosen egoistic or altruistic wants, but solely in terms of a practice or language of intercourse" (Oakeshott 1975, 182).[11] Could this postulate be converted into a principle and then be used to judge the correctness of a performance? In order to make this conversion, a state could not be a true civil association unless it was conceived of "solely in terms of a practice or language of intercourse." Ultimately, this would mean a kind of purposeless association. In the hands of a *theoretician,* such a principle could lead to the belief that true civil association requires the abandonment of all governmental distributive and welfare schemes. The "correct" government certified by this postulate-cum-principle would be a nightwatchman state.

Yet the idea of civil association has been abstracted and transformed in the theorization. Aside from the fact that few contemporary practitioners use the phrase "civil association," it is extremely unlikely that if they were to use the phrase, it would have the theoretical meaning given to it by Oakeshott. In other words, if one were to convert a postulate to a principle, it would not be a principle that applied to the practical world. If he has been successful, Oakeshott's theorizing has pared away the ambiguities and complexities of the modern state in order to understand more clearly the idea of civil association.

The weakness with this part of Oakeshott's argument is that there are those who believe that reality needs to be straightened out on the procrustean bed of theory. In order to do this, practitioners would have to begin to see the theoretical construction as something real and to regard its postulates as characteristics. This would entail exchanging a full-blooded, concrete, shared, practical understanding of some "going-on" for a bloodless, contestable, abstract construction held by one or a few individuals. Is this possible? Perhaps. Perhaps the ordinary identification of a going-on could be swapped for a theoretical construction: a carbon-based, featherless biped for a person, a parallelogram of forces for a balancing act in a circus, a purposeless association for a government. In so doing, the theoretician might convince us to rationalize, stabilize, and further discipline our practical understanding. Practitioners could engage in such an exchange despite the consequent impoverishment of our understanding. The possibility of such a transformation suggests that it may be a short step between understanding something through its postulates and seeing those postulates as the only legitimate understanding. It does not seem to be an impossible substitution.

If this conversion truly is possible, then the argument dividing theory and practice must either rest on a disconnection between principles and conduct or on some deeper problem of confusing the postulates of an identity with its features. Starting with the relationship between principles and conduct, what is the nature of the problem? According to Oakeshott, theorems "are incapable of specifying performances" (Oakeshott 1975, 26). In addition, principles "can neither direct nor 'justify' an adventure of doing" (Oakeshott 1975, 91). The problems raised by the concepts of "specify" and "direct" suggest that the broad character of theorems and principles cannot tell practitioners what to do given the specific circumstances they face. They cannot be "applied" in the sense of yielding a determinant course of action. But immediately after making this claim, Oakeshott suggests that they can be "used":

> Perhaps, in notably novel circumstances or in a situation of unusual obscurity, when persistent doubt about what to want or what to do has lost an agent his way, he may decide to fix his position by taking his bearings upon a general principle of conduct or a theorem of prudential lore. (Oakeshott 1975, 90–91)

In contrast, under normal circumstances, a competent practitioner diagnoses a situation and understands that the diagnosis prescribes certain conduct. For example, a competent medical practitioner does not need a principle of patient isolation in order to go from the diagnosis "This is a highly dangerous, easily communicable disease" to the prescription "Isolate the patient." When identification is itself diagnosis, the understanding contains the prescription. The prescription is itself part of the identification of the situation. This association of identification with prescription, of course, does not mean that practitioners are guaranteed to identify the situation correctly. But the quotation above suggests the possibility that a practitioner may find the principle "When one encounters a highly dangerous, easily communicable disease, isolate the patient" to be a useful way to get her bearings in a novel situation.

There may exist a connection between principles and conduct, but it is attenuated by the fact that even in a novel situation, there would not be a principle to tell the practitioner which principle to select. In addition, in order for a principle to be useful, the practitioner would need to know already what such terms as "dangerous," "easily communicable," and "isolation" mean. Principles are not "applied," if by application one means that by themselves they point to a specific course of action. Nevertheless, principles may be useful. Consequently, if the problem is that when postulates are converted into principles, there exists a gap between principles and conduct, then even for Oakeshott that gap may not preclude theory from being "useful."[12] We may regret what is lost in translation from postulates to principles, and we may find that the resulting principles are useful only in limited circumstances, but these regrets and limitations do not create a high wall separating theory from practice.

The theoretician's more significant error concerns mistaking or misrepresenting the character of postulates and hence the nature of theorizing. Oakeshott clearly rules out the possibility that postulates-cum-principles could certify or justify the correctness of performances. He rules it out because theorizing assumes a set of postulates that remain uncriticized in order to theorize. Presumably, if one made other sorts of assumptions, one would come away with a different theory. Thus, whatever "truth" emerges from theorizing will always be conditional. For Oakeshott, the truth of a theory depends upon the coherence of the platform of understanding that the theory occupies: Every attempt to understand an ideal character in terms of its postulates "is an autonomous adventure in theorizing, insular, inextinguishable, resistant to 'reduction', having its own conditional 'truth', and capable of its own conditional perfection" (Oakeshott 1975, 11). In order for the theoretician to be able to certify performances, the conditional truth of theory must be transferable to the practical world. If the theoretician is to forgo the standards of correctness available in practice, he must convince practitioners that the truth of a theory applies to their actions and performances. But an honest theorist can only offer a conditional claim to truth: Civil association is a purposeless association only if one accepts the postulates regarding the nature of moral practices, *lex, cives,* ruling, subjects, the public, authority, obligation, and so on. It is possible, of course, to assent to those postulates for the purposes of acting, but simple assent is not the criterion of truth. In order to establish the correctness of a postulate, one would have to take up the invitation to explore and theorize it. And presumably, because this additional theorizing would rest upon other postulates and assumptions, the theoretician would need to make good on (i.e., establish the truth of) those additional postulates. Theory cannot judge the correctness of our doings without providing an unconditional understanding. Paradoxically, it is the conditionality of unconditional theorizing that precludes it from being able to certify performances. Consequently, Oakeshott concludes, the theoretician's claims will be "acceptable only by those who share his belief in the truth of his theorems and share also his delusions about their character" (Oakeshott 1975, 26–27).

"But," the theoretician may respond, "our understanding of the practical world is also conditional—doesn't the same problem face ordinary criteria of correctness?" The response to this query is that the acceptability of those ordinary criteria does not turn upon demonstrating the truth of their conditions. From Oakeshott's perspective, practitioners can judge quite adeptly the correctness of their performances without even realizing the conditionality of their engagements. For example, whether one subscribes to a correspondence or a coherence theory of truth is irrelevant to understanding an oath in court to tell the truth, the whole truth, and nothing but the truth or to assessing whether a witness has committed perjury. The coherence of the practical platform of understanding provides practitioners, mapmakers, and conditional theorists with the wherewithal to judge doings when needed. Standards of correctness are ordinarily part and parcel of the practical engagements of practitioners.

Those who understand an ideal character through a set of postulates have an understanding superior to that of those mired in the unreflective ignorance of the practical world. But the price theorists pay for such knowledge is irrelevance.[13] One can try to evade paying the piper and obtain relevance only by according a theorem an unconditional standing. For those who are certain of themselves and of their theories, the temptation to become a theoretician will be great, but they will be listened to only by those who are convinced of the truth of the theoretician's claims and confused about the object of theoretical inquiry. Ultimately, Oakeshott's position may come down to the following: If theorists are true to their calling, then unconditional theorizing cannot direct or govern practice in any way. Only by selling unconditional theory in terms that it is not (that is, by portraying postulates as characteristics) can that gulf be bridged. Through such a deception, it may be possible to convince people to surrender their own lives for some theoretical ideal. These delusions may have enormous costs, rendering the prison of practice even more disciplined, but these "practical effects" of theory are entirely due to misconstruing its character and its truthfulness. In short, a properly understood form of theorizing is practically irrelevant.

Flathman's Response

Flathman's rejection of Oakeshottian skepticism is largely the product of an internal critique. Flathman argues that Oakeshott's own position shows that theorizing can inform practice. Oakeshott's position has negative consequences for practitioners: If we take his theory of theory and practice seriously, then as practitioners we will reject outright the conclusions and claims of theoreticians. In addition to this negative practical conclusion, Flathman believes that the theory-like character of practice and the importance of coherence to Oakeshott's philosophy enables theorists to contribute positively to practice. For actors and for theorists in Oakeshott's theory, "Coherence is the *criterion* of intelligibility and hence of truth, of reality, of all that is 'satisfactory' in experience" (Flathman 1989, 26–27). An incoherent understanding is a problem and a difficulty, but more important, it is an invitation to further exploration, refinement, and clarification. The real difference between theorists and others, on Flathman's interpretation, is the rigor with which theorists pursue coherence. Because actors in the practical world can be very successful despite the presence of "inconsistency, confusion, and misunderstanding" that is "unnoticed, unresolved, and even deliberately introduced and maintained" (Flathman 1989, 38), theorists can be identified by the single-mindedness with which they pursue the goal of coherence. Yet for both theorists and practitioners, coherence remains the central criterion of satisfactory understanding. The importance of coherence, combined with the theory-like nature of practices, leads Flathman to conclude that

> [p]hilosophers and theorists are specialists in detecting confusions and other maladies in the "theory" implicit in practice; practitioners specialize in acting on the invitations that theory extends. To the extent that philosophers and theorists identify and help to "cure" diseases of thought, they may contribute something that is—by standards practitioners also at least implicitly accept—of value to practice. (Flathman 1989, 39)

The "cure" entails not only identifying the maladies and confusions but also adding to the order and coherence of a practical engagement. This cure is possible because there is only one standard of intelligibility and one world of ideas to which it applies (Flathman 1989, 40–41).

As suggested above, the theoretical character of the practical world does license a very intimate connection between theorizing and doing. But this connection is limited to conditional theorizing and cannot be extended to unconditional adventures. At the heart of Flathman's position is the claim that coherence is powerful enough to enable unconditional theorizing to arbitrate performances. And Flathman is certainly right that coherence does play an important role in Oakeshott's philosophy. In *Experience and Its Modes,* Oakeshott notes that "experience or reality is not divisible into parts or departments; there are no distinct and separate areas of experience, no separate fields of knowledge" (Oakeshott 1933, 323). This claim suggests that if theorists can enhance the coherence of the postulates that underlie our practices, then surely that should be able to enhance the coherence of the practice itself.

Nevertheless, Oakeshott also argues in *Experience and Its Modes* that the practical mode of experience is a self-contained, homogeneous world of ideas exclusive of other modes of experience, such as science and history, as well as philosophy (Oakeshott 1933, 331). For Oakeshott, "practical thought is characterized by the acceptance of certain categories, certain postulates and a principle of homogeneity which are exclusive of those of all other modes of experience" (Oakeshott 1933, 338).[14] Coherence for the practical world can only be defined and understood from within the platform of understanding that it occupies (and this is true for the other modes as well). This is clearly implied when Oakeshott writes about the transferability of truths between modes, for "[w]hat is true or false for the one world is neither true nor false for the other, but meaningless and beside the point" (Oakeshott 1933, 349). If each mode of experience or each platform of understanding offers its own conditional truths, then coherence will also be conditional. The exception to this, in *Experience and Its Modes,* is the case of philosophy (as opposed to theory), which strives for complete or unconditional coherence. But this may be more of a logical requirement of his system than an actual possibility. The truths of practical life rest upon conditions and categories of that mode of experience. Although Oakeshott does not use the language of modes in *On Human Conduct,* what he says about the insular character of practice *vis-à-vis* other modes is transferable to the relationship between practice and various idioms of inquiry. Assuming that the distinction between characteristics and postulates holds, what satisfies the criterion of coherence in practice will not satisfy this criterion in theory. The conditionality of coherence means that there is no opening for unconditional theory to assist in the ordering or clarification of practical concepts and ideas.

Is Oakeshott's account of theorizing even of prophylactic value to practice, protecting it against the misconceptions of theoreticians? Flathman argues that to the extent that we accept Oakeshott's view, "practice is protected against the *claims,* commonplace in our civilization and culture, of 'theoreticians' and proponents of 'what used to be called philosophy' to the authority to dictate to all other practitioners" (Flathman 1989, 45). In other words, Oakeshott's condemnation of the theoretician is also a diagnosis that can at least rule out some performances. But Flathman's argument is mistaken: Oakeshott's theory of theory and practice is itself conditional, resting upon such assumptions as that the world is a world of ideas, that this world is one and whole, that coherence is the only criterion of intelligibility, and so on. Presumably, if we saw the world through a different set of lenses, we would also come to see a different relationship between theory and practice. Oakeshott's position could not have the prophylactic consequences suggested by Flathman without confusing postulates with characteristics or assumptions with principles. If practitioners resent and reject the theoretician, it is not because they have a theory of their own in their back pockets. The appropriate response to the theoretician is not to become a theoretician of a different sort.[15]

Refusing to draw even negative practical consequences from Oakeshott's view of theory results in a remarkably cramped, even extreme, position. Yet I believe that this *is* Oakeshott's position. Oakeshott also implicitly rejects the role of the theoretician through means that are more polemical, political, and practical. For example, it may be possible to read his essay "Rationalism in Politics" (1962) as a form of mapmaking, and not political philosophy (as he conceives of that term), which points to the peculiarities of a politics by the book. By operating within the shared beliefs and concepts of practical life, Oakeshott comes up with a similar view, one that should make political actors suspicious of political theorists armed with their certainties, ideals, and programs. The point here is that the basis for this diagnosis is not a form of unconditional theorizing. On this reading, "Rationalism and Politics" is itself a practical and not a theoretical intervention in politics.

There is much to recommend the prison of practical life: Its verdicts are useful and largely satisfying; its actors are sophisticated, adept, and certain; and its texture is open and extraordinarily mutable. It is upon this terrain that conditional forms of theorizing can provide normative guidance. But here the theorist simply does more systematically what the practitioner does unreflectively. By thinking within the conventional bounds, one operates within a prison erected in ignorance. There are plenty of good reasons why a theorist would want to break out of this prison. For unconditional theory does yield a deeper understanding of the ideal characters upon which practitioners rely. The enduring temptation, however, is to believe that remedying that ignorance also gives the unconditional theorist a warrant to arbitrate practices or judge performances. To the extent that Richard Flathman's vision of theory offers an ideal and a view of institutions, it has an unconditional quality to it that may enhance the coherence of our theories and deepen our understanding. According to Oakeshott, however, these gifts can never be practically employed without altering their character and deceiving their recipients. An unconditional theorist who breaks back into the prison of practice must inevitably distort both her theory and our practical engagements. Like Midas's touch, the unconditional theorist's contribution to practice is at once golden and destructive of life around her.

Notes

1. See, for example, pages 28–33 in his *Political Obligation* (1972), pages 5 and 32–34 in his introduction to *Concepts in Social and Political Philosophy* (1973), pages 17–29 in *The Practice of Rights* (1976), pages 225–236 in *The Practice of Political Authority* (1980), pages 8–11 in *The Philosophy and Politics of Freedom* (1987), pages 12–13 and 90–97 in *Willful Liberalism* (1992), pages xx–xxii in *Thomas Hobbes: Skepticism, Individuality, and Chastened Politics* (1993), and in the introduction to *Reflections of a Would-Be Anarchist* (1998). Flathman's most sustained treatment of this problem can be found in an essay entitled "Theory and Practice, Skepticism and Liberalism," in *Toward a Liberalism* (1989).

2. For an opposing view, see Anthony Stephen Gerenscer's *The Skeptic's Oakeshott* (2000). Very briefly, Gerenscer argues that Oakeshott's early skepticism was replaced by a view in which philosophy (or theory) could have a more contingent, conversational relationship to practical life. Those who choose to pick up the conclusions of philosophy could do so, but philosophy continues to have no authority over practice. Gerenscer's position, although closer to Flathman's view of theory, is not borne out in Oakeshott's *On Human Conduct* (1975). I will argue that Oakeshott continued to believe that an unbridgeable gap existed between theory and practice.

3. These terms ultimately provide an important entrance into how he differentiates theorizing from doing.

4. Oakeshott is well aware that recognition itself presupposes some level of identification and deployment of "rudimental ideal characters" (Oakeshott 1975, 4). The shapes, sounds, sights, and tastes that are characteristics are themselves ideal characters.

5. Oakeshott defines theorizing as "an inquiry designed and undertaken by a theorist in which he seeks to understand a 'going-on'" (Oakeshott 1975, 1).

6. As Oakeshott notes, "The condition (the uncriticized assumption) which constitutes this platform of conditional understanding is that every 'going-on' is what it is in respect of being understood in terms of an ideal character specified as a composition of characteristics" (1975, 6–7).

7. Indeed, the phrase that Flathman occasionally uses, that practice is "theory-like," seems too weak to accommodate fully the extent to which doing and the engagements of understanding are intertwined.

8. Oakeshott acknowledges that in many cases, particularly when we are trying to understand things that are themselves exhibitions of human intelligence, the theorist will find "his theoretic equipment unequal to his enterprise." He continues, "In this situation, the theorist must either do his best with what he has got, or he must himself re-engage in the different, more difficult, but also more interesting task of constructing an unambiguous theoretic character (a 'science') which might subsequently be used as an instrument of abstraction and understanding" (Oakeshott 1975, 20).

9. This claim is somewhat disingenuous, insofar as familiar identity becomes a great deal less familiar as it is purged of its ambiguous character. Consider the case of the game of tug-of-war.

10. Is an unconditional form of understanding possible? Oakeshott clearly believes one cannot question everything at once. The theorist "easily understands that nothing will come of questioning everything at the same time. Indeed, he recognizes this to be the condition of any specific achievement in understanding. He has a heavenly home, but he is in no hurry to reach it" (Oakeshott 1975, 25). Could we say that Oakeshott's understanding of theory and his claims regarding the relationship between theory and practice are unconditional? No, because Oakeshott clearly admits that his theory of theory and practice is conditioned in all sorts of ways and that in writing *On Human Conduct,* he had no desire to develop such a theory, suggesting that such a theory would itself be possible.

11. In contrast, associations that are in terms of purposes, affections, bargaining, and so on are called enterprise associations.

12. Oakeshott does see this gap as bridgeable to some degree at other levels of understanding. After all, the ability of practitioners to deploy ideal characters itself requires a coming together of particularity and "genericity." If Oakeshott believed the gap to be unbridgeable, then any form of understanding, including recognition and identification, would be impossible. Although it is true that these forms of understandings are not principles, they nevertheless involve an application of universals to particular situations.

13. To put it in terms of Oakeshott's earlier work, the price of philosophy is life itself: "Philosophy is not the enhancement of life, it is the denial of life" (Oakeshott 1933, 355).

14. In 1933, when Oakeshott wrote *Experience and Its Modes,* he had not formulated the distinction between postulates and characteristics upon which I am claiming so much depends.

15. A similar sentiment is found in Oakeshott's rejection of rationalism and social planning. In referring to the work of Friedrich Hayek, Oakeshott notes, "A plan

to resist all planning may be better than its opposite, but it belongs to the same style of politics" (Oakeshott 1962, 21).

References

Flathman, Richard E. 1972. *Political Obligation.* New York: Atheneum.
———. 1973. Introduction to *Concepts in Social and Political Philosophy,* ed. Richard E. Flathman. New York: Macmillan.
———. 1976. *The Practice of Rights.* Cambridge and New York: Cambridge University Press.
———. 1980. *The Practice of Political Authority: Authority and the Authoritative.* Chicago: Chicago University Press.
———. 1987. *The Philosophy and Politics of Freedom.* Chicago: Chicago University Press.
———. 1989. "Theory and Practice, Skepticism, and Liberalism." In *Toward a Liberalism.* Ithaca, N.Y.: Cornell University Press.
———. 1992. *Willful Liberalism: Voluntarism and Individuality in Political Theory and Practice.* Ithaca, N.Y.: Cornell University Press.
———. 1993. *Thomas Hobbes: Skepticism, Individuality, and Chastened Politics.* Newbury Park, Calif.: Sage.
———. 1998. *Reflections of a Would-Be Anarchist: Ideals and Institutions of Liberalism.* Minneapolis: University of Minnesota Press.
Gerenscer, Anthony Stephen. 2000. *The Skeptic's Oakeshott.* New York: St. Martin's.
Oakeshott, Michael. 1933. *Experience and Its Modes.* Cambridge: Cambridge University Press.
———. 1962. "Rationalism in Politics." In *Rationalism in Politics and Other Essays.* New York: Basic Books.
———. 1975. *On Human Conduct.* Oxford: Clarendon Press.

CHAPTER FOUR

Individuality and Egotism

George Kateb

This essay is written not only for Richard Flathman but to him. His theory of "willful liberalism," which is a theory of willful individualism, enriches thought about the aspiration to be or become an individual. As one who has been trying to work out a view of democratic individuality, I am naturally appreciative of Flathman's work. One particular question that interests me is the extent to which Flathman's theory is similar to the theory of democratic individuality. I believe that he would agree that there is considerable similarity. Especially in sections 3, 4, and 5 of part 2 of *Willful Liberalism*, there are pronounced similarities.[1] What I see Flathman doing in these sections is giving a truly instructive reading of the most humane qualities in Friedrich Nietzsche's thought concerning identity, autonomy, and authenticity. Salient is Flathman's discussion of such virtues as friendship, moderation, self-control, generosity, magnanimity, and even compassion as they appear in Nietzsche's earlier work and in *Thus Spoke Zarathustra*. Flathman also finds in Nietzsche and others, such as William James, an admirable emphasis on other human characteristics independent of character: inventiveness, creativity, spontaneity, and originality.[2] Furthermore, Flathman incorporates into his willful liberalism a determination to highlight the essential mystery, singularity, inexplicability, even the "limited mutual unintelligibility" of all human beings.[3] He composes a marvelous picture of the individual as actuality and aspiration.

It must be pointed out, however, that if Nietzsche is Flathman's main inspiration, it is a very Emersonian Nietzsche. Flathman rarely refers to

Ralph Waldo Emerson; that is no great matter. But it would be well to remember that Nietzsche, like James, is deeply indebted to Emerson. That certainly does not make Nietzsche into a theorist of democratic individuality, of course. Nevertheless, Nietzsche's work is undeniably valuable to later versions of democratic individuality, and Flathman has demonstrated that point better than anyone else has, even if he wants the term "willful liberalism" rather than "democratic individuality." Flathman is certainly closer to democratic individuality than he is to—how should we put it?—the aristocratic Nietzsche, the programmatic Nietzsche, or the wounded Nietzsche. This is not to deny that Emerson, to begin with, is radical in his rejection of the demotic and the populist: That rejection helps define his own theory of democratic individuality, as it does anyone else's. My point is that on the Nietzschean virtues, on human creativity, and on the irreducible and finally unsolvable human mystery, Flathman is very Emersonian. Flathman is thus fairly close to some version of the theory of democratic individuality.

But there are a few features of Flathman's view that I would ask him to think about again. I do not want to conscript him for Emersonian purposes, but I do want him to perfect his own system, sometimes with Emerson's help, and remove it further from self-insistence. First, I doubt that the words "will" and "willful" and the related word "voluntarist" best reflect the nature of Flathman's individualism. A strong will is a good thing for the right purposes. But to admire will as pure will is not likely to serve any individualism except one without limits or scruples. In ordinary usage, to be willful is to be stubborn in an almost perverse or self-indulgent and whimsical way. Emerson can say in "Self-Reliance" that "I would write on the lintels of the door-post, *Whim*," but he quickly adds, "I hope it is somewhat [that is, something] better than whim at last, but we cannot spend the day in explanation."[4] Will is strong, but willfulness is close to petulance; and when will is strong, it can be blind or cruel. Encouragement of egotism attaches itself to emphasis on the will, and with it, damage to the self. As it stands, such an emphasis does not go well with another and praiseworthy emphasis in Flathman's thinking, that on individual spontaneity and mystery, which are not phenomena of the will (understood as resolve and determination).

There is one other main issue that worries me. I notice that Flathman does not make much, if anything, of the place of self-examination and attempted self-knowledge in becoming an individual. The Socratic imperative remains binding in a democracy, even if nowhere else, because in a democracy, individuals matter more than their social roles. I grant that the emphasis on spontaneity and mystery places strict limits on the results of self-examination. We want to be self-surprising and are perhaps glad that we cannot get very far into ourselves. Still, self-examination, or what we would be more likely to call introspection, can deepen the sense of our own strangeness to ourselves and prepare us to expect the unexpected from ourselves (and from everybody else, of course) without being able to predict its content. Above all, self-exploration may acquaint us with our discontinuousness as well as with our internal vastness, the very sources of our spontaneity, mystery, and creativity.

But if egotism is to be resisted as harmful to the soul, it may be a mistake both for Flathman to place so much emphasis on the will and for him to turn away from introspection. These two traits are probably connected. The best Nietzschean elements in Flathman's conception are not willful, not self-insistent. In a word, they are far from egotism, even if some other elements are not. On the other hand, Flathman's omission of introspection may be a sign that his conception is not as strong in resistance to egotism as it could and should be. Egotism thrives in the absence of self-awareness: Self-insistence is often magnified by inattention to one's inner condition and can even be an escape from it. All in all, there are some risks of encouraged egotism in Flathman's theory.

In this chapter, I want to go on with the discussion of democratic individuality as an anti-egotistical aspiration. It has occurred to me with greater insistence recently that democratic individuality is, among other things, an ideal that is very much at odds with—in fact, at war with—egotism. I grant at the start that it is plausible to think that every kind of individualism must be entwined with egotism. After all, what is individualism supposed to be, if not a radical insistence on oneself and one's claims and, indeed, an insistence that often goes beyond one's rightful claims and recognizes no limits on them? Despite the plausibility, I believe that some kinds of individualism can be seen as sustained efforts to deal with self-insistent egotism: either to mitigate or refine or surpass it. To be sure, other kinds of individualism inflame egotism, or they appear to do so. But individualism, from its very nature, need not sponsor egotism; much less is it invariably the same as egotism. I see in democratic individuality the most powerful effort undertaken by any kind of individualism to battle egotism. I also believe that the theory of democratic individuality—the compound and complex conceptualization of what it means to be an individual in a rights-respecting democracy, as formulated by Emerson, Henry David Thoreau, Walt Whitman, and their heirs—is better at challenging egotism than even many anti- and non-individualist doctrines, which sometimes serve, in fact, as effective if disguised carriers of egotism.

What we need to do is to elaborate the distinction between egotism and individualism, if only crudely and provisionally. (One possible precedent is Aristotle's distinction between good and bad forms of self-love.)[5] By "egotism" I mean things like selfishness, intense self-centeredness, intense and even exclusive insistence on oneself. The claims and interests of others get short shrift wherever possible. An egotist makes no effort to take seriously other persons as persons, with their own inwardness and feeling for their own reality. Rather, for the egotist, others are aids and instruments or rivals and obstacles. In contrast, some kinds of individualism espouse self-concern, care of (or for) the self, and the effort to take oneself seriously in distinct ways. Self-insistence is not the same as self-concern; and each goes very well, goes best, without the other, paradoxical as that may sound. Perhaps I could say that self-insistence cannot absorb any element of proper self-concern, whereas most kinds of self-concern aim in theory to purge the self of as much selfishness or self-insistence as possible—an aim that of course can and never should be fully realized.

I take egotism, to some significant extent, to be inevitable in every society where there are at least the rudiments of self-consciousness, which is the ability to think of oneself as a self in some respects separate from all those around oneself and to engage in some minimal reflection about who one is, where one stands, what one wants, how one should live, and what may await at the end of life. There may once have been societies where self-consciousness did not exist; there may still be some such today. But my analysis does not reach to them, whether they were or are real or whether they are, instead, imaginary (critical or compensatory) constructions, such as, say, Socrates' "city of pigs" or Jean-Jacques Rousseau's original state of nature. Egotism, not just concern for self-preservation, is as close to being natural as anything psychological. The marvel is that some doctrines try to combat it in the name of individuals, of individual self-concern, not in the name of group or community or collectivity or deity and not in the name, either, of such idealistic aspirations as selflessness or altruism or self-sacrifice.

Egotism is the given. In other words, the vices of pride, vanity, jealousy, envy, and greed are to be taken as naturally occurring. Egotism is the comprehensive term for these and related vices, which existed well before any kind of individualism emerged. In civilization, each soul is inevitably afflicted, as Rousseau rightly taught. The affliction is a perpetual source of unhappiness in the egotist and hence a main source of the harm the egotist causes others. If we can say that individualism, as distinct from egotism, begins with the Socrates of Plato's *Apology,* we then have to say that it is a comparative latecomer. Thus, individualism did not invent egotism. The more important point is that some kinds of individualism, including Socrates' kind, do battle with egotism and its vices.

Ordinary self-interest is not egotism, either. The desire to preserve oneself, to improve one's life, to want love and friendship, and to want a decent life and the wish not to be treated unjustly or oppressed or abused or exploited or neglected—all this is modest and moderate; it is inseparable from being a person. In constitutional democracies, ordinariness is protected by guaranteed individual rights; it is rights-based individualism. If from some points of view—heroic or ascetic or religious or aesthetic—such ordinariness appears banal or unworthy or lowly or unimaginative, then so be it. What ordinariness should not be accused of is egotism; the vices of egotism should not be imputed to it. At the same time, ordinariness (rights-based individualism) is not yet a developed individualism; rather, it is still at the level of what Alexis de Tocqueville calls *individualisme,* by which he means the core of ordinariness in postaristocratic societies. Even he distinguishes *individualisme* from selfishness or self-centeredness *(égoïsme).*[6] There is no doubt that, as Tocqueville suggests, ordinariness—an everyday preoccupation with getting and keeping one's life in order, together with the lives of others to whom one is tied and for whom one is responsible—can become narrow and obsessive and turn into selfishness, or at least become outwardly similar to selfishness. But in theory, ordinary self-preoccupation (under the cover of protective rights) is not the same as inevitable egotism. Ordinariness is not far from Rousseau's idea of *amour de soi-meme;* and

I mean by egotism something like what he calls *amour-propre*.[7] Ordinariness in a constitutional democracy is a preliminary individualism (though immeasurably valuable in itself), and democratic individuality is its ideal fulfillment.

Contemporary discussions of individualism (including democratic individuality), understood as self-concern, rather than as self-insistence, have placed three concepts at the center: identity, autonomy, and authenticity. One cannot deny that other concepts, such as freedom (or liberty), self-realization, equal dignity, and personal integrity, regularly appear alongside the three I have mentioned, sometimes synonymously, sometimes catching a nuance missing from these three. It is also true that all these concepts figure in analyses and defenses of doctrines other than individualism. Yet I think it is fair to say that when we concentrate attention on identity, autonomy, and authenticity, we get to the nub of individualism. The concept of identity explores the fundamental questions Who am I? and How can I be myself? The concept of autonomy revolves around the meaning and worth of trying to take control of one's life rather than living submissively or at the mercy of externality. The concept of authenticity tries to determine the sense and significance of expressing oneself, one's inner truth and riches, in particular acts, episodes, and activities. Answers to these questions and problems can make up a doctrine of individualism; or at least, these concepts, taken together, make up a sufficiently complete framework for a doctrine of individualism.

The three concepts are not sharply distinct from one another. They all blend together. In fact, there are times when they are interchangeable designations. Furthermore, to think about any one of them is necessarily to think, immediately or eventually, about the other two. I will not try to offer a worked-out understanding of any of the concepts. Instead, I wish to suggest that each concept, when posited as an ideal and seen as essential to individualism, can be prized too much. The effect of overestimation is to encourage egotism, a more intense egotism than the natural egotism that is a given in any society in which self-consciousness exists. Such egotism would be, if practiced, an inflamed egotism. As such, it would be morally worse—if only in some respects—than the given or natural egotism.

I have already said that egotism is harmful to the soul. It is inescapable, but it can be either restrained or further inflamed. But even when not inflamed, it may lead to irrational behavior that can be destructive of the self as well as of others. It is by no means an exaggeration of ordinary self-interest; rather, it is a disposition that is often at odds with self-interest. When culturally inflamed, it is a primary source of magnified wickedness, especially the sorts of wickedness that stem from the desire to transgress for the sake of transgression or for the sake of expanding the realm of actualized possibility for the sake of expansion. It cannot be denied that an economically competive society inflames egotism. These psychological tendencies are latent in the given egotism of civilized life. They erupt when a cultivated egotism issues from the condition of society and receives encouragement from individualist concepts taken further than they should be or taken in the wrong direction. The upshot is that not only egotism is often at odds with ordinary preservative self-interest, it is at war with self-concern. And I hope to show that democratic individuality challenges egotistical self-insistence better than any other kind of individualism, better indeed than some anti- or nonindividualist doctrines. The reason to challenge egotism in the name of individualism is that egotism is loss of self. There are, of course, other, principally moral reasons to challenge it, but I will concentrate on loss of self.

The subject of egotism as loss of self pervades the work of the theorists of democratic individuality, Emerson, Thoreau, and Whitman. Their analysis begins with the damage done to individuals by conformist competition, but this analysis is only part of their general contribution to the project of urging persons in a democracy to use the inestimable advantage that comes from being free and possessed of rights in order, perhaps, to grow into democratic individuality. These writers have often been accused, however, of sponsoring an inflamed egotism or self-insistence that leads to unpurposive transgression or insatiable graspings. In other writings, I have tried to show that this charge is largely misleading. What I wish to do here is borrow from their work to suggest why these writers can help check the egotistical self-loss that can arise when the ideals of identity, autonomy, and authenticity are prized too much or in the wrong way. Emerson, Thoreau, and Whitman all help us think about self-loss and its connection to egotism, and they do so as defenders of individualism, as philosophers of democratic individuality. I turn first to the concept of identity and to the self-loss through encouraged egotism that sometimes results when the concept of identity figures prominently in the discussion.

What could be more individualist than an interest in personal identity? It turns out, however, that the attempt to defend too strenuously the centrality of the concept of identity fairly regularly encourages loss of self. I find two principal ways some defenders of individualism (wittingly or not) theorize identity into self-insistence, with all its risks of egotistical self-loss. The first defends a purely personal insistence on one's identity, and the second defends the rightness of mixing one's identity with that of a group. I want to say that in both cases, we find egotism inflamed and the self-loss that follows such inflammation. Emphases present in certain kinds of individualism lead away from the promise of individualism; and these emphases must be resisted in the name of an individualism that hopes to minimize self-loss. To this end, the resources of democratic individuality must be enlisted.

Insistence on one's identity comes down to the demand that one's identity be unmistakable, in one's own eyes and in the eyes of others, that is, to the demand that one be respected or honored for being who one is in particular. That is, I the egotist am special; I am radically different, unique. Perhaps other people are special, too. But that does not matter nearly as much to me as does my own specialness. If I am real only to myself, only I am real to myself. But I demand that those who are not quite real to me acknowledge my reality, my special and unique reality, even though I fail, or appear to fail, to acknowledge anyone else's. I want the world to take me on my own terms, to accede to my self-definition.

This version of egotistical self-insistence rests on the claim that I can know myself completely, that I can know who I am, that I can know my identity. I know all that there is to know about myself, and no one can know me as I know myself. Even if I am mysterious to others, at least in some respects, I am not mysterious, in any important respect, to myself. Whether or not others fully understand me when I say who I am, I fully understand what I mean. In who I am and what I do, I surprise others, but not myself. I can answer the question of my identity: I am not a puzzle or problem to myself.

What, then, is the interpretation of identity lodged in this version of egotistical self-insistence? Identity is personality, one's presence in the world, the sum of one's appearances and acts in it. Something may be kept back or hidden, and that is at one's disposal, but only what one chooses to reveal is anyone else's business. Take me as a rounded figure, just like a fully achieved character in a work of fiction. Only, I am self-authored; I write my own lines and also try to affect the lines, the appearances, and acts of those around me, so that my "character," my personality, can have its way. The wonder is that *I* exist, that the one I am, in my particular identity, my distinctive personality, exists; the wonder is *not* that I, a self-conscious creature among many such, exist, and exist together with everything else. The wonder is that this *special* me exists; the wonder is *not* that there is existence, that there is a world. The wonder that I in my special identity, in my distinctive personality, exist really means that I am necessary to the world, that I was called into existence to supply a deficiency or fill a niche: The world would be incomplete without me, without my unique self, which is my own personality. I am not an accident.

The sentiments that I have stated in the preceding few paragraphs make too much of the self, or make the wrong claims about the self. I do not deny—I wish to affirm—that some of these sentiments, though not all of them, are excesses of a fundamentally valuable sense of self, a sense of personal identity. The excesses are better than deficiency would be. Perhaps individualism could not get started or could not sustain itself without at least some of these sentiments. Indeed, Emerson's essay "Self-Reliance" gives voice to a number of them. But Emerson cannot be taken as presenting his whole view of personal identity in one essay, even if "Self-Reliance" is as great as any he wrote. In other essays, he qualifies and even takes back the self-insistence he impersonates so supremely well in this essay. He and Thoreau and Whitman, taken together (but surely not as a monolith), reject self-insistence of every sort, and most emphatically in the matter of wanting to think about oneself in the manner that any egotistical defender of personal identity would propose. Their ideas of self-concern, care for the self, prohibit self-insistence, especially when self-insistence is insistence on one's social personality. Or perhaps the matter should be put this way: They invite us to begin in excess, in egotistical self-insistence, so that we may awaken to our individual importance, but then they revise and refine their views of individualism, of democratic individuality, in order to induce in us a more truly individualist self-conception.

Of course, Emerson, the founding father of democratic individuality, is remembered very well for his encouragement of an inflamed egotism that seems to partake of the higher vices of self-enclosure, self-importance, perhaps even solipsism or narcissism. How can we think otherwise when such sentences as the following parade before our eyes as we read "Self-Reliance": "Whoso would be a man, must be a nonconformist." "Absolve you to yourself, and you shall have the suffrage of the world." "Few and mean as my gifts may be, I actually am, and do not need for my own assurance or the assurance of my fellows any secondary testimony." "No man can come near me but through my act." And last, "Insist on yourself; never imitate."[8] How can these sentences be read as anything but a philosophical intensification of normally present egotism, as an invitation to make as much as possible of one's distinctive personal identity, an invitation that comes dangerously close to self-worship?

The answer is that there is more to Emerson. He impersonates ideas and thus tries to see how far the implications of any serious idea extend. But then in the same essay or in other writings, he qualifies an idea by confronting the necessity of other, contrasting, and antagonistic, ideas, and impersonating them, too. The large tendency of Emerson's work, like that of Thoreau and Whitman, is to make a puzzle or problem of personal identity. These philosophers see excesses of self-insistence as signs of immature self-concern but certainly not definitive of it in its proper mode. The major notions of personal identity among the Emersonians finally endorse what they hold to be proper self-concern.

To insist on one's identity as a specific personality is, for the Emersonians, to sustain self-loss. A tenacious hold on oneself, on the peculiarities of one's personality, threatens an egotist with a serious loss of self because it obscures from one's own view one's richness and complexity and thus blocks the self-awareness and self-concern that the school of democratic individuality wishes to promote.

Democratic individuality can only (but may not) grow out of security in the possession of one's personal and political rights. Just by claiming rights, a person acknowledges the same rights for others. Democratic individuality begins in what Emerson calls "radical identity":[9] Each person deserves to be treated as an equal human being and is obliged to treat others in the same way. But to be recognized in one's basic rights is to be recognized not only as an equal but also as an individual. To take oneself seriously as an individual because one has equal individual rights is the beginning of the type of self-concern that is supposed to exist in constitutional democracies.

In working out the further meanings of equal individual rights, Emerson, Thoreau, and Whitman produce an unsurpassed richness of reflection, and on no subject more than that of personal identity. For example, Emerson says in *The Conduct of Life*, "be what you are."[10] That, at first sight, seems an egotistical imperative. But it is no such thing. The tone is not celebratory, or even strongly affirmative. To be sure, the words are not a counsel of resignation. The meaning is more like this: Just be what you are, be yourself, and do not fuss too much; take yourself as you really are, once you have some self-knowledge (which is always revisable and incomplete). The entire sentence reads: "Speak as you think, be what you are, pay your debts of all kinds." The whole sentence and its context make clear that being oneself is, above all, a rigorous avoidance of self-deception, dishonesty to oneself or others, and cowardice in the face of the demands of experience or conscience. The comprehensive self-generated or habitually obeyed enemy of proper concern for self, of proper concern for the best sense of one's identity, is the desire "to work and to live for appearances, in spite of our conviction, in all sane hours, that it is what we really are that avails with friends, with strangers, and with fate or fortune."[11] Emerson's view, which permeates his work, is at the furthest distance from the will to locate one's identity in one's personality and then to insist on identity as something invaluable, absolutely special. That would be "to work and to live for appearances," even if nonconformistically. One becomes completely socialized, with only a faint wish ever to detach oneself in order to take thought. It is self-loss.

But "be what you are" is only a small part of the Emersonian conceptualization of personal identity. "Be what you are" is, as it were, the negative part of the story: It means, Do not contort yourself into being what you are not, just by trying to be yourself, by trying to insist on the coherence of your social personality. The larger or affirmative part of the story deals with what Emerson calls the "infinitude" of each person and with Whitman's poetical conceptualization of the self. Then, if we add Thoreau on self-exploration, we have what almost amounts to a repudiation of the very idea of identity as social personality. The sense of self grows so large that identity as special or distinctive personality is relegated to a minor role, even if an inevitable and indispensable one.

The determined effort to spare oneself radical self-loss proceeds by way of turning attention away from personality. And the avoidance of self-loss—and hence the enlargement of the self to its true size, which is, as it were, infinite—does not conduce to self-magnification, that is, to thinking of oneself as superhuman while thinking of others as merely human, if that. Rather, thought of individual infinitude is meant to provoke every person to an awareness of all persons' richness, which no fixation on personal identity can ever permit anyone to see.

In "Self-Reliance" itself, the greatest Emersonian articulation of the claims of personal identity as one's special personality, Emerson speaks of the "internal ocean" in every person.[12] Latent in all people is every feeling or sentiment, every desire or passion, every impulse or notion, for good and bad. The aim is not to become indefinitely plastic—though Emerson gives a marvelous impersonation of radically rejecting fixed identity in "Circles"—but, instead, to learn how all of humanity is contained in every one of its members. This is the most important self-knowledge arising from self-examination. To be proud of one's particular identity is both to amputate part of oneself and to cut oneself off from the highest human solidarity, which is recognition of the vastness of every person. Everyone is immeasurably more than the personality, the persona, that he or she sustains in meeting the world. There must be personality, there must, of course, be a someone there, a definite entity. Not every latency can or should be made actual. But nothing human—no matter how good or evil—is alien, if only one would look carefully inside oneself, have the courage to explore oneself, undistracted by the exorbitant demands, self-imposed or supinely accepted, to sustain one's personal identity in the social world.

Thoreau says:

> If you would learn to speak all tongues and conform to the customs of all nations, if you would travel farther than all travellers, be naturalized in all climes, and cause the Sphinx to dash her head against a stone, even obey the precept of the old philosopher, and Explore thyself. Herein are demanded the eye and the nerve.[13]

It is unhappy that in the recent extensive literature about personal identity, so little attention has been paid to self-examination and the possibilities, more limited though they may be than Thoreau (for one) thought, of self-knowledge. The whole French-inspired critique of the subject has, I suppose, left people with the ideas that there is no self to examine and try to know and that the self is a fabrication, in both meanings of the word: a lie and a construction. But this critique goes astray by positing social personality as the whole self, oneself without remainder. Then, too, one aspect of the Freudian legacy is the sense that we cannot know ourselves without the trained and technical assistance of psychological specialists. These two tendencies are mutually hostile, but their combined effect is to denigrate the reality or worth of self-exploration. But the practice of self-acquaintance withstands all the hostility of various theories. The effort to know oneself is, of course, freighted with difficulties, some of them insurmountable. No one can get fully free of personality, nor should anyone want to. What is more, infinitude cannot be grasped. Each person is more than he or she can ever encompass. Yet what a difference the practice of self-acquaintance can make.

In contrast to encouraged egotism, which says or threatens to say that only I am real and others are mere phenomena, democratic individuality (if I may reify) says only that I can know myself as no one else can know me and that I, by necessary implication, can know no one else as well as I know myself. There is an unalterable difference between being privy to my inwardness and intuiting the inwardness of others as I watch them perform their lives (as they watch me). And what the Emersonians promise is that extensive self-acquaintance dispels the illusion of a fixed and well-defined personal identity. The observant self inspecting itself discovers frequent strangeness, much that is unexpected. Not only much of the worst but some of the best in each self remains suspended but kept in memory, lending itself as inward experience to future articulation, especially when we see elements of our inwardness suddenly made actual by others in their virtues and vices, gestures and deeds.

Surely, however, there must be concentration of the self. Is that not what identity is? Even if we grant the plausibility of the idea of individual infinitude, a person simply cannot live a life that is primarily, much less solely, self-absorbed, fascinated, or obsessed by the multitudinous events of one's inwardness. One must achieve definition, a shape, if only to oneself. One wants to get to the bottom of the reality of oneself, to discover by self-exploration what Whitman calls the "real Me."

What (or who), then, is the real me? The last thing it is, is one's personality. Nor is it either of two other things: The real me is not the infant self that never grows up, that exists before the onset of language, and that always leads a displaced life. Nor is it the ageless self that never changes but is already fully present in the infant; that would be essentially the same, no matter where and how the infant was brought up; and that does not need language to know itself self-consciously, because the ageless self is equivalent, or nearly so, to inborn temperament or disposition, or in a more religious term, to soul. Both these versions of the real me (neither is totally absent from Whitman, and both are commonly felt and forgivably vague, it must be said) fail to reach the most important matter, which is that the real me, the real identity, is the self disclosed to me in my recurrent or episodic recovery of myself, after having been overcome by experience, overcome even if I have been most active. In the words of Robert Frost in "Carpe Diem":

> But bid life seize the present?
> It lives less in the present
> Than in the future always,
> And less in both together
> Than in the past. The present
> Is too much for the senses,
> Too crowding, too confusing—
> Too present to imagine.[14]

We can no more seize the day than we can seize ourselves. We become real to ourselves when we are at one remove from reality: I know the real me only the second time around, when I relive an event in retrospective imagination. I become able to say to myself such things as So, that's what I did; So, that's what my involvement amounted to; So, that's what I meant; So, that's the meaning of what happened to me and around me. I have glimpses of the real me when I probe my experience part way down its depths. Do the glimpses add up to a whole picture? No. Do they add up to a coherent self? No; they reveal only a persistent self. Do I look to make a story or narrative of my experiences? No, certainly not; a real life is not a story, and the real me is not a character in a story. Should I aspire to become like a work of art? No; each of us is a shape only in shadow. I am only episodically my real self, and I know my real self only when I recollect myself and my experience in an uncommon moment of genuine sanity and lucidity. The real me relies on the series of interpretations of what I was in my experiences, inner and outer, with others or alone: my experience brought home to myself, so to speak. Let us add, however, that the idea of the episodic real me that is absolutely dependent on retrospective self-interpretation leaves unaffected the democratic imperative to treat others as fully real in the ordinary sense. They should be as objectively real to me as I cannot be to myself.

I would add that I am really myself when I act under pressure or act by a sudden eruptive impulse or improvised response. I am really myself mainly in unroutine circumstances, when there is no rehearsal or imitation—no (or less) conformity. It is precisely in unroutine circumstances that I disclose myself, I surprise myself, I use resources I was not fully sure I had. But on such occasions, I am ahead of myself, so to speak. I do not see myself on such occasions. Therefore, I must catch up with myself; I must manage to be retrospective. In short, I am the real me, I have achieved identity, only episodically, and I cannot know the real me if I do not make a practice, also episodic, of thinking back on my experience.

To be sure, Whitman can suggest that his (and everyone's) real me is not glimpsed from even my best words at all, that it is unexpressed and inexpressible and hence unknowable. He says,

> Oppress'd with myself that I have dared to open my mouth,
> Aware now that amid all that blab whose echoes recoil upon me I have
>   not once had the least idea who or what I am,
> But that before all my arrogant poems the real Me stands yet untouch'd,
>   untold, altogether unreach'd
> Withdrawn far, mocking me with mock-congratulatory signs and bows,
> With peals of distant ironical laughter at every word I have written,
> Pointing in silence to these songs, and then to the sand beneath.[15]

Let us content ourselves with thinking that the real me is always more than it can say about itself, always more than can be said about it in all of a person's most articulate moments.

But if the real me is a valid notion, an eligible view of it sees it as the composite of one's recurrent self-distillation, ever given to dilution and evaporation. It is certainly not to be confused with one's distinctive personality. In contrast, egotistical self-insistence, which is insistence on identity as special personality, is far from the real self. If one is trying to be oneself full-time (which one cannot really be), one has to put on an act and keep it going.

The unconquerable trouble is that un-self-examined persons—all of us most of the time—habitually feel most real, most really themselves, when they have lost sight of their infinitude and have accepted the shrinkage intrinsic to acceptable definition, to a desired definiteness. And they spurn the idea that they are only intermittently their real selves.

There is therefore a harsh truth to be faced: Attention to identity is not the invention of novelists, of philosophers, or of popular culture. Just as some level of egotism must be taken as a given in any society in which even rudimentary self-consciousness obtains, so the yearning to have an identity, in the sense of being defined and having definition as a personality, must be assuaged. The yearning is as intense as any desire for self-preservation, and often more so. And it is usually more intense than ordinary self-interest. Another truth to be faced is that the resources of democratic individuality, especially the notions of personal infinitude and the real me, are for the most part inadequate to combat the socially encouraged egotism of insistence on one's identity as a personality. In turn, however, this sort of self-insistence also cannot provide sufficient gratification of the yearning to have an identity. The murmur or roar of the internal ocean is too confused, and the real me is too hard to find. But even worse for egotism to bear is the smallness of one's own self. The attempted remedy, borrowed from societies that long preexisted any democracy and any individualist idea of self-concern but that contained an abundance of normal and inflamed egotism, is to foster group identity of various kinds. And only democratic individuality can hope to offer some theoretical resistance to this remedy.

Now, group identity is an intractably complex phenomenon. It has numerous sources and manifestations. It exists in various intensities, and its objects differ in scope and sector. I introduce the theme of group identity here because one of the principal sources of the strength of group identity is ungratified personal egotism, often enough unconsciously. One's group membership can, of course, promote one's ordinary self-interest, but it can also damage or destroy it. Yet when one's group identity is especially strong, the chances are good that something other than ordinary self-interest is in play. Egotistical self-insistence may be in play. And when thinkers promote a strong group identity, they are often indifferent to the ordinary self-interest of members of every and any group, just as they are hostile to individualism (however they understand it). That is to be expected. What is surprising is that we can find a thinker now and then (Charles Taylor is one example) who makes the case that good self-concern, unegotistical individualism of one kind or another, not only is compatible with strong group identity but should lead directly to it. Again, unconsciously, an attempted individualist defense of strong group identity promotes egotism, intensifying it beyond natural egotism and thereby aggravating the self-loss that encouraged egotism characteristically inflicts.

At the extreme end of participating in group identity, one transfers one's identity to the group. One cannot think of oneself apart from it. Questions about oneself are answered by reference to the actual or imagined shared attributes of the other members of the group. One is unburdened of a personal identity, which is felt to be incomplete and unimportant. One is not looking for one's other half or for another self, close to oneself that is strangely like and nicely unlike oneself. Rather, one is looking for enlargement, unconvinced that one's own ego is supplied with enough gratifications when it lives for itself, but also unconvinced that love and friendship suffice to finish the self, and of course unconvinced that one's internal ocean is big enough or that the real me is real enough. Group identity is a refuge from the frustrations of every degree of egotism, but also from the frustrations of the right kind of self-concern.

The group egotist absorbs the fellow members of the group as well as the abstract group into himself, with the result that when he looks at his fellow members he sees—that is, he thinks or imagines he sees—himself. They are not only like me, or appear to be, they are me, just about. They confirm my existence.

In group identity, one is enlarged by a kind of replication, especially when shared practices are performed in ritual, routine, or uniform. One me is not enough, but many of the same are enough, because I make them me, not simply mine. The delusion is a radical form of egotistical self-loss. With strong group identity, I lose sight of myself while imagining that I have at last found myself. Anti- or nonindividualist theorists who promote strong group identity are thus promoting a self-unaware egotism, while working to discredit the aspiration to a much less egotistical self-concern. Given this process of self-loss, it is a wonder that strong group identity can find defenders who claim to be sympathetic to individualism.

I have said that three concepts—identity, autonomy, and authenticity—make up a serviceable framework for discussions of individualism. The concept of identity seemed to be the place to start, and so I did. Some effort at self-knowledge, at ascertaining who one is and what one wants, is the precondition of both autonomy and authenticity. I also said that consideration of any of the concepts necessarily involves at least a little attention to the other two: The three concepts are interrelated and even merge. I therefore think that in what I have tried to say about the concept of identity, I have already suggested a few implications for the concepts of autonomy and authenticity. I cannot spend very much time on these latter two. As it is, the three concepts are not radically distinct from one another. But I do wish to amplify what I said at the start: The endorsement of autonomy and authenticity, which are indispensable to many kinds of individualism, including democratic individuality, can go so far as to convert self-concern into egotistical self-insistence and in consequence, lead to a measure of self-loss, just as the endorsement of identity can go too far.

What, then, follows for autonomy and authenticity from an understanding of personal identity that eschews personality as the true locus of identity and emphasizes individual infinitude and the episodic quality of my individual realness? Perhaps the most important conclusion, which I offer uncertainly, is that whenever autonomy is seen as a continuous, rather than as an occasional or episodic, state of the individual, then the danger of egotistical self-insistence grows, and with it, self-loss of one sort or another. The case may be somewhat different with authenticity, as I shall try to indicate. But in general I believe that continuous autonomy or authenticity is a project that cuts one off from the full extent of self-consciousness and consciousness of one's experience.

If this line of argument is defensible, then the concepts of autonomy and authenticity perforce undergo revision at the hands of democratic individuality. The heart of the revision is to see that autonomy and authenticity, like identity, are episodic and precarious, not pure and permanent achievements. (I think the notion of the episodic points to a more general fact of self-conscious life: the enormous importance for experience and instruction of moments, glimpses, and fragments.)

Concerning autonomy, I would say that the basic notion—that a person should be encouraged to try to take some control over the direction of his or her life—is indissociable from any individualism, including democratic individuality. Autonomy is self-direction rather than submission to the dictates of other agents and agencies. But certain interpretations of autonomy (whether or not the word itself is used) are more consonant with the notions of individual infinitude (multitudinous inwardness) and the recurrent real me than are other interpretations.

Without defending my assertions, I would say that the idea of having a plan of life (in John Stuart Mill's phrase) is not consonant, nor are the idea of trying to make oneself into a work of art or the idea of living one's life as an artistic process or as a story or patterned narrative. All these ideas exact a big loss in one's ability to encounter heterogeneous experience and to learn from it and distill it into one's best words. Openness to rebirth, a turn in a new direction, and abandonment are blocked. The self-loss involved is potentially great, while the self-insistence, the self-importance involved is likely to blind a person to the equal dignity and equal reality of other persons. More consonant with a sense of personal identity as revised by democratic individuality (and indeed flowing from it) are a few other interpretations of autonomy. One is Thoreau's incitement to live deliberately rather than remaining at the random mercy of conformity to fashion and its periodic shifts. Another valuable interpretation is found in Mill's itemization of commitments to pursue "the great objects of human life,"[16] which help keep us from sinking to "a lower grade of existence"[17] and also help give purpose in life by organizing one's energies. Mill singles out such commitments as the pursuit of power, wealth, or fame (or, we could add, beauty or culture). He favors a commitment to one's dignity, but his own life shows that he would not theoretically preclude mixtures, interruptions, and conversions.[18] Another is Nietzsche's idea of becoming who or what one is, with the warning (rather similar to the warning Emerson gives in "Circles") against a premature or false self-knowingness that seals a person in his or her identity:

> To become what one is, one must not have the faintest notion *what* one is. From this point of view even the blunders of life have their own meaning and value—the occasional side roads and wrong roads, the

delays, "modesties," seriousness wasted on tasks that are remote from *the* task. All this can express a great prudence, even the supreme prudence: where *nosce te ipsum* [know thyself] would be the recipe of ruin, forgetting oneself, *misunderstanding* oneself, making oneself smaller, narrower, mediocre, become reason itself.[19]

Self-knowledge will be misleading if it is not understood as always revisable and incomplete.

In a word, when the concept of autonomy is carried to the lengths of an individual's "perfectionism" (once and for all), which is a fundamentally aristocratic idea, we approach egotistical self-insistence and consequent self-loss or self-diminishment.

Concerning authenticity, I think, again, that some interpretations go well with democratic individuality, and others tend to encourage egotism and all its surplus damage to the self. I find the core of authenticity in public or social expression that is true to oneself: the effort to express oneself honestly in speech and act, to reveal oneself to others, to show what one is made of. (Obviously, the concept of authenticity is, in some respects, almost interchangeable with the concept of identity as the real me.) Authenticity, like autonomy, is indissociable from individualism in its several kinds, including democratic individuality. To live a completely repressed, hidden, or closeted life or a conformist life bound to custom or convention in every main respect could hardly comport with individualism. Nor could a life dominated by hypocrisy, dishonesty, or fear in the face of one's desire or conscience. But as with autonomy, a number of interpretations of authenticity do not square with the reconceptualization of identity effected by democratic individuality, and hence, they threaten to encourage egotistical self-insistence and loss of self.

Emerson speaks the truth in "The Poet" when he says,

> For all men live by truth, and stand in need of expression. In love, in art, in avarice, in politics, in labor, in games, we study to utter our painful secret. The man is only half himself, the other half is his expression.[20]

But then he makes a sober confession:

> Notwithstanding this necessity to be published, adequate expression is rare.... Too feeble fall the impressions on us to make us artists.... Every man should be so much an artist, that he could report in conversation what had befallen him.... The poet is the person in whom these powers are in balance, the man without impediment.[21]

Emerson thus introduces standards that are not self-generated to measure the quality of individual expression. The average level is not very high, and despite hope and every social reform, it never will be. That is to say, the average level of all the attempts that people make to express their authentic responses to their experiences of themselves and their world is not very high and never will be. Either experience registers feebly on us, or we cannot manage to express our responses adequately. Geniuses of expression are rare. The encouragement of authenticity as a widespread purpose is an encouragement to display what is not of much interest to others and is probably not of much interest to oneself, after a while. Persisting, insisting on oneself as a revealer of what lies within, will probably lead to embarrassment, and with it, eventual frustration. The public revelation of what is within may not only fail of an adequate articulation; it may be, instead, a revelation merely of one's personality. One's tastes, consumer preferences, slight idiosyncracies of manner or style, and whimsical hobbies and interests are brought forth; but one's inner eye is always on the expectations of others and the impression made on them. We become performance artists of ourselves. Authenticity can turn into loss of authenticity, loss of self, fueled by vanity. Care must be taken to encourage authenticity only on certain terms, so that egotism is not encouraged.

In general, an authenticity that grows out of the revision of personal identity made by the theorists of democratic individuality may be characterized in this way: Anyone can hope for episodes or moments of being able to express oneself in speech and acts that become memorable to oneself and to others in one's circle and beyond. Now and then, and not very often, one concentrates what is inside oneself and sends it out in a perfectly adequate representation of oneself. A whole life cannot be spent authentically, however. Even the greatest honesty and courage flag and fail, as does the enormous talent that is required but that is available only infrequently. A few exceptional moments of authentically expressive speech and conduct cannot justify a whole life, perhaps, but they may make all the difference to one's ability to think that one has occasionally been all there, has risen to the occasion.

Could there be some more continuous manner of authenticity? Of the three constitutive concepts of individualism, authenticity is the only one that holds the promise of being continuous without self-loss. The most eligible proposal may be found in the idea of task or vocation, as theorized by Emerson and Thoreau, with ample precedents before them and numerous versions of the same idea after them and not even influenced by them. The idea of vocation is venerable and pervasive. It is worth noticing, however, that it plays a significant role in the work of theorists of democratic individuality. One can express oneself authentically by doing one's work in a certain spirit. Not every kind of work lends itself to the spirit of vocation if that spirit is not religiously ascetic. But some kinds do. What matters is that one finds congenial work and does it with a whole heart. One expresses oneself authentically by devotion to work that has rules, traditions, and models of its own; one could not have originated them. They frame one's energies and talents, but they do not dictate the full content or result of one's efforts.

Pursuing a vocation is not like following a recipe; rather, it is like committing oneself to a project that requires continuous acts of adaptation, some improvisation, one's own angle of vision, some virtue, and some departure from what has been done routinely. These requirements, if even only partly met, comprise a creativity that mates one's best resources and the work to be done. In the work that is best for oneself, one is taken outside oneself, out of one's social personality. One is enabled to leave a mark outside oneself. One becomes attentive, even submissive, to the work to be done. The work gets done when one forgets everything but the work. In such self-forgetfulness, aspects of oneself are enlisted and employed that the process of expressing social personality does not begin to reach. This, or something like this, would be a more continuous authenticity.

"But do your work," says Emerson in "Self-Reliance," "and I shall know you. Do your work and you shall reinforce yourself."[22] Also, "[d]o that which is assigned you, and you cannot hope too much or dare too much."[23] Thoreau says that "what is once well done is done forever";[24] "[a] man's whole life is taxed for the least thing well done";[25] and "[l]et every one mind his own business, and endeavor to be what he was made."[26]

The tragedy is that most people do not have work that lends itself to the ideal of vocation. The formulations of Emerson and Thoreau most appropriately suit the task of producing one's best sentences. One lives to articulate and formulate. Most people do not live for such an end; more important, their work lends itself only to occasional fulfilling moments or episodes in otherwise unfulfilling jobs. Or is even so much too much to hope for? If so, the conclusion must be that the idea of authenticity as vocation cannot now (or ever?) be consistent with democratic individuality. Vocation is not egotistical self-loss; it is actually one of the best interpretations of care for the self. But it seems available only to a comparative few. An equally important point is that only rarely do theorists of authenticity locate in vocation one of authenticity's true sites. When vocation is not the center, the tie between authenticity and egotistical self-loss is likely to be strong.

My overall contention is that identity, autonomy, and authenticity tend to be, when reimagined by the theory of democratic individuality, episodic rather than continuous and secure. I would add that if episodes do not suffice, we must face the following consequences of our determination to understand the main constitutive concepts of individualism as continuous states of being: We will equate *identity* with what turns out to be the completely socialized personality, and we will be compelled to license the untrammeled and hubristic assertiveness of a few. We will be forced to conclude that only a few can plausibly aspire to *autonomy* (a tight control over the plan of one's life) or to *authenticity* (a frequent, unimpeded, and intrinsically valuable personal expressiveness). If theorists want identity, autonomy, and authenticity to be continuous, they are led, willingly or not, to aristocracy or some other elitism. And they also encourage egotism, willingly or not. Then, too, the move to realize these concepts through immersion in group identity is only confusion and moral disaster. The three concepts that help constitute individualism, when they are not democratically revised, may even rationalize aspirations to kinds of individualism that may not be better, morally or existentially, than some kinds of anti- and nonindividualism, provided these latter are unarmed, unmobilized, and noninterventionist practices, like the practices of isolated and freely associated enclaves and communes. I will not, however, befriend "my station and its duties" in order to combat inflamed egotism, as some have done. The aim is to see in the aspiration to democratic individuality a brave attempt to battle self-loss in its several egotistical forms.

Notes

1. Richard E. Flathman, *Willful Liberalism: Voluntarism and Individuality in Political Theory and Practice* (Ithaca, N.Y.: Cornell University Press, 1992), 166–224.

See also his *Reflections of a Would-Be Anarchist: Ideals and Institutions of Liberalism* (Minneapolis: University of Minnesota Press, 1998), esp. chaps. 1, 6.

2. Flathman, *Willful Liberalism,* 216–17.

3. Ibid., 216.

4. Ralph Waldo Emerson, "Self-Reliance" (1841), in *Essays and Lectures* (New York: Literary Classics of the United States, 1983), 262.

5. Aristotle, *Nicomachean Ethics,* trans. Terence Irwin (Indianapolis: Hackett, 1985), IX: 4, 8, pp. 245–47, 253–55. Also of special relevance is the critique of egotism in D. H. Lawrence, "Democracy" (c. 1923), in *Phoenix: The Posthumous Papers of D. H. Lawrence* (New York: Viking, 1972), 699–718.

6. Alexis de Tocqueville, *Democracy in America* (1835), 2 vols., trans. Henry Reeve, rev. Francis Bowen, and ed. Phillips Bradley (New York: Vintage, 1959), vol. 2, bk. 2, chap. 2, p. 104.

7. Jean-Jacques Rousseau, "Discourse on the Origins and Foundations of Inequality Among Men," in *The First and Second Discourses* (1755), ed. Roger D. Masters (New York: St. Martin's Press, 1964), esp. 128–51.

8. Emerson, "Self-Reliance," 261, 261, 263, 273, 278.

9. Stephen E. Whicher, Robert E. Spiller, and Wallace E. Williams, eds., *The Early Lectures of Ralph Waldo Emerson* (Cambridge, Mass.: Harvard University Press, 1964), vol. 2, 285–86.

10. Ralph Waldo Emerson, "Illusions" (1860), in *The Conduct of Life,* in *Essays and Lectures,* 1122.

11. Ibid.

12. Emerson, "Self-Reliance," 272.

13. Henry David Thoreau, conclusion to *Walden* (1854), in *Walden and Other Writings* (New York: Modern Library, 1937), 286–87.

14. Robert Frost, "Carpe Diem" (1949), in *Collected Poems, Prose, and Plays* (New York: Literary Classics of the United States, 1995), 305.

15. Walt Whitman, *Complete Poetry and Collected Prose* (New York: Literary Classics of the United States, 1982), 395. Compare the discussion of the real me in Richard Poirier, "In Praise of Mess," *London Review of Books,* 4 June 1998, 20.

16. John Stuart Mill, "Utilitarianism" (1863), in *Essays on Ethics, Religion, and Society: Collected Works of John Stuart Mill,* vol. 10 (Toronto: University of Toronto Press, 1969), 236.

17. Ibid., 212.

18. Ibid., 212, 235–36.

19. Friedrich Nietzsche, *Ecce Homo* (1908), in *On the Genealogy of Morals and Ecce Homo,* trans. Walter Kaufmann (New York: Vintage, 1969), 254. There are interesting sentences on being oneself, on becoming oneself, and on forgetting oneself in Nietzsche's "Schopenhauer as Educator" (1874), in *Untimely Meditations,* trans. R. J. Hollingdale (Cambridge: Cambridge University Press, 1983), 127, 133, 155, and passim. Of special relevance is the remark that "men have now become so complex and many-sided they are bound to become dishonest whenever they speak at all, make assertions and try to act in accordance with them" (133). For a discussion of Nietzsche's concept of becoming oneself, see Alexander Nehamas, *Nietzsche: Life as Literature* (Cambridge, Mass.: Harvard University Press, 1985), 171–72.

20. Emerson, "The Poet" (1844), in *Essays and Lectures,* 448.

21. Ibid.

22. Emerson, "Self-Reliance," 264.
23. Ibid., 279.
24. Henry David Thoreau, "Civil Disobedience" (1849), in *Walden and Other Writings*, 646.
25. Henry David Thoreau, *A Week on the Concord and Merrimack Rivers* (1849) (New York: Crowell, 1961), 125.
26. Thoreau, conclusion to *Walden*, 290.

CHAPTER FIVE

The Fetish of Individuality:
Richard Flathman's Willfully Liberal Politics

Ronald Beiner

The intention that animates Richard Flathman's liberalism lacks nothing for clarity: It is to push the idea of liberalism as far as it will go in the direction of a minimalist conception of political community, short of ceasing to be liberalism and turning into an anarchist or libertarian politics.[1] The motivation behind this theoretical project is equally clear: His political philosophy is motivated by an intense and sometimes hysterical fear of the agencies of state power, as well as a fear that a strongly politicized conception of human purposes will constrain and diminish the otherwise much more expansive range of human possibilities. I confess that when I look at the political characteristics of contemporary liberal societies, what I see is radically different from what Flathman perceives: not a hyperpoliticized experience of life that threatens to crowd out concerns beyond the boundaries of politics but an underpoliticized existence that leaves most citizens disempowered and indifferent; not a monster state that politicizes everything but a state that is fairly diffident in applying political power to desirable public purposes (for instance, with respect to public regulation of the economy and the amelioration of material inequalities). In one of his more apocalyptic moments, Flathman writes, "[T]he fires of state power burn hot and destructively among us" (*Reflections*, 102). I honestly cannot square this judgment with my own perception of the ambitions of the liberal state, and when Flathman refers to "the rage to legislate and administer that is rampant in the modern state" (*Reflections*, 175, n. 12), I wish he would specify precisely what domains of legislation and administration he would like to see expunged from liberal statecraft.

It is tempting to jump to the (unwarranted) conclusion that Flathman's real agenda is to slander the state in order to impugn its welfare functions (which is the purpose of most, though not all, contemporary enemies of state authority).[2] There are some suggestions in this direction in chapter 1 of *Reflections of a Would-Be Anarchist:* Willful liberalism, according to Flathman, presupposes "a substantial number of associates who for the most part 'take care of themselves,' who do not need to be 'cared for' by others or by society. And there must be associates who, by cultivating virtuosities such as civility and especially magnanimity, care for others in the [emphatically minimalist!] sense of not inflicting themselves harmfully or destructively on the latter" (*Reflections,* 15–16). He also complains that proponents of what he calls "virtue liberalism" place too much emphasis on the problem of social equality, at the cost of what ought to be the dominant liberal concern, namely, themes of free agency and self-enactment (*Reflections,* 9–11, 131; *Willful Liberalism,* 4–5). On the other hand, in his book on Thomas Hobbes he concedes that "use of governmental authority and power is sometimes the least objectionable way to combat unjustifiable inequalities" (*Thomas Hobbes,* 170; unfortunately, he fails to specify the kinds of situations for which this resort to state power is or is not appropriate); and he at least hints that he has little sympathy for neoconservative critics of the welfare state (*Reflections,* 123–24, 178, n. 11).

In *Willful Liberalism,* we get the same tension between, on the one hand, Flathman's reluctance to commit himself to any particular set of political-economic prescriptions, and on the other hand, his insinuation that contemporary liberalism's preoccupation with social equality and the defense of the welfare state constitutes a betrayal of what fundamentally defines the liberal vision of politics. He writes that "[s]trong voluntarism doesn't attempt to provide, in advance and on the basis of (say) a theory of political economy, a recipe for determining what the state or other aspects of public life can and cannot, should and should not do.... Accordingly, there may be circumstances under which the measures characteristic of socialist and welfare states will be appropriate" (210–11), contrary to the libertarian dogma that such measures are never appropriate. Yet there are repeated hints that he disapproves strongly of the welfarist thrust of much of the most influential versions of recent liberal theory (see *Willful Liberalism,* 128, n. 2, where Flathman makes explicit that "welfare liberalism and the welfare state" embody a failure of nerve in relation to the robustly "voluntarist" version of liberalism that he favors and on whose behalf he argues throughout the book). Again, it is in Flathman's most Oakeshottian moments that his antipathy to the welfarist version of liberalism is most apparent. He appeals to Michael Oakeshott in trying to clarify what he finds repellent and what he finds attractive in Friedrich Nietzsche's antiegalitarianism (Nietzsche "crystallizes resistances that I have come to have concerning liberalism as it has evolved" [*Willful Liberalism,* 181, n. 77] during the last century). According to Oakeshott, liberalism properly understood is concerned with "the menace of 'sovereign' authority and with constitutional devices [namely, institutionally embodied "natural rights"] to reduce it.... the menace was identified as the propensity of rulers to inhibit the enjoyment of these rights by the exercise of lordship."[3]

> But these "natural rights" came to include the enjoyment of certain substantive conditions of things capable of being assured only in the exercise of lordship (e.g. employment, medical attention, education) and consequently what was menacing became, not a lordly managerial government, but a government which failed in its lordly office of assuring to subjects the enjoyment of these conditions. (*Willful Liberalism,* 181, n. 77)

When one puts this sympathetic appeal to Oakeshott together with Flathman's earlier suggestion (in *Willful Liberalism,* at the end of part 2, section 1) that the authentic understanding of liberalism is the voluntarist one—that social agents should make their own lives without paternalistic intervention by the state—and that recent liberals have caved in to leftist and communitarian challenges "by altering that understanding and sometimes by questioning their own commitment to it" (*Willful Liberalism,* 127), one can discern a definite doctrine concerning the relation between liberalism and the pursuit of social justice, however reluctant Flathman may be to profess it openly.

In fact, however, concerns about political economy and issues of distributive justice cannot be what is driving Flathman's central preoccupations as a liberal, for if they were, these topics would be better represented in his writings.[4] It is clear that something else lies at the core of his reflections, namely, the idea of an unbounded art of living, the self's commitment to the project of its own self-design or self-fabrication, and how this existential enterprise relates to both philosophy and politics, or how philosophy, morality, and politics might constrain or inhibit the self's joy in its own self-creation. Flathman thinks that libertarianism (with which he otherwise has so much in common) has been corrupted by its vulgar "preoccupation with truck and barter" and by its failure to see that the fundamental concern of the philosophical individualist should be "with the making and living of lives, not with 'making a living'" (*Willful Liberalism*, 211, n. 110; he cites the authority of Nietzsche in this context). The catchword of Flathman's political philosophy is self-making, and it is for individuals to make their individuality, not for collectivities or individuals in concert to make their collective or citizenly identity.[5] Like Michel Foucault in the last phase of his work, Flathman conceives, as the supreme end of life, an aesthetics of the self whereby self-designing individuals fashion the authentic singularity of themselves, and the chief purpose of political reflection is to identify threats that politics might pose to this extravaganza of self-making.[6]

Indeed, politics poses such a threat, from Flathman's point of view, that the very status of citizen is regarded as suspect. Citizenship, he writes, is "an office" and thus is implicitly a function of "a politically organized and governed society" (*Reflections*, 157). Therefore, to assume this office is already to be "enmeshed" or "embroiled" in the state (182–83, n. 22). "To become a citizen is to submit to political rule; it is to yield to rule that aims to make one into what the regime wants one to be" (157). Contrary to the deluded imaginings of participatory democrats, who pretend that citizenship can involve "all citizens [ruling] all of the time," membership in political community can never be free of "the sting of the submission that is involved in acquiring the office of citizenship" (158). In fact, for most individuals, the reality of citizenship (obscured by "the moraline language of legitimacy and obligation") consists in more or less steady submission to an elite (158).

Embracing the office of citizenship therefore implicates us in a structure of authoritative rule, however much we may delude ourselves that we are partners in an enterprise of self-rule (or of ruling-and-being-ruled-in-turn):

> [W]hen we identify ourselves first and foremost as citizens we conscript ourselves to the state that creates that office; in making the activities of citizenship our primary commitment we risk adding the force of our thinking and acting to the authority and power of the state. To the extent that politics becomes avidly participatory and government widely

popular, political rule [perniciously] extends its range and deepens its [otherwise already too deep] penetrations. (158)[7]

Or as Flathman elsewhere puts it:

> [C]itizenship is inseparable from authority.... [Authority] has a role to play only when we disagree concerning the merits of the actions we should and should not take, the policies we should and should not adopt.... either authority has no work to do or it works to give us a reason for an action that we would not otherwise (that is, in the absence of authority) take. To subscribe to authority is to commit oneself to take actions that one would not take if considered exclusively on the merits of the actions themselves [a commitment one can never make without regret].... [Consequently,] citizenship implicates us in the perhaps necessary but nevertheless objectionable mode of relationship that is subscription to political authority. ("Citizenship and Authority," 143–44, 147)

Flathman's remarks concerning citizenship in *Willful Liberalism*, though brief, help a lot to elucidate just how profoundly hostile he is to what he calls our society's "morally charged and therefore onerous politicality" (*Willful Liberalism*, 198, n. 99; strangely, be claims that it is not just our own society that is pervaded by this onerous politicality; Michel Montaigne's, Hobbes's, and Nietzsche's societies are also pervaded by it). The discussion of citizenship occurs in the context of Flathman's important critique of Tocquevillean liberalism in part 1, chapter 2 of *Willful Liberalism* (74–80). Alexis de Tocqueville, like other liberals, is worried that the seeming liberty and pluralism of democratic life in the United States masks a deeper conformism, "a new physiognomy of servitude."[8] "Variety is disappearing from the human race; the same ways of acting, thinking, and feeling are to be met with all over the world" (quoted in *Willful Liberalism*, 77). Genuine independence is therefore in deep peril in this new egalitarian age and is in need of rescue. The means of rescue, for Tocqueville, is a heightened sense of citizen engagement; a strong experience of citizenship and civic-mindedness will rebuild the cultural resources for individuality that other aspects of modern life dissolve. As Flathman sums up the Tocquevillean analysis: "[I]ndependence or individuality requires *political* activity.... Tocqueville looked to politics rather than government to check these tendencies and to invigorate independence and diversity" (*Willful Liberalism*, 78). Flathman makes the observation here (which will turn out to be a key one) that Tocqueville is relying in this analysis on "a distinction [the politics/government distinction] that requires scrutiny" (78). As Flathman correctly perceives, the Tocquevillean strategy is to push liberalism as far as possible in the direction of civic republicanism, so far, in fact, that Tocqueville's proposed cure for U.S. conformism and sameness reads like a direct anticipation of Hannah Arendt's political vision (see *Willful Liberalism*, 78). Flathman himself, of course, wishes to push liberalism in precisely the opposite direction, hence the crucial importance of his debate with Tocqueville on the topic of citizenship.

Why does Flathman say that the politics/government distinction requires scrutiny? As a good liberal, Tocqueville is extremely anxious about the centralizing momentum of modern government and the danger that it will turn citizens into passive receptacles of state power; the more individual citizens can retain civic power in their own hands and assume their civic responsibilities with vigor and commitment, the greater the prospect that individuality and plurality will survive the threats to which modern life exposes them. Why does Flathman resist this analysis? The answer to this question will clarify further the force intended by Flathman when he speaks of citizenship (deprecatingly) as "an office." Flathman argues against Tocqueville that political activity cannot be adequately separated from government (and therefore cannot be an adequate prophylactic against too much government) precisely because "citizenship is an office in, or rather of, government.... Accordingly, to act as a citizen is in part to discharge the duties or fulfill the responsibilities established and defined by an entity that, on Tocqueville's view, those holding that office should be trying to act against. [This generates a t]ension between acting against that which one is acting within" (*Willful Liberalism*, 80). What results is a "*complicity* of citizenship and political activity" with "government and its immense and immensely dangerous authority and power" (80; emphasis added). In the next paragraph, Flathman refers to the futile "reach for politics *and hence government* to protect and enhance individuality" (80; emphasis added). Flathman means this to be a refutation of the Tocquevillean cure for conformity-enforcing and individuality-contracting government: Because political activity puts into practice the "office" of citizenship and because this office is a function of governmental authority, what is meant to counter centralized authority actually reinforces it; no matter how hard one tries to direct one's civic energies *against* the established regime, one cannot escape "complicity" with it. Given the concision of Flathman's account here, it is easy to miss just how paradoxical his argument is. Suppose one asserts one's sense of civic responsibility by joining with fellow citizens in protest marches against the policies of a heavy-handed or mean-spirited government. Flathman sees this as complicity in the threat to individuality embodied in government per se. How so? I suppose he could reply that if the efforts of the protesters ultimately prevailed, they would simply succeed in substituting a new regime, legislating a new set of policies that would presume to install an authoritative regulation of civic life for all citizens (true!), that is, that the very act of participating politically aspires to government, or to contributing to the authoritative regulation of the life of fellow citizens (true again). But this simply restates the claim that Flathman wishes to establish, which is that the real threat to individuality and plurality does not reside simply in oppressive or excessive government; rather, it is implicit in civic involvement generally. Governmental constraint of individuality is coterminous with civic activity as such (which is what Flathman means by the reference to "politics and hence government").[9]

As Flathman emphasizes throughout his work, anyone who has read Ludwig Wittgenstein with care and attention (as he himself certainly has) knows that language and social convention thoroughly constitute human experience, and therefore no reasonable liberal will regard "atomism"—the idea that individuals are self-sufficient units rather than products of socialization, tradition, and constitution by linguistic and historical communities—as anything other than an entirely unpersuasive myth. On the other hand, the rhetoric of self-making and the notion that it should be the ideal of liberal politics to leave individuals as much as possible to their own devices reinscribe the idea that individuals can make a life for themselves in abstraction from social relations and larger political realities. It seems almost as if the purpose of Flathman's persistent fascination with Wittgenstein is to keep reminding himself of a reality that he is constantly tempted to wish away, namely, the social constitution of individual experience. It is, as the great voices of liberalism since the nineteenth century have forcefully brought to our attention, certainly true that for those living in a mass society, autonomy and meaningful individuality are continually in jeopardy. And it is also undoubtedly the case that it is a leading purpose of Flathman's celebration of individuality to respond to the powerful critics of the social conformism reigning within a mass society (see *Willful Liberalism,* 107:

Flathman cites Tocqueville, Thoreau, William James, Nietzsche, Max Weber, José Ortega y Gasset, Arendt, Erving Goffman, and Oakeshott). But when Flathman echoes Oakeshott's indictment of the "individual manqué" created by the statist and paternalistic political culture of the modern age (*Willful Liberalism*, 203), he is invoking a more radically individualistic—and more emphatically anticivic—social ideal than the conceptions of individuality appealed to by Tocqueville, by John Stuart Mill in his more Tocquevillean moments, or by Arendt.[10] Unlike the more civic-minded nineteenth-century liberals, who shared Flathman's concerns about individuality and plurality, Flathman's preferred liberalism "would favor public arrangements and institutions exclusively to the extent that they serve private values" (*Willful Liberalism*, 208). This commitment to hyperindividuality and the corresponding dismissal of political life as a "self-diminishing activity" (*Willful Liberalism*, 205) helps explain why Nietzsche looms so large in *Willful Liberalism*—and not just this or that aspect of Nietzsche, but specifically Nietzsche in his most antipolitical and hyperindividualistic guise.[11] (Flathman knows that there are dramatically different sides to Nietzsche's thought, but he deliberately highlights the side of Nietzsche that he thinks can be most suitably appropriated to his own conception of voluntaristic liberalism.) It is striking that the epigram that is quoted most frequently in the three books upon which I have focused in this chapter is from Nietzsche, and it expresses a thought that is brutally individualistic: "This is what *I* am; this is what *I* want:—*you* can go to hell!" (quoted in *Willful Liberalism*, 177, 190; *Thomas Hobbes*, 50, n. 15; *Reflections*, 167, n. 9, 168, n. 3).[12]

What does it mean to "favor public arrangements and institutions exclusively to the extent that they serve private values"? Which "private values"? Flathman knows that politics is inescapable (otherwise one would be able to opt for anarchism rather than liberalism), and he surely knows that any form of politics (including liberal politics) enforces a particular ranking of ideals and aspirations, social practices and moral priorities, ways of life and human possibilities. Yet he recurrently appeals to an experience of individuality that would simply turn its back on the political realm and presume to "make itself" in a social vacuum that actually, as Flathman knows, cannot exist. (As quoted earlier, Flathman conjures up the impossible dream—his exemplars here are Montaigne, Hobbes, and Nietzsche—of withdrawal from "societies that are pervaded with a morally charged and therefore onerous politicality" [*Willful Liberalism*, 198, n. 99]: One cannot fully achieve this withdrawal, Flathman concedes, but there is in the mere attempt to accomplish the impossible a genuine pathos.) Flathman's political ideal is nicely encapsulated in a formulation he borrows from William James: "Hands off: ... It is enough to ask of each of us that he should be faithful to his own opportunities and make the most of his own blessings, without presuming to regulate the rest of the vast field" (*Willful Liberalism*, 66).[13] Whether or not we are openly presuming this, or willing or not to acknowledge this presumption, the fact is that the vast field *is* being regulated (that is what politics is, and again, Flathman concedes that politics is inescapable), and therefore the promise of a hands-off policy that simply leaves individuals to pursue their own opportunities and develop their own blessings is one that cannot be fulfilled.

Flathman recognizes that it is not easy to carry through in a thoroughgoing way the voluntarist impulse that forms the essence of liberalism as Flathman conceives it. As he writes, "The fundamental and abiding commitment of liberalism is to the most disturbing moral and political idea of all, the idea that each and every human being should be free to think and act as she sees fit. This idea is no more than barely intelligible, and the ideal of implementing it fully is manifestly impossible to achieve" (*Willful Liberalism*, 14). But (leaving aside the question of how to implement fully one's normative principles and sticking with the question of what those ultimate normative commitments should be), Flathman never satisfactorily answers the question his inquiry naturally generates: If unconstrained self-enactment is the core liberal ideal, if uninhibitedly free agency is what gives liberalism its normative power, why stop with liberalism? Why not carry forward all the way to libertarianism? Why not be an anarchist rather than merely a would-be anarchist? Why not scrap institutionalizations and institutionalisms rather than merely abide them grudgingly? Flathman is explicitly and deliberately reluctant to apply his principles to concrete policy questions, and I have considerable sympathy for the reasons that underlie this reluctance.[14] Nonetheless, I think it would help a lot to clarify the content of Flathman's normative vision if he allowed himself to illustrate in more detail how these theoretical commitments might translate into practical commitments. Let me offer an example of how the puzzle I have presented is left unanswered by Flathman—for reasons, I think, that go to the heart of his not-fully-coherent normative commitments. In *Reflections*, (133–34), he lets it be known that he favors gun control legislation "because it might restrict somewhat the distribution of weapons among folks like you and me [as opposed to criminals, who will manage to acquire guns in any case]." If individuality and plurality are the supreme liberal goods, why allow the state to prevent individuals from expressing their individuality by purchasing a wonderful plurality of different kinds of guns? Should not a strongly voluntarist liberal celebrate a liberal society where "folks like you and me" (as opposed to criminals) exercise their powers of self-enactment through their diverse taste in guns, rather than being boringly, monotonously gun-averse? In a liberal society governed by will rather than by reason, one should be fully open to (i.e., relish the excitement of) being surprised at any moment by what one's willful and exuberantly unpredictable fellow citizens will spring on one. Again, why liberalism and not libertarianism?

Flathman's liberalism is situated at the threshold that divides liberalism from libertarianism, and he exposes his thought to the full force of the tension between the warring normative ideals that pull on one from both sides of this threshold. Flathman's liberalism, as he openly admits, is composed within the intellectual space of the strong temptation to step outside liberalism, to come down on the anarchist or libertarian side of the threshold.[15] In order to articulate a more persuasive social philosophy, Flathman needs to spell out why, on an issue like gun control, his appreciation of agencies of social regulation allows him to remain true to his genuinely liberal (or even "virtue liberal") impulses, to fight off the temptation to give in to his libertarian impulses. But to give such an account, he would have to start to flesh out more substantive conceptions of shared human goods and would thus violate his "individuality-oriented," "agency-oriented," voluntarist ideal (which tries to avoid substantive teleological arguments at all costs). It seems to me that Flathman simply evades this predicament by refusing to spell out his own commitments.

It is hopeless to think that on major issues like gun control, social welfare policies, education, or environmental policies, the outcomes can be "left for each of us to determine for ourselves" (*Willful Liberalism*, 13). Rather, as Flathman sometimes concedes, such issues are inescapably matters for political determination, and it makes sense to empower the broadest range of citizens so that as many of them as possible can contribute to the political determination of outcomes that will shape a public life shared by all. By urging us to settle for a minimalist conception of citizenship, Flathman's politics would have the effect of getting us to resign ourselves to less control over our collective destiny than is tolerable, given the magnitude of what is, willy-nilly, at stake in political life. By encouraging us to think that the major spheres of life-praxis can and should be largely privatized, the idea of self-enacting individuality misconstrues our existential situation and mystifies our relationship to our society.

I want to conclude with two reflections on Flathman's relationship to the discipline of political philosophy, one paying tribute to his fidelity to the vocation of the political philosopher and the other criticizing a kind of resistance on his part to the rationalist predisposition, as it were, of the political philosopher as such. Let me present the latter reflection first (which will allow me to end on a note appreciative of Flathman's substantial intellectual contribution).

The main theme of Flathman's recent work in political philosophy is the idea that political philosophers (or at least liberal political philosophers who cherish individuality as much as he does) should give less emphasis to notions of shared rationality and considerably more emphasis to the notion of incommensurable wills. In general, we think of as liberals thinkers, like John Rawls and Jürgen Habermas, who, in their vision of politics, aspire to public reason and mutual transparency. We think of as antiliberal, on the other hand, thinkers, like Nietzsche and Martin Heidegger, who disdain liberal democracy because it banishes the sense of mystery and quasi-religious impenetrability that gives depth to human experience. Flathman's purpose in *Willful Liberalism* is to offer a version of liberalism that embraces the opacities and impenetrabilities that liberals typically fear and antiliberals typically relish. As he puts it, his purpose in the book is to foreground and valorize "not only difference, separation and incompatibility but indeterminacy, opacity, and incomprehensibility... features of human affairs that have no better than an insecure place in liberal thinking [and] that are accorded much greater prominence in doctrines and outlooks widely regarded to be illiberal" (*Willful Liberalism*, 119). Hence the appeal of "voluntarism": "Perhaps [liberals'] frequent insistence on the rational, reasonable, mutually intelligible character of action itself serves to make voluntary conduct vulnerable to control and to diminution? Do liberal attempts to augment these characteristics of action serve rather to enhance the possibilities for intrusion and manipulation?" (*Willful Liberalism*, 128). These questions are given greater urgency, for Flathman, by the rise of new versions of liberal theory—what he generically labels "virtue liberalism"—that place the idea of public reason and public deliberation at the center of the liberal idea. Rawls offers a weak and ambiguous species of virtue liberalism; "more uncompromisingly virtue-oriented" varieties of liberal theory include the liberalisms formulated by William Galston, Amy Gutmann, and Stephen Macedo, "all of whom share Habermas's view that, ideally, no domain of thought and action would be exempt from the requirements of deliberative rationality and morality" (*Reflections*, 10). If citizens of a liberal political community are required to be rational deliberators, then what is philosophically salient are the features of human experience that are shareable and mutually accessible; if we deliberate in common about rational norms of public life, then in principle, once those norms are rationally defined, they are binding upon all of us. The purpose of political philosophy, on this view, is to pursue a rational dialogue concerning the character of suitable public norms, desirable public goods, and the public virtues necessary to sustain this rational dialogue and secure its appointed ends.

This is the conception of liberal political philosophy that causes Flathman the most grief. He relishes opacity and diversities of experience sufficiently far-removed from each other as to render the human beings who are the subjects of these experiences well-nigh mutually unintelligible to each other, and he strenuously rejects those versions of rationalist liberalism that interpret such diversities and opacities as a problem to be overcome rather than as something to be welcomed and embraced.[16] This set of ideas is nicely expressed in the following commentary on William James:

> [G]roup relationships must be, in part, relationships of mutual intelligibility or comprehension. The actions of numbers of people who are unfathomable to one another may come together to produce consequences that they severally recognize or not, intend or seek to prevent, welcome or regret, and so forth, but some measure of mutual intelligibility is a necessary condition of groups and group activity. One of the charms of

James's thinking is his relish for cases in which this condition goes unsatisfied. (*Willful Liberalism*, 72)

Flathman's central idea is that individuality (and therefore plurality as well) flourishes where there is a form of social order that favors the emergence of individuals who are unique bundles of desire, passion, and purpose; who can be only inadequately fathomed by applying the rational categories generally available for the understanding of human beings; who vitiate general norms and rules; and who are perhaps barely intelligible.[17] The flourishing of individuality is the flourishing of existential mystery, which defeats (or at least eludes) the rational comprehension of human beings by each other.[18] To Flathman's credit, this is a radical social vision. The problem with all of this, quite apart from whether it represents a fully attractive conception of social order, is that there is something in this philosophical idea that runs against the very idea of political philosophy as an enterprise of rational understanding and public reason-giving. If the most desirable social order is one that spawns individuals who are essentially unfathomable, does this not undercut the possibility of political philosophy as a discipline of rational reflection on desirable human purposes and desirable social orders? If will rather than reason constitutes the core human reality, would there not seem to be something misguided about the whole enterprise of political philosophy as the pursuit of rational argument and rational dialogue about the best way for human beings to live their lives, individually and collectively? Flathman's brief comments concerning postmodernism (namely, that its adherents postulate "the claim ... that every presumption of more or less definite mutual or even self-understanding can and should be exposed as illusory" [*Willful Liberalism*, 171]) show that he is aware of this risk. Like the postmodernists, does Flathman's celebration of will pull the rug out from under his own activity as a reason-seeking political philosopher?

I promised two reflections on Flathman's relationship to political philosophy; now for the second of these:

Political philosophy in its most ambitious sense consists in the relentless pursuit of a few favored themes. It is a form of reflection that is uncompromisingly focused on an intellectual epicenter; it then radiates outward, extending to every dimension of social and moral life. Richard Flathman's work meets these highest standards of political philosophy, and the idea of individuality, whether it is or is not ultimately defensible as the supreme political-philosophical norm, is unlikely to find a more articulate champion or a more genuinely philosophical advocate.

Notes

1. Richard Flathman's works cited in this chapter, and their abbreviations, are *Willful Liberalism: Voluntarism and Individuality in Political Theory and Practice* (Ithaca, N.Y.: Cornell University Press, 1992); hereafter *Willful Liberalism*. *Thomas Hobbes: Skepticism, Individuality, and Chastened Politics* (Newbury Park, Calif.: Sage Publications, 1993); hereafter *Thomas Hobbes*. "Citizenship and Authority: A Chastened View of Citizenship," in *Theorizing Citizenship*, ed. R. Beiner (Albany: State University of New York Press, 1995), 105–51; originally published in *Toward a Liberalism* (Ithaca, N.Y.: Cornell University Press, 1989); hereafter "Citizenship and Authority." *Reflections of a Would-Be Anarchist: Ideals and Institutions of Liberalism* (Minneapolis: University of Minnesota Press, 1998); hereafter *Reflections*.

2. One of the notable features of Flathman's thought that prompts this suspicion is the strong sympathy for Michael Oakeshott's efforts as a political philosopher, expressed consistently throughout Flathman's work. Oakeshott, of course, was committed to what he called "the political economy of freedom," that is, a laissez-faire understanding of the relation between state and economy; see Michael Oakeshott, "The Political Economy of Freedom," in *Rationalism and Other Essays* (London: Methuen, 1977), 37–58. That Oakeshott is the major intellectual influence upon Flathman's notions of individuality and self-enactment and that Oakeshott hugely shapes Flathman's reading of Hobbes (*Thomas Hobbes*, 174; *Willful Liberalism*, 2) are incontestable; what impact Oakeshott has on Flathman's thinking concerning the relation between liberty and social justice is much less clear.

3. Michael Oakeshott, *On Human Conduct* (Oxford: Clarendon Press, 1990), 245, n. 2.

4. In *Willful Liberalism*, 9, n. 3, Flathman recognizes that his readers will be curious where he stands on these issues, but he does little to satisfy their curiosity. What we get are tortuous equivocations: On the one hand, welfarist liberalism diminishes the voluntarist aspect of liberalism that Flathman desires to augment; on the other hand, antiwelfarist doctrines are distinct from Flathman's preferred version of liberalism because libertarianism is by definition a nonliberal doctrine. The most that Flathman can say by way of clarification is that his willful liberalism "partly overlaps with, but in fundamental respects is in opposition to, libertarianism," which falls well short of being sufficiently helpful.

5. *Willful Liberalism*, 14: "[S]elf-making and self-command wherever possible; mutual, collective, and above all governmental and political disciplines only as necessary or manifestly contributive to the former."

6. Cf. *Willful Liberalism*, 79, for Flathman's strong endorsement of Foucault's "persuasively advanced" critique of "pervasive social control ... abetted and intensified by democrat government."

7. My interpolations make explicit the judgments that are implicit throughout Flathman's text.

8. Alexis de Tocqueville, *Democracy in America*, 2 vol., ed. Phillips Bradley (New York: Vintage Books, 1957), vol. 1: 240.

9. Cf. *Reflections*, 150: "that species of state official called a citizen"!

10. Cf. *Willful Liberalism*, 50: Contrary to liberalism's critics, "my inclination is increasingly to think that liberalism is *insufficiently* individualistic."

11. Cf. *Willful Liberalism*, 166: "A liberalism that appropriated something like Nietzsche's affirmation of 'the will' would be less avid for commonality, transparency, and cooperation; it would be more appreciative and celebratory of diversity, disagreement, and mutual indifference. Perhaps it would even diminish somewhat liberalism's notorious ambivalence concerning politics, the state, and the rule of some over others that politics and the state invariably involve," that is, resolve this ambiguity in the direction of greater hostility toward politics.

12. Friedrich Nietzsche, *Will to Power* (1901) (New York: Vintage Books, 1967), para. 349.

13. Cf. *Willful Liberalism*, 79, where Flathman rebukes Tocqueville, Arendt, and participationist democrats generally for violating the hands-off rule.

14. *Willful Liberalism*, 9, n. 3: "[T]his analysis doesn't settle any of the questions concerning public policy that are debated between liberals and libertarians [nor does a suitable understanding of the relationship between theory and practice oblige the theorist to settle these questions]." *Willful Liberalism*, 13: "[S]trong voluntarism leaves open most of the issues of public policy.... the particular ways in which [our selves and our lives, our affairs and our activities] will change [as a result of embracing a more voluntarist liberalism], the shapes and characters they will acquire and assume, are left indeterminate—that is, are left for each of us to determine for ourselves." *Reflections*, 133: "If a theorist claims that her theory answers [questions of policy] she becomes, in Oakeshott's derisive sense, a 'theoretician,' an 'impudent mountebank.'"

15. *Reflections*, 79: The best liberal thinking is haunted by the thoughts of antinomians and individualist anarchists. *Reflections*, 161: "[L]iberal political theory at its best is enticed by but cannot fully embrace anarchist or antinomian thinking." *Reflections*, 180, n. 9: The best proponents of moral and political liberalism are haunted by libertarianism, anarchism, and antinomianism. Cf. *Willful Liberalism*, 208, n. 106: Anarchism and antinomianism "haunt all forms of liberalism and particularly its strongly voluntarist formulations." In "Citizenship and Authority," 151, n. 45, Flathman refers to "the immense attractiveness" of philosophical anarchism.

16. The problem with virtue liberalism, as Flathman sees it, is that it puts too much emphasis on what is public (and therefore general, shareable, and implicitly oriented to the demands of citizenship) and fails to put enough emphasis on what is private (therefore unique and inaccessible to shared experience). Cf. *Willful Liberalism*, 173: "Claims on behalf of the private realm typically valorize will and spontaneity, independence and autonomy, individuality and diversity, and are accompanied by skepticism concerning the reach of rationality, reasoning, and the principles and rules, duties, and responsibilities that the human abilities sometimes allow us to delineate and to justify to one another. In contrast, argumentation concerning the public domain stresses already-established commonalities as well as the possibilities for extending them through knowing, judging, mutually convincing justification, and the like."

17. Flathman cites three main exemplars of this philosophical ideal: Jamesian zest, Nietzschean free-spiritedness, and Oakeshottian self-enactment (*Reflections*, 153).

18. See *Willful Liberalism*, 130: Just as theological voluntarists "sought to restore the majesty of God" by emphasizing the inscrutability of divine will, so secular voluntarists attempt to elevate human self-regard by emphasizing the inscrutability of human volition ("insisting that we human beings are—or could become—what each of us chooses to make ourselves by our own acts of will"). See also, *Willful Liberalism*, 158, n. 46: The "conception of human action as wonder-ful," as involving a miracle of creativity analogous to divine action, is "the single most important idea in strong voluntarism, the idea—and ideal—in strong voluntarism that is most valuable to a liberalism with a heightened sense of and commitment to individuality."

CHAPTER SIX

Freedom, Flathman, and Feminism

Nancy J. Hirschmann

Although Richard Flathman would never call himself a feminist in the intellectual or theoretical sense nor would most of his colleagues—in a personal sense, he has been consistently supportive of colleagues and students interested in feminist concerns; he has supervised several feminist dissertations, and quite a few feminists—Nancy Hartsock, Susan Hekman, Bonnie Honig, and I—have considered him an extremely helpful and inspiring mentor.[1]

Of course, this is much more likely to be testimony to his liberalism—though I disagree with what you say, I will defend to the death your right to say it (and maybe even help you figure out *how* to say it)—than to feminism per se; for Flathman's personal support and help to feminist scholars is matched by a political theory that is in many ways antagonistic to certain popular schools of feminist thought, particularly those in the care-centered vein, because he believes they display too much affinity with communitarian political theory—to which, as every follower of Flathman's work knows, he is strongly opposed. This antagonism is most pronounced in his work on freedom and strong or "willful" liberalism because feminists have sought to reconfigure freedom and individualism along lines that are consistent with communitarian ideas and ideals.[2]

Yet at the same time, significant *aspects* of his work can be seen to lend themselves to feminist utilization and application, which is what lies at the heart of his ability to mentor feminist theorists with whom he may, for the most part, disagree. In this chapter, I want to look at the apparent ambivalence, or perhaps duality, Flathman displays on "the feminist question" by identifying another ambivalence in his work, between freedom and liberalism. I will begin by considering his theory of freedom, which is generally taken to be the hallmark of liberal theory, and indeed, for Flathman, it is a central liberal value. Specifically, freedom is for Flathman the central value of the individualism and agency that sit at the core of his liberalism. But I will then seek to complicate the relationship between liberalism and freedom by pointing out the tensions between his theory of freedom and his more recent work on liberalism, which gives important place to a notion of subjectivity that resonates with feminist ideals and concerns. Indeed, in the early pages of *Reflections of a Would-Be Anarchist,* Flathman suggests the possibility "that the ideas or ideals of willful or virtuosity liberalism have a particular pertinence to thinking currently being pressed by the oppositional forces most important to the liberal societies of our time, that is, the racial, feminist, and gay and lesbian liberation movements."[3] Part of my project here is to explore that possibility. But another part is more specifically to inquire whether rereading his theory of freedom in light of this vision of liberalism produces a more feminist-friendly interpretation of Flathman's work. Since his feminist-friendliness, I believe, is less obvious and apparent when one looks at his theory of freedom than when one considers his vision of liberalism, I want to suggest that despite the keen interdependence of freedom and liberalism in his work, his vision of the latter may have outgrown the former, and that this growth illustrates greater openness to feminist perspectives and arguments than is obvious at first glance.

Flathman's Idea of Freedom

In *The Philosophy and Politics of Freedom,* Flathman fairly overtly follows the lead of Isaiah Berlin, with his conception of "negative liberty."[4] According to Berlin, negative liberty consists in an absence of external constraints. The individual is free to the extent that she is not restrained by external forces, primarily viewed as law, physical force, and other overt coercion. "By being free in this sense I mean not being interfered with by others. The wider the area of non-interference, the wider my freedom."[5] Berlin's general notion that restraints come from outside and are alien to the self is an important basic tenet of negative liberty; specifically, other humans' direct (or, in some cases, indirect) participation "in frustrating my wishes"[6] is the relevant criterion in determining restraint.

And these "wishes," or desires, preferences, interests, and needs, which I must be able to pursue unimpeded if I am to be free, on Berlin's account, are seen as coming from me and from me alone. Flathman particularly seems to bolster this aspect of Berlin's theory; as he says in *The Practice of Rights*, what is important is that rights "serve the interests of the A's as they understand them," not as others define them.[7] For both Berlin and Flathman, desires do not need to be "brute," that is, immediate, physical, and compelling;[8] desire can just as easily be seen as long term, well thought out, and rational. The point for negative liberty, however, is that whether the desires are long term or immediate, "brute" or "rational," they are desires that the agent has formulated herself. That is, the desires may be formed in reaction to external stimuli—I may not want a brownie until I smell the ones you take out of the oven—but what matters is that this desire is mine, and I am responsible for acting on or resisting the desire.

Similarly, these desires are conscious in the sense that I have to know I have them. Certainly, desires may be responses to unconscious feelings—my yearning for the brownie may stem from repressed memories of my mother's baking and a repressed desire for the security of childhood that the smell invokes—but the relevant point again is that I want it and that I know I want it, not necessarily that I know why I want it. Thus, negative liberty draws clear-cut lines between inner and outer, subject and object, self and other. This kind of freedom, as Charles Taylor puts it, is tough-minded because of the strict notions of individual responsibility and accountability that it finds necessary to choice.[9]

It is also tough-minded, however, in the way it starkly differentiates between freedom and various other political concepts, such as equality and justice. As Berlin says, "Everything is what it is: liberty is liberty, not equality or fairness or justice or culture, or human happiness or a quiet conscience,"[10] a sentiment Flathman echoes. For instance, in their rejection of positive liberty, both Flathman and Berlin argue that values such as autonomy, rationality, and so forth, which are seen as part of liberty to theorists like Jean-Jacques Rousseau, are in fact simply other things that are being confused with liberty. Thus, negative liberty defines itself in opposition to concepts such as obligation and authority; these things, although perhaps necessary to human society, or even to individuals' pursuit of their desires, are nonetheless limitations on freedom.[11] They may even produce greater freedom in the future, but of themselves, they are immediate constraints on liberty.

In these senses, as I have already indicated, I read Flathman's vision of freedom as cohering closely with Berlin's. In *The Philosophy and Politics of Freedom,* however, Flathman goes beyond the strict "two concepts" model to hypothesize five kinds of freedom. These range from a Hobbesian freedom of movement (freedom$_1$), to freedom of agency (freedom$_2$), to autonomy (freedom$_3$), to the communitarian idea of freedom (freedom$_4$), to the transcendent notion of freedom (freedom$_5$). The first he rejects—despite his professed affinity with Hobbes—on the basis that specifically human freedom is about *action,* while *movement* is about objects. (Or insofar as "movement" pertains to humans, freedom is not a relevant consideration: If a doctor checking my reflexes hammers my knee but stands directly in front of my leg so that it cannot swing out, the movement of my leg is hindered, but not "unfree.") The remaining four notions of freedom Flathman considers possibly more plausible, though in the end he concludes that only freedom of agency is truly a valid conception of freedom.[12] This close relationship between agency and negative liberty is one that persists through his work on "willful liberalism."[13]

But there is, not surprisingly perhaps, a twist: Flathman also insists on seeing liberty as "situated." Rejecting the abstract individualism often associated with a Hobbesian state of nature, Flathman operates instead from a Wittgensteinian framework, holding that humans have "shared language, common traditions and beliefs, norms and rules that are more or less settled among persons who make up a community or association, institutions and practices invested with some species of legitimacy or authority."[14] That is, all freedom is situated in that all choices we make are limited by the context in which we live; freedom and choice are never completely abstract. This situatedness is important to freedom because it provides the context for the choices and actions that people take: "Actions take their identifications and much of their character from these features of the situations in which they occur.... actions are influenced, limited, and perhaps directed by elements external and possibly alien to the agents who take them."[15]

The situated character of freedom might seem to ally Flathman with positive liberty, despite his protestations to the contrary, particularly in his allowance of the possibility of external "direction." Positive liberty specifically seeks to include what might be called "internal barriers": fears, addictions, compulsions, desires, and thoughts that are at odds with my "true" self. Positive liberty advocates believe that we can have "second order desires," or "desires about desires."[16] Humans' conceptions of the good, both for themselves as individuals and in general, reflect and work from our capacity for reasoned reflection and rational thought, and many of our immediate or visceral desires can run contrary to these conceptions. Because of these conflicting capacities, however, it is not enough to experience an absence of external restraints, because the immediate desires I have may prevent me from achieving what I truly want. For instance, let us say that I am struggling to quit smoking, and a fight with a colleague initiates a craving for a cigarette. It could be argued that my immediate, short-term desire to smoke violates my larger, longer-term desire (say, to improve my health or to protect the well-being of the fetus I am carrying), which I honestly feel is more important to me. Being able to smoke uninhibitedly does not mean I am free (after all, smoking will not resolve the dispute with my colleague, so we cannot even argue for a trade-off between competing goals).

In his account of willful liberalism, Flathman does seem to express some affinity with the notion of conflicting desires, and he argues that what "willfulness" involves is precisely one's ability to choose between desires, to take responsibility for such choice and for directing one's self. But positive liberty often goes further, and logically, it also allows this "strong evaluation" to be performed by others, who may know my true will better than I, particularly when I am in the grip of these self-destructive desires.[17] (Hence Flathman's association of positive liberty with what he calls the "virtue liberalism" of John Rawls and Immanuel Kant.)[18] This second-guessing is the crux of Flathman's objection to positive liberty: Others can prevent me from doing certain things that will (according to them) violate my deepest desires and highest purposes, or they can force me to do other things that will (again, according to them) help me realize these purposes, in the name of freedom. Hence, Berlin defines positive liberty as a paradox: To coerce A to do X because it is for her own good is a logical impossibility, because if it is for her own good then she really wants it and therefore is not being coerced. A has willed X whether she knows it or not.[19]

Flathman says positive liberty is worse than a paradox: It is an outright contradiction to the very essence of liberty. Forcing others to be free he finds particularly repugnant, as do many others. Flathman situates himself squarely in the negative liberty camp, and indeed he says that positive liberty is not a theory of freedom at all.[20] Instead, he argues (much as does Berlin and much as I indicated earlier), positive liberty is really about something else, such as virtue, goodness, or truth (or to be more cynical, power, domination, or control). Indeed, insofar as positive variants *are* about freedom, he implies, they adopt a negative liberty model; I may have a desire both to smoke and not to smoke, but freedom involves my ability to make a choice between those two options and to take responsibility for that choice, without outside interference. The fact that positive freedom theories also contain other notions, such as autonomy, virtue, or community, does not mean they really have a different take on freedom per se, he maintains; it only means they add other things to a basic concept of freedom. But these other things are *other*, they are not about freedom.

What freedom is about in Flathman's view, then—to twist the words of his much-admired Hobbes a little—is an absence of external impediments to *action*. As Flathman says in *Toward a Liberalism*:

> "Freedom" and "unfreedom" are predicates of human actions. Roughly, actions are taken by (and hence talk of both freedom and unfreedom presupposes) persons who are "agents," that is, persons who, in the setting of a commmunity with a shared language and the elements that Wittgenstein and others have identified as necessary to such a language, form and hold beliefs; form desires and interests, objectives and purposes, that are influenced by their beliefs; frame intentions to act to satisfy their desires, interests, and so forth; and attempt to act on their intentions. Agents and actions are free insofar as their attempts to act are not prevented, impeded, or deflected from their objectives by the actions of other agents, and are unfree insofar as they are prevented, impeded, or deflected by the actions (including deliberate refusals to act) of other agents. In the absence of agency or action there is no "freedom evaluability," nothing of which either freedom or unfreedom can be predicated.[21]

This expands beyond Hobbes's "absence of impediments to motion" by focusing on the notion of an agent as a person who lives within a "form of life," who, in order not only to pursue and satisfy desires and preferences but to *form* desires and preferences in the first place, needs a social context with language that gives meaning to who she is and what she wants. A coherence with the classic negative liberty view is evident in the emphasis on the lack of coercion and the delineations between inner/self and outer/other, but Flathman notes that freedom is never abstract and must always be situated. At the same time, however, the fact that situatedness may "influence or direct" my actions, because all actions must take place in social contexts wherein others take actions that may conflict with mine, does not cross the positive liberty line of affecting the motivating desire itself. I am the subject of my own freedom in that I am the determinative force arbitrating among competing desires, as well as between these desires and the context that makes fulfilling them result in particular consequences.

Situatedness is of particular importance to the notion that freedom is about having and making choices, which is a classic aspect of Berlin's vision of negative liberty. As Flathman construes it, agency is about the ability to formulate desires and act on them, and central to this is choice. What Flathman despises most about positive liberty's "*forcer d'être libre*" [to force to be free] is the notion that one must do what another tells one to do in order to be free; the central ability to make one's own choices, for good or ill, is taken away, and along with it, freedom. Hence, he allies negative liberty with what he calls "agency liberalism" and even more strongly, "willful liberalism." Freedom is only an "instrumental good," serving the end of "acting on passions and desires, and . . . pursuing ends and purposes chosen to satisfy passions and desires."[22] The "individuality and . . . self-enactment" that he envisions as a "formal but not substantive end" demands "the widest possible freedom of individual action as a necessary but not sufficient condition of effective pursuit of this ideal."[23]

It is this need for preserving choice that delineates negative liberty in a political context. As Flathman particularly articulates in *Reflections of a Would-Be Anarchist*, he is only a "would-be" anarchist because he recognizes, albeit reluctantly, the need for laws if liberty is to be preserved;[24] absolute negative liberty would result in chaos, thus jeopardizing not only other things of importance to humans—security, justice, fairness—but freedom as well, in that one would have to spend so much time defending what one has that one would be prevented from seeking other things one wants. Laws can restore a balance between each person's liberty and others' equal liberty.[25] But even given the need for law and political society, negative liberty requires, in Berlin's words, "a certain minimum area of personal freedom which must on no account be violated.... a frontier must be drawn between the area of private life and that of public authority,"[26] an ideal with which I believe Flathman agrees.

Thus, in negative liberty, government is meant to protect individuals from each other, to preserve individuals' liberty from the external interference of other individuals' pursuit of *their* liberty. And indeed, all but Hobbes go even further to articulate a structure of government that must restrict *itself*, for it is an additional, and potentially more potent, threat to citizens' liberty as well, a sentiment Flathman strongly endorses. Government and political structures must thus serve the ends of liberty, rather than justice or equality; or rather, they serve those only insofar as they serve—or at the very least do not conflict with—liberty. Flathman's work on policing in particular brings home his suspicions of a state with a broader mandate to serve, rather than simply protect, because of the potential power of "normalization" (à la Michel Foucault) that policing and state authority holds.[27] In this, Flathman seeks to hold onto a notion of the "choosing subject," a subject who, though situated, is nevertheless strongly individualistic, not at all communitarian.

Subjectivity, Choice, and the Meaning of Constraint

Feminists who have struggled against centuries of second-guessing by men about what it is that "women want" should be sympathetic to the objections Flathman raises about positive liberty. They also, in their attention to relationship and context, have much to admire in Flathman's insistence on the situatedness of freedom and the need to understand agency and choice in appropriate contexts. However, feminists would also note that once we recognize the centrality of people's ability to make choices and to pursue "passions and desires," then two factors become prominent: the external dimensions of the barriers to liberty (those things that may be preventing me from pursuing my passions and desires); and the internal factors of desire, preference, and passions themselves (why and how it is that I come to want the things I want and to make the choices I make, and how I become a choosing subject). I will consider the latter element first, because it feeds into the former.

In his "willful liberal" configuration of situated freedom, Flathman ostensibly rejects consideration of the internal factors involved in the construction of the choosing subject as somewhat beside the point of freedom; in true negative liberty fashion, as I have said, he believes that one's desires are one's own, wherever they come from. This does not mean that he believes that subjectivity is unimportant, of course; indeed, his discussion of Foucault in *Reflections of a Would-Be Anarchist* and in his current work in progress[28] both suggest that subjectivity is a newly emerging concern for Flathman. Rather, it means he believes that subjectivity is not part of the meaning of *freedom,* which, by focusing on the absence of impediments to action, must take the subject as we find her.

Yet I wonder if Flathman is not too hard on positive liberty, and if his Wittgensteinian recognition of situatedness does not in fact demonstrate a certain affinity with it. In its focus on the internal barriers to liberty, positive liberty demands that we attend precisely to the choosing subject in freedom theory. This issue is important to feminism, for it acknowledges that freedom does not simply involve the question of whether anyone or anything is preventing one from doing what one wants to do; rather, it also involves the question of how it is that one comes to want the things one wants, to make the choices one makes. The social construction of choice—both in the sense of what choices are available in any given context and why, and in the sense of what "choice" means and how desire comes to be felt and expressed—are important to feminist attempts to intervene in the questions of freedom and agency.

Indeed, though Flathman seems to follow Berlin, who insists that positive liberty unquestionably involves external determinations of the will, specifically determination by the state (as in Rousseau's infamous *forcer d'être libre*), there are actually several levels to positive liberty, only some of which involve forcing one to be free; others involve an individual's self-assessment of competing desires. For instance, Charles Taylor—whom Flathman frequently, and perhaps justifiably, disparages as a "communitarian"[29]—interprets the positive liberty notion of following one's own true will, and "freedom from" internal desires and passions that do not represent the true self, as indicating a "divided self," a self that has—and knows it has—mutually exclusive desires that are better and worse. He focuses on internal barriers to realizing the better or higher desire rather than on the external mechanism that directs one to that desire, and he does so in an individualist fashion: In his examples, the subject always seems to know that she has a higher and lower desire and is struggling to achieve the former.[30] These examples seem to me consistent with Flathman's view. The recognition that subjectivity is important suggests that he might benefit from, even be forced to allow certain aspects of positive liberty into his account.

This question may be approached by considering the relationship between choice, which involves issues of subjectivity, and barrier or constraint, which introduces what might be called the "objective" or "descriptive" view of freedom: Freedom can be determined not by how an individual subjectively experiences reality but by an objective determination of reality. Thus, Berlin holds that freedom is determined by "the number of doors open to me"; the more doors that are open, regardless of whether I go through any of them, or even *want* to go through them, the freer I am. Berlin does concede that "the extent to which [doors] are open," as well as the relative importance of these various doors and paths, are relevant to freedom; but given the necessarily subjective dimensions of such evaluations, "the number of doors" is ultimately determinative. Freedom is thus, in an important sense, quantitative on the negative liberty model, even measurable.[31]

The advantage of defining freedom in the more objective terms of available options is that definition's ability to circumvent the fact that subjective desire is almost always contingent on social circumstances. For instance, one could not claim that a black slave was free simply because she said she did not want to leave the plantation, because this desire could be seen as the final effects of colonization. But at the same time, this shift from subjective to objective evaluation is problematic and leads to some obviously clumsy constructions. For instance, if what I want is the only option available—say to eat chocolate chip ice cream when that is the only flavor made—Berlin and many other negative liberty theorists would nevertheless insist that I am less free than I would be if I could choose between that flavor and two others, even though in both scenarios I get to eat the flavor that I want. The foreclosure of the possibility that I *might* want something other than chocolate chip, or that I could have this other flavor if I *did* want it, seems to be more important than what I actually *do* want at any given point in time.

But if we carry this logic to its conclusion, I would seem to be less free if the local convenience store carries *only* my preferred flavor of chocolate chip than if the store carried ten flavors, *none* of which are chocolate chip and *none* of which I like. This seems at best counterintuitive; even worse, it carries strong overtones of second-guessing, which is the problem of positive liberty that Berlin is the most anxious to avoid. And indeed, Flathman seems to reject the "objective" assessment of choices available that Berlin adopts—what Berlin calls the "open options" approach—precisely because of this second-guessing problem. To say I am "freer" in the latter scenario than in the former, regardless of my preferences, betrays and even undermines the individualist core on which negative liberty is based.

As I read Flathman, it is for this reason that he—along with some others, such as Stanley Benn[32]—brings notions of subjective desire back into his otherwise negative theory of freedom by emphasizing the importance of the notion of "autarchy," which refers to an agent who makes choices that are "rational" in the weak sense of "having reasons." The strong sense of rationality—having very particular reasons, the "right" reasons—transcends freedom to the realm of autonomy, which is the following of self-prescribed laws, the establishment of a *nomos* by which individuals guide their behavior. For Flathman, autonomy is an ideal *related to* freedom, but given the fact that autonomy is rarely achieved, autarchy is the best necessary condition for freedom. For without autarchy or the freedom to choose (including the freedom to choose one's own *nomos*), we can never hope to achieve autonomy.

In locating freedom in the realm of "autarchy"—the freely choosing, independent subject—Flathman (along with Benn) completely rejects heterarchy, the idea of acting on and for the desires and preferences of another. Heterarchy can only be explained in terms of coercion (which directly makes one unfree; the removal of the coercion will restore the freedom) or domination (which involves a more systematic control of another's will and desire such that the immediate coercive threat could be removed without changing her behavior or restoring it to freedom). However, the requirement that one offer reasons for one's choices means that the subjective elements fall well short of the Hobbesian pursuit of desire. Reasons require an agent to be able to articulate her preferences and evaluations within a language, as Flathman particularly notes, that puts certain limitations on choice, placing it between the objective notion that Berlin puts forth (the number of "open doors") and the subjective expression of desire (what I want).

This recognition of the importance of the subjective to freedom is significant, for it also highlights the issue of what counts as a "barrier to" or a "constraint on" liberty, specifically, whether one must consider strictly external barriers to action, or whether one must be concerned with internal barriers such as learned emotional responses. But it also raises a further question: Even if one sticks with external barriers, how far can these be pushed? Can poverty, for instance, be considered an obstacle to liberty? Can patriarchy or sexism? Certainly, an expanded view of what counts as a barrier produces more choice in an objective sense; for instance, if poverty is seen as a barrier, the number of activities that I am "unfree" to do goes up—to go out to dinner, buy a new coat, pay my utility bill—whereas if poverty is seen as a natural consequence of any economic structure, I am not "unfree" but only "unable" to do those same things. As Benn notes, "[B]y extending the range of restrictive conditions judged capable of alteration, the range of freedom-related contexts can itself be extended. Conditions formerly accepted as necessary may be called progressively into question."[33]

Moreover, the idea that the concept of a barrier can be read extremely broadly to include social conditions, political contexts, and economic structures brings into question the division between internal and external, as well as between subjective and objective, because one's structural placement in social systems, such as the economy or the sex/gender system, interacts with one's subjective experience and perception of that placement. It is the complicated divisions between specific and systemic and between internal and external that prove so heuristically useful to understanding different notions of freedom and that provide feminism with its critical purchase. In particular, these divisions enable feminists to point out ways in which customs, practices, and beliefs that men and women have accepted as "normal" in fact encode beliefs that are deeply sexist and restrict women and men in illegitimate, unjustified, and unnecessary ways, but that are internalized and construct the subjectivity of gendered individuals. Such a view allows feminists to see patriarchy as a social structure that is so wide-ranging and pervasive as to inhibit women's choices and freedom on a multiplicity of levels—from advancing in one's job or career, to going out of the house at night, to being able to develop a self-conception and range of desires not predetermined by what patriarchy tells us to want—without there being a specific identifiable act of intentional sexism.

Yet this is where Flathman's potential feminism hits some roadblocks. Given the clear emphasis on choice as essential to liberty; given the tendency Flathman displays to shy away from both an "objective" account of freedom and a narrowly subjectivist, individualized conception of choice; given his emphasis on the notion of situatedness—all this seems to suggest that he should be responsive to a fairly generous notion of "constraint" as well. On the contrary, however, Flathman seems to maintain that such an expansive reformulation of "constraint" contradicts the fundamental underpinnings of negative liberty. The central issues for him turn on notions of intentionality, assignability, accountability, and agency. And here, it seems, Flathman is at his most conservative, and here he is most opposed to feminist projects. For he says that negative liberty requires that barriers be the result of "intentional and purposive actions by identifiable agents"; barriers to liberty must involve "the possibility of obstacles deliberately placed or left by other intentional or purposive agents."[34]

The requirements of intentionality and purposiveness, Flathman suggests, eliminate from consideration impediments that are not deliberately placed but are nevertheless socially generated and constructed, such as poverty and lack of employment opportunity or inhibitive social norms for women; rather, these are part of our "form of life," basic background conditions that must be taken as given. In a footnote, he says that the idea of "social arrangements as impediments to liberty if they are alterable or remediable by human agency" is somewhat allowable but very problematic, because claims for freedom involve a "charge of responsibility for deliberate interference, not merely with causal influence."[35] There must be an identifiable moral agent who can be held accountable, and that agent must have used her agency—that is, acted deliberately, intentionally, purposively—in erecting the barrier to others' freedom. Such requirements still allow us to see *specific* sexist behavior by specific individuals as potential barriers to particular women's liberty, of course: A boss insisting on sex in exchange for a promotion, a husband beating up his wife, or a rapist in the middle of his crime can still be seen, in Flathman's conception, as engaged in specific acts of restraining an individual woman's liberty. But Flathman implicitly rejects the notion that feminists have argued for, that what makes these kinds of actions possible to begin with is a generalized background condition of sexism and male privilege that has not only allowed men to engage in such behavior with impunity but has at least tacitly (and sometimes overtly) condoned it.

The reason for Flathman's high threshold hinges on the concept of a self that he adopts, a concept that is strongly allied to the traditional liberal view that is so central to the classic forms of negative liberty. His arguments about situatedness notwithstanding, he argues that "unequivocal identifiability, assignability, and responsibility" are necessary to the concept of a self. Flathman insists that we need to take an agent "as we find her—that is as she discloses herself to us through her thought and action."[36] His emphasis on situatedness does not deny—indeed, it insists—that past interactions produce who an agent is. But this takes our social construction as given, not as problematic: "Generic situatedness ... establishes a 'structure' which is a necessary condition of meaningful action and hence of a set of possible actions."[37] Since meaning cannot exist outside of such a structure, we must accept the structure as a given, like gravity or the laws of physics, and as such it would be nonsensical to consider such structures as barriers to freedom. The "general facts of nature" Flathman introduces set limits on what it is possible to do and hence on freedom: We are not able "to jump, unaided, twenty-five feet straight up from the surface of the earth, to develop gills instead of or in addition to lungs.... Few if any of us decide to stand upright, to walk by moving first one foot and then the other, or to see figures three-dimensionally."[38]

Such facts set the context for freedom, for even thinking about freedom: "Conduct that is mutually meaningful—and hence *possibly* freedom-evaluable—is conduct within these general facts as they are accepted by the 'reasonable' participants in a form of life. These facts, and the limits they 'impose' on our conduct, are for the most part beyond our powers to change,"[39] and hence, they do not really "impose limits" at all. Rather, they merely define the parameters of possible action. Certainly, some of an agent's "interactions" within such structures may be "deeply objectionable from the standpoint of freedom," but this is so only from the standpoint of the agent's preexisting "situation." "The notion that situatedness is an obstacle to or restriction upon freedom is incoherent."[40]

But note the qualitative shift Flathman has made from the examples of gravity and bipedalism to "form of life"; in this shift lies the implication that the "laws" that are "given" are not merely the laws of physics but are more deeply cultural in that they set the *parameters for* forms of life. If he were limiting his remarks to the former, his point would be not only extremely weak—for few, if any, theories of freedom take serious issue with gravity as a barrier to one's freedom—but also off the point, to the extent that he is trying to counter the possibility that social contexts can restrict liberty even though they are not the result of the deliberate action of an agent. In this, the "inability" to change aspects of a form of life without becoming incomprehensible takes on a different meaning, as Flathman ends up endorsing a more traditional conception of negative liberty than would seem to follow from his premises about the situatedness of freedom.

This orientation is a long-standing one in Flathman's work, dating back at least to his 1972 book *Political Obligation*. I have elsewhere argued that in *Political Obligation*, he fails to acknowledge that certain forms of life can not only be oppressive or unjust but can also enmesh people so deeply in their forms of life that people are prevented from seeing their injustice. Although human life takes place within language and community, so does our ability to think about and critically assess that life. This enmeshment can provide certain absolute limits to our ability to see exactly what is wrong with our form of life and can prevent us from being able to offer, or even articulate, "good reasons" for disobeying or even changing our form of life. This obviously can result in the endless perpetuation of certain injustices—against women, for example—that are built into the structure of a society and language. Values of care, connection, and relationship, for instance, which are important to women's historical experience, are systematically obliterated from political obligation because they are not considered part of "our" form of life and hence do not enter the discourse.[41]

In his more recent work, Flathman seems to acknowledge this problem, noting that "[t]here may nevertheless be respects in which individuals are inassimilable to, will resist or attempt to resist subsumption under, the concepts and categories that inform and organize the main features of cultural, social, and political life."[42] But even this welcome acknowledgment points to a difficulty in Flathman's theory from a feminist perspective: Namely, he needs to acknowledge more fully the social construction of the choosing subject in his understanding of freedom. Consider domestic violence, for instance; Flathman would agree that a man beating up his girlfriend or wife is restricting her freedom (among other things), but this agreement does not attend to the context within which battering occurs and in which the subject is produced. A "battered woman" is "produced" by the relations of power between her and her batterer, but those relations are enabled by the broader system of patriarchy that allows many batterers to get away with their behavior. A focus on individual agency, intentionality, accountability, and assignability ignores the broader context of male privilege that make an incident of domestic violence *not* just the actions of an identifiable individual. Many victims of domestic violence do try to "liberate" themselves in the way Flathman defines as "freedom"—choosing to leave the batterer—but find structural constraints thwart their efforts. What if she has called the police but they will not arrest because they think the batterer just needs to calm down? Or the police arrest but the district attorney will not press charges because he thinks that, as often happens, she will change her mind at the last minute and refuse to testify?[43] What about judges who accept the "cultural defense" wherein men are excused for the abuse and murder of their wives because they come from cultures where such reactions are normal and expected expressions of honor?[44] Do these judges also limit her freedom?

Flathman might respond, "Well of course, all of those things would constitute constraints on freedom because they involve the actions of individuals—the husband, the police, the prosecutor, the judge—who are preventing the woman from attaining her goal of physical safety." That would be arguable, however, for at the very least, the notions of identifiable and purposive agency, assignability, and intentionality are called into question in these accounts: Police who do not arrest, for instance, often do not realize that they may be condemning the woman to further violence; they think they are intervening in a positive way. Or worse, they know from sad experience that the batterer will be free on bail in a few hours and be angrier than ever, putting her in even greater danger, and so they advise the woman against pressing charges.[45] They may be also be constrained by other structural limitations on their official behavior, limitations that Flathman might well be expected to uphold, given not only his strong voluntarism version of negative liberty, but his critique of policing as well:[46] They may be prevented from arresting unless the victim presses charges, which she may be unwilling to do because, with several children to support and minimal job experience, she is economically dependent on her abusive partner. Similarly, judges may be caught between the demands of respect for cultural difference and the preservation of women's safety. They do not "intend" to limit the woman's freedom; indeed, by respecting cultural difference they may think they are enhancing choice.

These examples, of course, remind us of Flathman's approach to state power, which serves as the all-important background for his conception of the self and his theory of freedom. Flathman is "deeply suspicious" of state authority and is, in classical liberal style, interested in keeping state power minimal. Though many feminists share this deep suspicion, many others have noted that the ideal of the noninterventionist state that characterizes liberalism holds true only from the perspective of privilege; from the perspective of powerlessness, the liberal state is highly interventionist, as any welfare mother or woman seeking an abortion can attest.[47] Flathman might agree with that, and he might argue that such states in fact fail to uphold (willful) liberal ideals. But other liberals would point out that even a minimalist state often intervenes most intrusively and egregiously precisely when it claims to be doing the contrary, for example, when its failure to arrest and prosecute domestic abusers under the rubric of respect for the privacy of the family results in the ruination of women's and children's lives.

What this suggests is that in terms of defining barriers to freedom, purposive, intentional, assignable, accountable agency is too narrow to accommodate the complexity of women's unfreedom within sexist societies. This becomes even more apparent when we consider the agency of the (un)free subject herself. For instance, a mother who is a battered woman may not be able to think only of her individual self; if she kills herself, will her children be victimized by her husband? If she kills him, will she go to jail and lose her kids to foster care? Even women who have no children may be subject to such barriers: Batterers often use threats of violence against pets and other family members, such as women's parents, in order to control them.[48] It is not just that a woman may "want" to protect these other beings and may sacrifice herself to that end; it is that none of us, or at least few of us, can separate our own safety from the safety of those we love. Their well-being is often tied into our own. Such relationships, as a constituent part of a person's social construction as a woman, may be a fundamental, though unacknowledged, part of the structure of her identity as a choosing subject. The individualist model—even Flathman's nonatomistic individualism—fails to acknowledge the profundity of relationship in the construction of identity.

But even in terms of a woman's individuality, social context is vital. For instance, perhaps a woman will not press charges against her batterer because the emotional abuse that generally accompanies physical abuse has constructed her sense of self in such a way that she believes she is somehow responsible for the batterer's actions, that she "deserves" the beating, or that resistance is futile (the Martin E. P. Seligman "learned helplessness" response).[49] Or perhaps more generalized notions of "femininity" and criteria that define a "good wife" in terms of relationship make her take on more responsibility for her husband's well-being and actions than makes sense in terms of her safety. Or maybe she is not even able to accept the fact that she *is* being abused, that she is "one of those women," because of social norms that view domestic violence, like sexual assault, as something that women should be ashamed of. Such cultural norms may construct women into "choosing" the very things that they are in fact restricted to.[50]

Similarly, how we *interpret* the agency of the (un)free subject is relevant. For instance, consider a battered woman who goes limp and becomes passive during a beating. Although some might see such behavior as enabling the batterer—going along with or putting up with his treatment of her rather than challenging his right to hit her—from the battered woman's perspective, given the structural difficulties of getting out of an abusive relationship, such passivity can be seen as a way to resist the batterer because it often minimizes her injuries and may defuse his anger more quickly. But though such resistance may display her "agency"—she assesses her limited options and chooses among them—it does not produce freedom because it does nothing to stop the violence.

Clearly, for Flathman, agency and freedom are distinct entities: It is extremely important to see the battered woman's agency operating even within severely constrained circumstances and to note that though she displays agency, she is not free.[51] But what this example highlights is the need to understand how agency and freedom are also related, and how context sets the terms for both. Particularly if we reject the strict "objective" account of freedom as measured by the number of "doors" that are "open" and recognize the relevance of subjective elements, such as desire, then the agency of the (un)free subject needs to be understood in the context of the structural factors that foster the formation of desire and motivate choice. Similarly, barriers to freedom need to be expanded to allow for the evaluation of those contexts to see how their construction of subjectivity may operate in ways contrary to the assumptions underlying willful liberal ideals of freedom.

Toward a Feminist Liberalism?

Why Flathman does not recognize these sorts of structural factors as restrictions on liberty has to do, once again, with the concept of the self he employs; despite his rejection of atomism, it is decidedly the Enlightenment self. But this concept of the self does not completely make sense. And indeed, Flathman's concept of the self may have changed—and with it, his take on freedom—since he wrote *The Philosophy and Politics of Freedom*. For instance, in *Willful Liberalism*, he makes the point that difference and individuality require social relationships, in a literal sense: "Even if I could know, realize, or somehow experience my own characteristics, my inability to know or understand the characteristics of anyone else would prevent me from regarding my self as distinctive, from viewing myself as characterized by individuality."[52] And again, in *Reflections of a Would-Be Anarchist:* "I cannot form a conception of who I am or of who I might hope to become without attention to my historical, cultural, or sociological inheritances and circumstances."[53] At the same time, however, social relations require difference and individuality: There must be distinction between individuals if they are to be able to "relate" to one another rather than simply melt into each other in an organic community love-fest (not Flathman's words, but his scornful sentiments toward communitarianism nonetheless).

This approach to individualism and liberalism reveals considerable coherence with feminist approaches and values. In particular, this interdependency between individuality and relationship is (as I and other feminists, including Susan Hekman and Susan Okin have argued) central to Carol Gilligan's theory (contrary to the most common readings of her theory).[54] These tensions suggest that Flathman's position is more ambivalent than he would care to admit; but in that ambivalence, I believe, lies space for feminists to enter and borrow from some of his insights.

Certainly, many feminists have been suspicious of, and have even staunchly rejected, liberalism as a racist, classist, and sexist ideology that holds no hope of accommodating gender differences and women's particular history and material experiences. They maintain that its individualism and rights were constructed specifically for propertied white men and are sustainable only through the subservience of white women, landless workers, people of color, and the poor. They would particularly take issue with Flathman's claim, following José Ortega y Gasset, that liberalism is "generous," in that majorities could but do not "repress the expressions, concerns, and objectives of minorities."[55] The question of difference is an especially significant issue in such debates: Despite liberalism's apparent emphasis on individuality, it is often accused of ignoring the specificity of gendered experience that systematically disadvantages women under the definition of equality as sameness, resulting in the extreme difficulty that women have had in obtaining equality, in liberal terms, in the workplace, in public policy, and in the courts. Indeed, many blame liberalism for feminism's own difficulties, particularly feminism's tendency to talk in quasi-universal terms of "women," which allows middle-class, heterosexual, white women to deny that they are really only talking about themselves and are excluding the experiences and needs of women of color, lesbians, and poor women.[56]

Yet many feminists at least implicitly agree that the *ideals* of freedom and equality, so central to historical liberalism, are also historically important to women, who have been systematically denied both equality under the law and the freedom to control their lives, make choices, and act as agents in the world. The importance of these ideals suggests that certain *aspects* of liberalism that Flathman emphasizes—the importance of individuality and difference, the notion that individuals have social and political meaning and significance, the need for people to exert at least some degree of control over their bodies, relationships, and lives—are vital to most, perhaps all, kinds of feminism. And indeed, the emphasis on "difference" that lies at the heart of many feminist *critiques* of liberalism is what, in Flathman's view, provides the heart of liberalism itself. Flathman's take on liberalism—or more accurately, his long-standing effort to *restore* liberalism to its rightful meaning, to bring it back from what he considers reductive misreadings, and in particular from the now-dominant strain of "virtue liberalism," which he believes has many affinities with the much-despised positive liberty[57]—in fact addresses many of these feminist concerns. His assertions that liberalism is neither "anything" nor "nothing," that it is, instead, a "something" in the Wittgensteinian sense—a multiplicity of positions that share a "family resemblance"—in particular complements the notion that freedom is situated, because *as* a "something," it requires a fuller account of situatedness to give it meaning. What we might call a "feminist liberalism," for instance, starts from a situation of patriarchy within which women are oppressed and constrained; liberalism becomes the framework through which resistance is lodged and freedom is struggled for. But feminist liberalism also requires a contrasting situation—a "woman-defined space," if you will—that enables the challenge and resistance to patriarchy and that enables women to imagine things differently. Feminism has revealed that women do not just wake up one day and declare, "Hey, I'm unfree!" Rather, feminist critique of and resistance to patriarchy has required a long-range strategy of theoretical analysis and political activism, a strategy of large-scale social and legal reform as well as "consciousness-raising" and individual-based "micro-resistance" activities, to reveal the multiple levels and ways in which women are not only limited by sexist laws, practices, customs, norms, attitudes, and beliefs but are also constructed to be the kinds of people who accept this sexism as "normal," as their "form of life."

This suggests again the need to understand the social construction of the choosing subject, or as Flathman puts it, the autarchic agent. I believe that in contrast to his writings on freedom, Flathman's account of liberalism as open to a multiplicity of views allows for the entrance of this constructedness. Flathman's claim that "as idea(s), as an array of practices, and especially as a multiplicitous set of ideals, liberalism is a many-splendored thing"[58] suggests that a variety of things are *consistent with* liberalism, though not *required by* them; and this complements the feminist emphasis on difference and diversity among women and between women and men.

Feminists have argued that the supposed neutrality that liberalism has always claimed in fact contains a very specific politics, one that not coincidentally coheres with the interests of propertied white men. This crucial observation has been the source of many feminists' rejection of liberalism. By denying that they contain this politics, mainstream liberal theories in effect erase their tacit modifiers: Oppositional liberalisms, like welfare liberalism, become labeled, but other liberalisms make their modifiers invisible. Thus, for example, white liberalism, patriarchal liberalism, or capitalist liberalism, each of which adapts the general liberal ideals of freedom and equality to specific political purposes, interests, and visions, appropriate the generic term "liberalism." If feminist critiques of "liberal" theorists are correct—as I believe they are—that the ideals of freedom and equality are often used to advance the political power and agendas of particular groups, most often economically privileged white males, at the expense of other groups, usually white women, men and women of color, and poor people of all races and genders, then to call such theory an unmodified "liberalism," rather than, say, "patriarchal liberalism" or "white masculinist liberalism," involves the erasure of this political power and the denial of this agenda. Moreover, it is an erasure and denial so effective as to be hidden even from its very perpetrators, who, in circular fashion, are protected by the supposed "neutrality" of their position from having to listen to feminist (and other) critiques at all. But just as a generalized "feminism" often ends up really talking about white Western middle-class women, so is "liberalism" often really talking about privileged white Western males.

As with feminism, however, this neutral facade for dominance does not mean that other groups cannot access its ideals. Hence, as feminists have created and subdivided into Third World feminism, black U.S. feminism, and lesbian feminism, to name just a few, there can be black liberalism, socialist liberalism, or feminist liberalism, just as there can be patriarchal or capitalist or white liberalism. Such specifications and refinements reflect not essential being but political positionalities; And liberalism, as a vague but flexible cluster of abstract concepts, can be tailored to a variety of experiences and needs, as the meaning of "the individual" is particularized in those terms. By understanding liberalism in this way, the essence of the debate does not center on liberalism per se but, rather, on the various political positionalities attempting to lay claim to liberal ideals. The debate, then, should not be between feminism and liberalism, or even between different kinds of feminism, such as liberal and socialist, but between feminism and patriarchy, or racial equality and white privilege, or workers' control and capitalism—each of which can adapt liberal ideals to its own ends. On this reading, liberalism merely provides the framework within which such political battles are carried out. It is in this sense that liberalism is "neutral," but such neutrality calls out for more particular content, a content that is provided by politics.

I believe that something like this is what Flathman advocates in his categories of "agency liberalism" and "virtue liberalism," even if it is not an exact parallel to them. What he is talking about in such differences among approaches to liberalism is not simply morals—though it is in part that—but politics: a vision of what society should look like, the structuring of power relations and institutions, the advocacy of ideals and preferences not just for oneself but for everyone. Even though the crux of agency liberalism involves letting people determine those things for themselves, that position itself is a political one: to structure a society in which everyone is permitted to make a wide range of decisions about their own lives.

But if so, then reading his theory of freedom through his theory of liberalism suggests that freedom itself may be more "political" than Flathman acknowledges. Certainly he wants freedom, like liberalism, to be open-ended and multiplicitous; the negative liberty approach seeks to fend off attempts to give freedom a particular content, to allow individuals to do what they want. Hence as I quoted earlier, "liberalism as I envision it is committed to the ideal of individuality and hence self-enactment as formal but not substantive end and to the widest possible freedom of individual action as a necessary but not sufficient condition of effective pursuit of this ideal."[59] And as Flathman argues forcefully, these "individuals" are not "abstract" or "atomistic"; rather, they are situated in language, context, and forms of life, all of which will of necessity involve political content. Therefore, the content that I as an individual wish to give my own personal "freedom" must similarly be seen in context or situation; and these contexts are never neutral; they are intensely political.

Thus, though Flathman might object morally or politically to certain feminist ideals, this view of freedom would be very consistent with many of the specific freedoms feminists tend to demand: not only with negative liberties such as freedom from sexual violence, equal pay, an end to gender and racial discrimination, and abortion on demand, but also, one could claim, with arguably positive liberties as well, such as adequate child care and comparable worth, and even with care-centered communitarian liberties, such as entitlements to welfare payments for primary caretakers. The line, for him, is drawn at the classical liberal position of not interfering with another's freedom. But up to that point, virtually anything goes, and much of it is political. To invoke Rawls's terminology, Flathman's "concept" of liberal freedom is compatible with many different, and perhaps even competing, "conceptions" of freedom.

But at the same time, the diversity of these conceptions is not unlimited: If freedom is neither "anything" nor "nothing" but is, rather, a "something," then we must attend to those all-important parameters, the "family resemblance" that contains the conceptual boundaries to what can be considered a version of "freedom." By saying that these parameters are set by politics, I am suggesting that politics is a vital component of the social constructedness of the choosing subject. Various political positionalities, such as feminism, or strong voluntarism, or virtue, set the parameters for meaningful choice, selfhood, and identity; they provide a framework for possibilities of meaning, which in turn have an impact on the identity and signification of the choosing subject, which in their turn will have an impact on the choices that are made. And just as the crux of agency liberalism entails the vision that those choices will be various and multiplicitous, rather than uniform, so does feminism, in its emphasis on difference, similarly entail a vision of varying outcomes of the choice-making processes that individuals engage in daily.

This means that, just as reconciling freedom with Flathman's liberalism would require him to be open to a variety of feminist freedoms, feminism, in order to be consistent with Flathman's liberalism, would similarly have to be open to a much broader diversity of views than it has generally allowed. For instance, diverse political goals ranging from support for lesbian marriage (based on freedom of association and rights to privacy) to opposition to abortion (based on the argument that many abortions result from economic hardship and social stigma perpetrated by a sexist society, such that to talk of "women's choice" is hypocritical at best)[60] could be reconciled with the broad and generic "liberal" outlines of individual freedom, equality, and rights within recognizably feminist parameters. Such parameters are crucial, however; for example, in contrast to the antiabortion argument I just offered, which was based on *women's* rights to economic subsistence and freedom from sexist stigma, the more common pro-life argument for a "right to life" for the "unborn" could be legitimated through appeal to *liberal* ideals by couching its claims in terms of "rights" for the fetus, but not through appeal to *feminist* ones, because fetuses take unilateral precedence over women in such a view. By contrast, the argument that abortion is wrong because women are destined by Scripture to reproduce can be reconciled with *neither* liberalism *nor* feminism. Thus, the importance of feminist parameters lies in the recognition that not just anything can count as "feminist"; there is a "family resemblance" among political and normative ideals that can be called feminist. The same can be said for liberalism as well.

Using Flathman's vision of liberalism to expand what can be labeled a "feminist" position enhances freedom, not only enlarging the feminist tent to allow for a greater diversity of voices but also fostering such diversity. Again, the feminist attention to relationship suggests that a context that allows and even encourages a broader diversity of views will not simply tolerate views that are developed independently; rather, it will provide the means for the development of such views by constructing subjectivities that are able to think and see in different directions. The central importance of social relationships to the context within which individual identities are constructed means that freedom cannot simply be a more robust version of letting others alone; it must logically involve the recognition that those others come to be who they are through the social contexts in which they exist.

Thus, feminism can benefit from Flathman's vision of liberalism; and recasting his theory of freedom in light of that liberalism could similarly aid feminist projects. At the same time, however, I have no illusions that such arguments will actually cause Flathman to alter his conception of the self; he has taught his students well that the conception of the self is an important foundation for a theorist's approach to politics and political theory. And in my heart of hearts, I would not really want to win this argument, because Flathman's unique brand of individualism has contributed to the irascibility his students and colleagues have come to know and love. But Flathman is something of a stickler for consistency, and so I hope at least to nudge him in my direction by raising these objections. It would also be gratifying to see tangible evidence that his decades of mentoring feminists has had some impact on him. It certainly has had an impact on us, and I suppose that is what really counts.

Notes

1. This chapter was written while I was a National Endowment for the Humanities (NEH)–sponsored fellow at the Institute for Advanced Study in Princeton, New Jersey. Thanks to the institute and the NEH, as well as to Cornell University for the sabbatical that enabled me to be at the institute and to write this chapter. Thanks also to Bonnie Honig and David Mapel for their comments and suggestions. Finally, thanks to Richard Flathman for always challenging me to think more clearly; I hope this chapter fulfills that demand.

2. See, for instance, Seyla Benhabib, "The Generalized and the Concrete Other: The Kohlberg-Gilligan Controversy and Feminist Theory," in *Feminism as Critique,* ed. Seyla Benhabib and Drucilla Cornell (Minneapolis: University of Minnesota Press, 1988).

3. Richard E. Flathman, *Reflections of a Would-Be Anarchist: Ideals and Institutions of Liberalism* (Minneapolis: University of Minnesota Press, 1998), 16.

4. Isaiah Berlin, "Two Concepts of Liberty," in *Four Essays on Liberty* (New York: Oxford University Press, 1971).

5. Ibid., 123.

6. Ibid.

7. Richard E. Flathman, *The Practice of Rights* (Cambridge and New York: Cambridge University Press, 1976), 201.

8. See Charles Taylor, "What's Wrong with Negative Liberty," in *The Idea of Freedom: Essays in Honor of Isaiah Berlin,* ed. Alan Ryan (New York: Oxford University Press, 1979).

9. Ibid., 176.

10. Berlin, "Two Concepts of Liberty," 125.

11. Though obligation, through the social contract and consent, is a limitation on freedom that is also an expression of freedom and free will, via choice, it is its opposition to liberty that yields "the problem of political obligation" as the paradox of modern political theory. I have elsewhere discussed the tension between freedom and obligation in Nancy J. Hirschmann, *Rethinking Obligation: A Feminist Method for Political Theory* (Ithaca, N.Y.: Cornell University Press, 1992); see also Carole Pateman, *The Problem of Political Obligation: A Critical Analysis of Liberal Theory* (New York: John Wiley, 1979); and Carole Pateman and Nancy J. Hirschmann, "Political Obligation, Freedom, and Feminism," *American Political Science Review* 85, no. 1 (March 1992): 179–88.

12. See Richard E. Flathman, *The Philosophy and Politics of Freedom* (Chicago: University of Chicago Press, 1987), chaps. 1–4.

13. See Flathman, *Reflections,* 8 et passim.

14. Flathman, *Philosophy and Politics,* 112.

15. Ibid.

16. Taylor, "What's Wrong with Negative Liberty," 184.

17. Ibid., 185–88.

18. Flathman, *Reflections,* 9–10.

19. Berlin, "Two Concepts of Liberty," 133–34.

20. Flathman, *Philosophy and Politics,* chap. 4.

21. Richard E. Flathman, *Toward a Liberalism* (Ithaca, N.Y.: Cornell University Press, 1989), 113–14.

22. Flathman, *Reflections,* 5.

23. Ibid., 31.

24. "[A]gency-oriented liberals allow the necessity of restrictions on liberty, but they are as congenitally wary of such restrictions as they are skeptical of foundationalist accounts of liberty or its value," Flathman, *Reflections,* 8; see also xv–xvi, 49, and chap. 6 more generally.

25. Ibid., 7.

26. Berlin, "Two Concepts of Liberty," 124.

27. Flathman, *Reflections,* chap. 6.

28. Richard E. Flathman, "Discipline, Freedom, and Resistance: Preliminary Reflections by Way of an Engagement with Foucault," paper presented at the 1998 annual meeting of the American Political Science Association, 3–6 September 1998, Boston, Massachusetts.

29. For example, see Flathman, *Reflections,* 34.

30. For instance, consider Taylor's example of spite in "What's Wrong with Negative Liberty." He believes his true will is not to "lash out" at his companion, but his "brute desire" keeps getting in the way and harming the relationship, which his true will wants to maintain. But if Taylor were truly engaging in the second-guessing form of positive liberty, he would not be able to make such an assertion because second-guessing falls into infinite regress. For instance, how would he know that spite is not his subconscious's way of telling him that the relationship is in fact bad for him, not his "true will" at all? This reveals an acontextual approach to desire and the desiring subject: We do not know where the spite comes from, what his particular desires are for the relationship, and where they come from. Nor are we told of the criteria for determining the "importance" of the relationship, and how they are established. These are all key issues, questions that Taylor fails not only to address but even to think of, and in this, he and Flathman demonstrate some problematic affinities in the individualism that underlies their respective conceptions of freedom.

31. Berlin, "Two Concepts of Liberty," 191. Berlin's emphasis on retaining the distinction between "unfree" and "unable" involves a commitment to defining freedom in such quantitative terms. See Hillel Steiner for an argument for a mathematical formula for comparing "Red" (Soviet) and "Blue" (British) freedom in "How Free? Computing Personal Liberty," in *Of Liberty,* ed. A. Phillip Griffiths (New York: Cambridge University Press, 1983), 73; see also Ian Carter, "The Measurement of Pure Negative Liberty," *Political Studies,* 40 (1992): 38–50.

32. Stanley I. Benn, *A Theory of Freedom* (New York: Cambridge University Press, 1988).

33. Ibid., 133.

34. Flathman, *Philosophy and Politics,* 17.

35. Ibid., 324.

36. Ibid., 225.

37. Ibid., 180.

38. Ibid., 139.

39. Ibid.

40. Ibid., 147.

41. See Hirschmann, *Rethinking Obligation,* 94–98; Richard E. Flathman, *Political Obligation* (New York: Atheneum, 1972).

42. Flathman, *Reflections,* 23–24.

43. Angela Brown, *When Battered Women Kill* (New York: Macmillan, 1987); Mildred Pagelow, *Woman Battering: Victims and Their Experiences* (Beverly Hills, Calif.: Sage, 1981). I detail the issues discussed in these few paragraphs at greater length in "Domestic Violence and the Theoretical Discourse of Freedom," *Frontiers: A Journal of Women's Studies* 16, no. 1 (1996): 126–51.

44. Sherene Razack, "What Is to Be Gained by Looking White People in the Eye? Culture, Race, and Gender in Cases of Sexual Violence." *Signs: Journal of Women in Culture and Society* 19, no. 2 (1994): 894–923, 918.

45. Kathleen Ferraro, "Cops, Courts, and Battered Women," in *Violence against Women: The Bloody Footprints,* ed. Pauline Bart and Eileen Moran (Newbury Park, Calif.: Sage, 1993).

46. Flathman, *Reflections,* chap. 6.

47. For instance, see Martha Fineman, *The Neutered Mother, the Sexual Family, and Other Twentieth Century Tragedies* (New York: Routledge, 1995).

48. Martha R. Mahoney, "Legal Images of Battered Women: Redefining the Issue of Separation," *Michigan Law Review* 90, no. 1 (1991): 1–94.

49. Lenore Walker, *The Battered Woman Syndrome* (New York: Springer, 1984).

50. Diana Coole, "Constructing and Deconstructing Liberty: A Feminist and Poststructuralist Analysis," *Political Studies,* 51, no. 1 (1993): 83–95.

51. Indeed, I have argued this myself in "Domestic Violence and the Theoretical Discourse of Freedom."

52. Richard E. Flathman, *Willful Liberalism: Voluntarism and Individuality in Political Theory and Practice* (Ithaca, N.Y.: Cornell University Press, 1992), 114.

53. Flathman, *Reflections,* 35.

54. See Susan Hekman, *Moral Voices, Moral Selves: Carol Gilligan and Feminist Moral Theory* (Cambridge: Polity Press, 1993); Susan Moller Okin, "Reason and Feeling in Thinking about Justice," in *Feminism and Political Theory,* ed. Cass R. Sunstein (Chicago: University of Chicago Press, 1990); Nancy J. Hirschmann, "Difference as an Occasion for Rights: A Feminist Rethinking of Rights, Liberalism, and Difference," *Critical Review of International Social and Political Philosophy: Special Issue on Feminism, Identity, and Difference* 2, no. 1 (1999): 27–55; and Hirschmann, *Rethinking Obligation,* chap. 3.

55. Flathman, *Reflections,* 19.

56. bell hooks, *Feminist Theory: From Margin to Center* (Boston: South End Press, 1984).

57. Flathman, *Reflections,* 11.

58. Ibid., 105.

59. Ibid., 31.

60. Kay Castonguay, "Pro-Life Feminism," in *Feminist Philosophies,* 2nd ed., ed. Janet A. Kourany, James P. Sterba, and Rosemarie Tong (Upper Saddle River, N.J.: Prentice Hall, 1999).

CHAPTER SEVEN

Liberty Conceived as the Opposite of Slavery

Richard Friedman

The Issue

In *The Philosophy and Politics of Freedom,* Richard Flathman identified a wide range of issues implicated in the debate over the two concepts of liberty, raising the suspicion that perhaps that debate does not stage the problem in a satisfactory manner by allowing for only two alternatives: either "negative liberty," as the absence of external coercion, or else "positive liberty" as self-government. The following discussion of the liberty/slavery polarity is an attempt to carry forward what Flathman's book suggests. More specifically, the particular issue to be considered is whether the "liberty" that is "incompatible with slavery" (Flathman 1987, 18) is captured by the negative concept of liberty or whether it embodies a distinct type of liberty that is irreducible to the absence of coercion.

Versions of what may be called the irreducibility thesis do crop up in histories of servitude, especially those dealing with ancient slavery. In his influential article "Theorie de l'esclavage" (1931), Henri Levy-Bruhl contended that the ancient Roman juridical notion of *libertas,* when viewed in opposition to slavery, is not the same as unconstrained action (163)—a claim echoed in several works on Roman law. Recently, Philip Pettit, in *Republicanism: A Theory of Government,* and Quentin Skinner, in *Liberty before Liberalism,* have argued that when liberty is pitted against slavery, then an understanding of liberty can be brought to light that is equivalent neither to the absence of coercion nor to the standard alternative of positive liberty as self-determination. In support of this position, both authors pursue a historical agenda, presenting the case for a distinct conception of liberty ("nondomination") by showing how it is inscribed in certain traditions of political and legal thought, including the "legal tradition of ancient Rome" (Skinner 1998, 38).

These studies suggest the approach adopted here, which is to zero in on the liberty/slavery opposition expressly articulated in ancient Roman law (in *The Digest of Justinian*) rather than to assume or stipulate a definition of slavery, as is done in contemporary philosophical works on freedom. There is indeed something odd about the latter procedure. In philosophical writing on freedom, slavery, when it is mentioned, is always presented as the paradigm case of unfreedom; yet what slavery is comes to be taken for granted, as though the type of control involved in slavery is obvious. This assumption must be challenged if the conceptual issue about liberty posed at the outset of this chapter is to be resolved.

Liberty and slavery are certainly played off against each other as oppositional terms in the opening pages of *The Digest of Justinian* (1985; hereafter *Digest*). They are explicitly presented as mutually exclusive legal statuses in a series of pronouncements from several jurists, most conspicuously in the fundamental division ("*summa divisio*") of the law of persons: "[T]he great division in the law of persons is this: that all humans are either free or slave" (*Digest*, 1.5.3). Moreover, what has been called a "brutal opposition" (Didier 1991, 248) between *jus gentium* and *jus naturale* is set up over slavery in the first book of the *Digest*. In that text, along with all the other surviving works of Roman jurisprudence, slavery is always said to be *jus gentium* and never *jus naturale* (*Digest*, 1.1.4.). *Jus gentium* is an expression with several meanings, but here it is used to refer to the laws and institutions established within every society. All peoples have slavery; there is no society in which everyone is free. But that is not all. Some jurists also declare liberty for all human beings as *jus naturale* (*Digest*, 1.1.4; 50.17.32; 12.6.64; 1.5.5.1), and at one point slavery is even declared *contra-naturam* ("against nature") (*Digest*, 1.5.4.1.), the one case in which an institution of *jus gentium* is so described.

So the liberty/slavery antimony is given a prominent place in the *Digest*, and a massive literature has developed on this matter, with much controversy over both meaning and significance. The delimited aims of this chapter have, therefore, to be noted at the outset. No attempt will be made to confront the many issues raised by the juristic pronouncements. The limited purpose of this discussion is to concentrate on the meaning, or rather, meanings, of liberty when situated in the liberty/

slavery polarity of Roman law and to show that an analysis of that polarity can provide a way of resolving the issue indicated at the beginning of this chapter.

The point of departure for this analysis will be a consideration stressed by Roman legal historians, that slavery is defined in two branches of Roman law. Roman law was divided (in *The Institute of Gaius,* hereafter *Gaius*) into three branches: the law of persons, the law of things, and the law of actions. Slavery in turn was defined in two of these branches: In the law of things, slavery was defined as being property, and in the law of persons, slavery was defined as a legal status that is the polar opposite of *status libertas*. A slave is property, and a slave lacks liberty. It is essential to bear in mind this focus on two aspects of a single entity because this duality is crucial to the kind of control to which a slave is subjected and hence crucial to identifying the "unfreedom" of slavery.

What follows is complex, and the analysis has been broken down into sections beginning with the law of persons. The terms *libertas* and *servi* have been retained at certain points, rather than translated, in order to keep the main issue up front and to help avoid reading back modern preconceptions.

A First Type of *Libertas* as a Legal Status

In the Roman law of persons, *libertas* and *servi* are presented as mutually exclusive legal statuses. So the initial question is what it meant for *libertas* to be a legal status in contradistinction to *servi* as a status.

Status as a Roman juridical category referred to the legal position of the individual: the particular bundle of legal powers, duties, rights, immunities, privileges, disabilities, and so on with which the law recognized him to be endowed. But in this regard, the law of persons recognized striking differences in legal capacity, depending on various factors, including birth, gender, and citizenship. Thus, among those accounted free, Roman law distinguished the legal position of those born free from that of those manumitted from slavery. Again, women who were free were nevertheless not in their own power *(sui juris)* but in the power of another *(alieni juris)*, namely, the male head of the household to which they belonged. Roman law also distinguished the legal position of Roman citizens from that of noncitizens. Citizens had exclusive access to *jus civile* as the body of law regulating relations among Roman citizens, whereas foreigners, or at any rate some foreigners, eventually came to have juridical standing and protection under *jus gentium* in yet another sense of that expression (for example, see *Gaius*, 3.93; *Digest*, 2.14.5.7).

The Roman legal world was, then, characterized by pronounced differences in legal identity even among those who were free. Nevertheless, status *servi* stood out starkly in this world of legal unequals (at least in the classical pronouncements) because the slave was excluded entirely from the legal community as a subject with powers, rights, and duties, and so was explicitly deprived of legal capacity. This negation of juridical personality is manifest in classical jurisprudence. The slave enjoyed no legal powers; that is, he had no capacity to perform acts with juridical effects. A slave could not marry, make a will, or inherit unless also freed. "A slave cannot owe anything or be owed" (*Digest*, 15.1.41). "A slave cannot incur or have obligations" (*Digest*, 50.17.22) or enter a contract on his own behalf or that of his master. "A slave cannot have property" (*Digest*, 50.16.182), and what he acquires belongs to his master. A slave lacked the protection of the law. He could neither sue nor be sued; "there is no action with a slave" (*Digest*, 50.17.107). He was in the power of his master, who was even said to have the power of life and death over him (*Digest*, 1.6.1.1), though some limitations seem eventually to have been established (*Digest*, 1.6.1.2). A slave was thus declared a legal null: "[S]lavery is akin to death" (*Digest*, 50.17.209); "a slave is dead" (*Digest*, 35.1.59.2); "slaves are regarded as not existing" so far as *jus civile* is concerned (*Digest*, 50.17.32); "slaves have no *jus*" (*Digest*, 4.5.3).

The distinguishing feature of *servi* as a status was, then, the total deprivation of juridical capacity: There were no other human beings with whom a slave was recognized to have a reciprocal relationship governed by law.

By contrast with the position of a slave as legally "dead," *libertas* as a status referred to the legal position of any human recognized to have access to some body of law regulating his or her interactions with others. This meaning of *libertas* is strikingly displayed in the Roman law dealing with status change, which could take place in either direction, up or down. Thus, an individual could be deprived of *libertas*, and this change was categorized as the greatest possible diminishment of status that could be imposed by law because it was the complete extinction of legal capacity. A citizen could be stripped of his citizenship without also losing his *libertas*, which meant he lost access to *jus civile* because *jus civile* was reserved to Roman citizens. However, because he remained free, he had access to another body of law, *jus gentium* (*Digest*, 48.22.15). Because he was still free, he was still legally alive. Then there was the remarkable *postliminium* (recovery of legal status): A Roman captured by the enemy was regarded by Roman law as reduced to slavery and consequently as devoid of juridical capacity in Roman law. Accordingly, he could no longer perform acts, such as making a will, that he could have previously performed, when free. But under the law of *postliminium,* if he somehow escaped and returned across Roman lines, then he was restored to his antecedent legal position as a citizen with access to *jus civile* and was thus said to have reacquired the *libertas* that he had lost (*Digest*, 49.15.5.1). To be free meant to have access to some law; to be a slave meant to have no law.

From this standpoint, it is possible to recognize why the law of persons presented the *libertas/servi* dichotomy as a mutually exclusive and jointly exhaustive division: "[A]ll humans are either free or slave" (*Digest*, 1.5.3). A human being either belonged to some legal community, so that his interactions with others were governed by law, or else he was outside legal community, having no reciprocal legal relation with others. A slave had no reciprocal relation with others governed by law, including his master. He did, of course, have a legally recognized connection to his master. However, this connection was not a legal relation between fellow-subjects but, rather, a property connection between an owner and the thing lawfully owned. (I will consider what this extra-legal property relation was, further on.)

At this point, it is necessary to stress that this stark binary opposition between *libertas* and *servi* is a conceptualization of classical Roman jurisprudence, and like any legal conceptualization it cannot be automatically assumed to correspond to the actual situation of any human. On this score, there has been much discussion by Roman historians as to how far the classical statements accord with the actual condition of those classified as slaves. For example, J.-C. Dumont has argued at length that the *libertas/servi* bifurcation in the law of persons was an "oversimplification" (1989, 20) and that both the juridical and extra-juridical evidence (such as that provided by Roman theater) shows that slaves did have a recognized, though watery, legal existence. Again, Philippe Didier has argued that there was "an affirmation of the personality of the slave in Roman law" (1991, 275–76) in that he was recognized to have limited legal standing (e.g., he could incur "natural obligations" or have a certain type of property called *peculium*). The thesis has also been advanced that although the classical statements are presented as timeless, obtaining throughout Roman history, or as *jus gentium*, obtaining universally among all peoples, and thus as "pretending to be outside history" (Amiranti 1981, 35), it is crucial for the historian to resist the temptation to read them back into Roman history prior to the massive expansion of Roman imperial power, with its influx of foreign captives reduced to slavery by conquest.

Thus, there is a good deal of skepticism about the fit between the classical law of slavery and what is called "social reality." For purposes of this chapter, however, it is not necessary to challenge this skepticism or to enter into an inquiry into the problem it poses. The aim of this chapter is to work through the logic of the *libertas/servi* polarity as articulated in Roman law, keeping in mind that, as logic, it leaves open the historical issues just indicated. In this regard, there is indeed a crucial problem of historical perspective. In ancient law, membership in some legal community conferred personality, and membership in turn depended on such factors as birth, citizenship, and ethnicity, but not on merely being human. The idea that being human and being recognized as a juridical person were coextensive should not be attributed to this premodern legal world; to be outside legal community was not to be free but, rather, to be totally vulnerable.

Relation of *Status Libertas* to the Lawful Use of Force

The preceding account of *libertas* as a legal status raises an obvious question. That account is formal in the sense that it says nothing about the specific character of the particular bundle of powers, duties, and rights carried around by a human recognized as free. And it is also silent about the scope of legal regulation of those accounted free, and about whether this or that act is prohibited, prescribed, or permitted by law, or whether there are any areas of human affairs regarded as exempt from legal intervention. In short, *libertas* as a status concept is (at least so far) noncommittal about liberty as a noninterference concept.

Merely conceiving *libertas* as a legal status thus seems to leave lots of questions up in the air. But to start with, it is essential to clarify one crucial issue: the relation between the lawful use of force and a human's status as free or slave.

To be free as a matter of status meant to belong to some recognized legal community as a person who, in relation to others, was protected by law. This protection afforded by law did not, however, mean that a person was exempt from being lawfully coerced or that there was no lawful justification for resort to force. The use of force was, however, subordinated to law in that recourse to force was lawful only as to punish a prior legal offense or to enforce a law, that is, to prevent the violation of law. By contrast, *servi* as a status involved a distinct basis for the lawful use of force. Since a slave was legally "dead," he was not afforded the protection of the law, and consequently the use of force was not subordinated to law in the way it was in the case of a juridical person. A slave did not have to have committed a legal wrong in order for recourse to force by his owner to be lawful. Thus, what was the height of illegal behavior in the relation between fellow subjects within a legal community was transformed into lawful behavior in the relation of master to slave.

The first book of the *Digest* provides a striking expression of the lawfulness of this power possessed by a master over his slaves: "Slaves, then, are in the *potestas* of their master, this form of *potestas* being power in virtue of the *jus gentium*. For we can observe that equally among all nations, masters have had the power of life or death over their slaves" (1.6.1). That is, it is the universal condition of servitude, recognized in the legal arrangements of all peoples, that masters have the lawful power to preserve or kill those humans who are their slaves.

According to Hans Kelsen, it is part of the essence of a legal system that every act of force is either a sanction or a delict (1970, 39). The master-slave relation is not, however, a legal relation between persons; rather, it is an extra-legal relation of force. The use of force by the master is neither a sanction imposed on his slave for an offense committed by the slave, nor yet is it a delict committed by the master against his slave, a delict that is itself subject by law to a sanction. And this is so because a human reduced to slavery is excluded from the community of law and deprived of juridical personality. Slavery as a legal institution thus involves the release of force from the constraint of law.

There is a refrain that has been long associated with the liberty/slavery polarity that captures this distinction about the lawful use of force. Liberty, it is said, involves "immunity from arbitrary coercion and punishment," whereas slavery involves "subjection to the arbitrary will of another" (Brunt 1988, 297). The meaning of "arbitrary" here is crucial. What it means when applied to slavery, in contrast to liberty, is that the use of force by the master does not have to meet the independent test of whether force violates the law in order to be lawful. Furthermore, "will of another" means that it is the will of the master to do as he pleases, independent of any action willed by his slave, that is alone required to justify the use of force. Again, the basic theme is the release of force from subordination to law.

To sum up, the relation between *libertas* as a status concept and liberty as a noninterference concept is that the former specifies the conditions that must be satisfied for coercive intervention to be lawful. *Libertas* as a status concept has to do with a distinct type of rule—rule by law, in contrast to arbitrary rule, over slaves—rather than with the scope of rule by law over those recognized as free.

A Second Type of *Libertas* as the Absence of Law and Force

Up to this point, this discussion has been concerned with *libertas* as a juridical status concept, and as P. A. Brunt says, "[I]n all legal writings *libertas* generally means the status of one who is not a slave" (1988, 282). Brunt's statement expresses a widely held view not only about *libertas* in ancient Rome but also about *eleutheria* among the ancient Greeks. *Eleutheria*, like *libertas*, was a status concept or membership concept whose meaning was inseparable from its opposite: the position of a slave (cf. Finley 1983; Pitkin 1988; Ostwald 1995).

It is surprising, then, to discover that the first book of the *Digest* contains a distinct definition of *libertas* that does not appear to be a status definition, even though it is placed in *Digest*, 1.5, "Human Status," directly after Gaius's fundamental division in the law of persons between *libertas* and *servi* as statuses: [L]*ibertas* is one's natural power of doing what one pleases, except insofar as one's action is ruled out by force *(vi)* or prohibited by law *(jure)*" (*Digest*, 1.5.4: Florentinus, *Institutes*, book 9).

This passage defines *libertas* as being of a logically different order than *libertas* as a status concept. As Giuliano Crifò points out, Florentinus's statement about *libertas* "refers not to juridical liberty but to 'material liberty' as the 'fact' of the absence of violence or law" (1958, 67; my translation). This valid observation points up the consideration that Florentinus's definition is a "factual" definition that is negative in form and that applies to individual actions, not to legal positions. It is factual in that it makes the criterion of whether or not an act is free consist of the absence or the presence of either of two empirically ascertainable conditions in the environment of the actor. It is negative in the sense that it focuses on two conditions that prevent or attempt to prevent an act from occurring. And finally, it is quantitative in the sense that the scope or amount of liberty of action possessed by any given individual varies inversely with the scope of law and coercion to which he is subjected. In this regard, the word *libertas* can be applied to the actions of any human being, irrespective of his legal status as free or slave, making the difference quantitative. The difference between free and slave, on this meaning of *libertas*, consists in the extent to which the actions of each are or are not in fact restricted by law or coercion.

Thus, two logically distinct meanings of the word *libertas* coexist side by side in the first book of the *Digest:* The first is a status concept in which *libertas* is placed in opposition not to law but to slavery, and the second is a negative act concept in which *libertas* is explicitly placed in opposition to both law and coercion. The question, then, is how to account for both definitions, or more precisely, how to account for the presence of the negative act definition of *libertas* given the valid claim that "*libertas* generally means the status of one who is not a slave" (Brunt 1988, 282).

In modern political and legal thought, the context in which a negative definition of liberty is usually offered is to stage the question of the proper scope of individual liberty: how far law and government may justifiably intervene in the affairs of the individual and whether there are areas that ought to be immune from intervention. It is imperative, however, to resist reading this modern context back into the ancient situation. Thus, if Florentinus's definition of *libertas* as unrestricted action is contextualized, it may be seen to be concerned with a very different matter, which is after all centered on the *libertas/servi* polarity.

The entire passage from Florentinus's *Institutes* incorporated into the *Digest* reintroduces slavery. This passage has been much discussed and needs to be seen in its entirety:

> *Libertas* is one's natural power of doing what one pleases, except insofar as one's action is ruled out by force *(vi)* or prohibited by law *(jure)*.
> 1. Slavery *(servitus)* is an institution of *juris gentium*, whereby someone is against nature *(contra naturam)* made subject to the ownership of another. 2. Slaves *(servi)* are so-called, because generals have a custom of

selling their captives and thereby *preserving* rather than killing them; and indeed, they are said to be *mancipia,* because they are captives in the hand *(manus)* of their enemies. (*Digest,* 1.5.4: Florentinus, *Institutes,* book 9)

This statement offers a context in which Florentinus's negative definition may be understood; in fact, it acquires a highly specific meaning. In the first place, Florentinus focuses on the property component of slavery and records the fact that this type of property is lawful among all peoples. It is *jus gentium.* But furthermore, because the slave is here recognized as in fact lawful property and because the possession of something can be lawful only if it is acquired by a lawful method, Florentinus goes on to identify the method in question: conquest. Putting aside Florentinus's peculiar etymology of the word *servi,* enslavement is here treated as the end result of a war of conquest in which the victorious power chooses to preserve and sell his captives rather than kill them and thus to reduce those previously free to the property of the purchaser.

In Roman law, this method of acquisition of property, including humans as property, was repeatedly acknowledged as lawful and assigned to *jus gentium. Digest,* 1.5, immediately following the passage from Florentinus, includes this passage:

> People are brought under our power as slaves either by *jus civile* or by *jus gentium.* This happens by civil law if someone over twenty allows himself to be sold with a view to sharing in the price [i.e., fraudulently]. By *jus gentium,* people become slaves on being captured by enemies or by birth to a female slave. (*Digest,* 1.5.5.1: Marcian, *Institutes,* book 1)

Again, at *Digest* 41.1, devoted to the enumeration of various methods of lawful acquisition, conquest as a legal method of acquiring slaves is recognized as *jus gentium* (*Digest,* 41.1.1.7). Statements of this "law of conquest" may also be found in several other places in Roman jurisprudence (cf. *Justinian's Institutes,* 11.2.2, 1.3.4).

The Roman jurists are here referring to a "law" widely recognized in Greek and Roman antiquity. Perhaps the best-known statement of this "law" appears in Aristotle's *Politics,* in the course of his report of the controversy over the justice of slavery: "By law, a person can be a slave, and in a state of slavery. The law *[nomos]* is a kind of agreement, by which people say that things conquered in war belong to the conquerors" (I, 1255a 5–7). Expressions of this *nomos* can be found in many other Greek authors, such as Xenophon (*Cyropaedia*, 7.5.73) and Polybius (2.58.9–10). In ancient Rome, it is found not only in the legal literature but also in extra-juridical works, where it is referred to as *juri belli* (law of war), as in Livy (34.57.7) and Caesar (*Gallic Wars* I.36).

There are certainly interesting variations in the ancient formulations of this law, variations that are beyond the scope of this chapter. But two aspects of this law, shared by all formulations, need to be noted here, and together they constitute the reason for dwelling on this matter.

The first has to do with the content of this law. In all formulations, the conqueror is acknowledged to have the lawful power to do anything to the captive, across a wide spectrum of possible options, from killing him or enslaving him, extinguishing the independent existence of his community and annexing its territory, to, at the opposite extreme, freeing him, permitting the continued existence of his community, allowing him to retain his property, and even granting him citizenship. The conqueror is under no legal limitation or duty to select among these options but, instead, has the lawful discretion to decide the fate of his captives. In short, such a captive is not to be confounded with a prisoner-of-war under recent international law, who is a human being with rights the conqueror is obligated to respect.

The second point has to do with the universal use of legal language in the formulations of this law. In all formulations, *nomos* or *jus/jure* are employed, and they are used from the internal point of view of the actors in order to justify their actions as lawful. This consideration needs to be stressed because the kind of legal phenomenon that this so-called law of conquest or right of conquest is, has proved puzzling in modern scholarship. This puzzle is well worth study on another occasion. Suffice it to say here that this "law" was invoked to justify the conqueror's discretion to do as he pleased with his captive and that conquest was explicitly recognized in Roman law as a lawful method of acquiring property, including humans as slaves.

From the perspective provided by this law of conquest, a specific contextual explanation of Florentinus's negative definition of *libertas* may be offered: The conqueror is, from within the purview of this law, subject to neither coercion nor law with respect to his relation to his captive. Following a conquest, the relation of conqueror to captive is this: (1) The captive has surrendered, laid down his arms, and become defenseless, and he is at the mercy of the conqueror. The capacity to coerce has become unilateral, flowing in one direction only, from the victor toward the vanquished, whereas prior to capitulation, during hostilities, the ability to employ force was bilateral, even if unequal. Thus, the actions of the conqueror toward the captive cannot be prevented by force; the conqueror is free insofar as one of the preventative conditions of action has been removed from the scene. (2) The conqueror is under no obligation imposed by law in deciding the fate of the vanquished. He can lawfully kill him or preserve and sell him into slavery or restore him to his prior status as free. In short, the conqueror is legally unlimited; he may do as he pleases. The second of the two preventative conditions of action has also been removed.

If Florentinus's definition of *libertas* is read in this fashion, then we can see he has chosen his wording with care. He explicitly picks out two external conditions—the absence of force and the absence of legal restriction—that must be satisfied in order for *libertas*, as "doing what one pleases," to obtain. This reflects with precision the legal and factual position of conqueror in relation to captive. What Brunt refers to as the "concept of freedom as per se unrestricted" (1988, 290) applies to a specific human relation recognized by law. Moreover, if the conqueror chooses to reduce the captive to slavery and sell him, then the two basic features of the conqueror's position, that he is legally unlimited and can employ force with impunity, are transferred to another human, the purchaser. In this regard, the status of a slave as legally dead may be seen as the perpetuation of the conqueror-captive relation in the master-slave relation in society. This is the extreme or limiting case of negative liberty in a relation between two human beings. On this interpretation, Florentinus invoked a negative definition of liberty, which the compilers of the *Digest* incorporated, because the law itself recognized the legality of a relation between human beings in which one of them could do as he pleased to the other.

The key point for this chapter, then, is that *libertas* is once again being conceived as the polar opposite to slavery. However, the binary opposition in this case is not the fundamental division in the law of persons between *libertas* and *servi* as legal statuses but, rather, a distinct binary opposition between master (or conqueror) and slave (or captive). Here, the *libertas* that is the antithesis of slavery is the liberty to do anything one pleases to another human, not *libertas* as the status of a juridical person to be ruled only by law and hence to be protected against being the plaything of other human beings, including rulers.

Two Types of *Libertas* Because Two Types of Rule

The word *libertas* had, then, two logically distinct meanings in the first book of the *Digest*, and these two meanings were instantiated in two distinct *libertas/servi* polarities.

The presence of these two types of *libertas* in the same text is not the product of a disagreement between the jurists about what *libertas* is nor the result of confusion among the compilers of *The Digest of Justinian*, whose mandate was to bring harmony to Roman law. The explanation is Aristotelian, and it is to be sought in the dualistic character of the ancient legal world. This was a world in which some humans were ruled by law and other humans were ruled by masters. There existed two distinct types of rule, both of which were recognized as lawful, with each yielding a different experience called *libertas*—two distinct conceptions of the way a human being could be understood to be free in relation to other human beings.

The two kinds of *libertas* were associated with two different human figures: with the ruler when he ruled in a certain fashion, and with the ruled when he was ruled in a distinct fashion.

In one case, the word *libertas* applied to the position of the ruler when the type of rule he possessed was that of a conqueror or master. Here *libertas* was placed in opposition to both law and slavery: in opposition to law because it consisted of being unimpeded by law in acting as one pleased toward one's own slaves, and in opposition to slavery because the slave was powerless to do what he pleased to his master. The articulation of a *libertas/servi* antinomy in this case reflected the recognition of a human relation in which one human was placed by law above the law and another human was placed by law outside the protection of law.

In the second case, the word *libertas* applied to the position of the ruled when the kind of rule to which he was subject was rule by law. Like the *libertas* of a master, this type of *libertas* was also defined in relation to law, on the one hand, and to slavery, on the other. But in contrast to the *libertas* of a master, this *libertas* was placed in opposition not to law but only to slavery because this *libertas* consisted of being ruled only by law and consequently stood in stark contrast to the kind of power exercised over a slave.

Both types of *libertas* have in common that they were both defined in opposition to slavery. But there is a fundamental difference. Mastery and slavery are relational concepts, each requiring the existence of the other. There can be no masters without slaves, no human to whom one can lawfully act as one pleases unless that human is legally dead. The *libertas* possessed by a human recognized as a juridical person is also defined in opposition to slavery, but it does not notionally require slavery. Juridical personality is also a relational concept, but the relation whose existence it requires is that of a legal order properly so-called, that is, in which interactions between human beings are mediated by rules of law. The juridical subject requires fellow subjects, not slaves.

Liberty, Slavery, and Property

The preceding analysis, although multifaceted, still does not complete the account of the type of control exercised over a slave because "[i]n classical Roman law, the power over a slave has a double aspect" (Kaser 1993, 76): In the law of persons, the slave was a legal null, and in the law of things, the slave was property. It is necessary, then, to turn attention next to the property component of slavery.

In Roman law, slavery, in its property aspect, was characterized by what A. M. Honore called "the standard incidents of ownership" (1961, 108). The owner of the slave had the exclusive use of his human property; others could use the slave only with the consent of the owner. As with any of his other property, the owner was protected in his possession by laws prohibiting theft, fraud, and injury. And in the law of things, the slave was categorized as movable property that was "*in commercium*" (in lawful commerce). The slave could be bought and sold, given as a gift, bequeathed in a will and inherited, mortgaged, rented, and used as collateral on a loan, with all these transfers being the product of the owner's will. So none of the standard features of property, as set out in recent philosophical analysis, appear to be missing from the case of slavery.

There are several general treatments of Roman property law that include discussions of slavery, and the specific purpose here is to concentrate on that feature of this form of lawful property that is fundamental to understanding the type of control exercised over a slave. In this regard, it is essential to focus on "use," what it means for an owner to be able to use what he owns. Whatever else property involves, it certainly involves the use of the thing owned.

The core idea involved in an owner lawfully using the property he owns is that he is legally entitled to engage in a wide range of physical actions or movements directed toward his property. To use a horse, a house, a chair, or for that matter, an automobile is to ride it, enter it, occupy it, sit on it, touch it, push it, pull it, turn it on, turn it off, lock it up, throw a party in it, paint it, inscribe a name into it, remodel it, position and reposition it, and so on. All these actions are so many instances of the employment of bodily force exercised by the owner on the thing he owns (or which the owner permits to a user). This is no less the case if the activity of "labor" is added to the list of physical actions constituting the use of a thing. "Use," then, is a relational concept in which one term of the relation, the user, can physically act on the other term of the relation, the usable.

It will be readily recognized that to engage in any of the aforementioned actions toward a fellow member of a legal community constitutes the height of illegal behavior—indeed, nothing less than violence. That is, on this conception of "use" in a property relation, the thing used cannot be a juridical person unless these bodily actions are somehow understood as either sanctions for a legal wrong committed by the thing so used or else done with the consent of the thing so used. The relation between juridical persons is mediated by rules of law, and the condition that must be satisfied in order for the unwelcome use of such physical actions to be lawful is the prior commission of a legal offense by the person on whom the bodily force is exercised. In a property relation, however, no such condition has to be satisfied in order for the user to use what he owns. The usable does not have to break the law to legitimate its use; because the usable is not a person, this condition is removed. From this standpoint, then, the person/thing dichotomy may also be recognized as stating a mutually exclusive and jointly exhaustive classification of legal conditions paralleling the binary opposition *libertas/servi* as legal statuses.

Parenthetically, it should be noted that the preceding remarks are not intended to suggest that there are no limitations imposed by law on the kinds of physical actions that an owner can direct toward his property. In the exercise of force that constitutes the use of a thing, the owner is not entitled to violate the laws protecting other members of the legal community. But this limitation on the owner's treatment of his property arises from the legal status of other persons, not from the legal status of the thing owned. In a legal relation between persons, the use of force is limited by the standing of the parties whose interactions are governed by law; in a property relation, the use of force is limited by its side effects on other members of the legal community.

To return to slavery, the same concept of "use" is applicable to a human being reduced to property. The meaning of "use" does not change because the property is human. It still consists in physically acting on the thing owned. However, the legal condition of this use of a human being is the negation of juridical personality. The person so used must be excluded from the legal community so that the physical actions involved in using him do not count as unlawful conduct. Thus, the denial of *status libertas* to a slave in the law of persons is, from the perspective of law, a necessary condition of the use of a human as property, because it is only that denial that releases the owner from the fundamental constraint imposed by law on the treatment of a juridical person: that the use of force is either a delict or a sanction.

To sum up, slavery as a legal institution may once again be recognized to involve the legal release of force from the constraints of law. But in this second aspect of slavery, the focus is on enabling the owner to use his property without that use being conditional on some prior legitimating act of the human so used.

The Two Dimensions of Slavery as a Legally Defined Condition

A good deal of attention has recently been devoted by historians and social scientists to the question of the adequacy of juridical definitions of slavery articulated within societies in which slavery is a legally established institution and to the connected question of how to go about constructing a conception of slavery that is free from dependence on such internally articulated definitions. This is a highly contentious issue in contemporary thought. Suffice it to say here that it has become apparent why, in Roman law, slavery was defined two-dimensionally, both as a status whose polar opposite is *libertas* and as property. The reason lies in the type of control required to turn a human being into a usable that can be exploited as property. If a human is to be subjected to use as a thing, it is necessary to cut that human off from all legal ties with other humans so that he will be unprotected by law from his owner's use of force. If one human is to be the lawful instrument of action belonging to another human, he must be delegalized, deprived of his natural capacity to enter into legal relations with others. He must be placed by the law outside the law, and therefore there must be a law of persons that expressly denies him *libertas* as a status. The existence of a law of persons that defines servitude as legal death is internal to the type of control involved in slavery.

By contrast, there is no need for the law to place a nonrational animal outside the law, no need for a law of persons to deprive an animal of *status libertas*. To control an animal in order to use it as property, the animal may well have to be hunted, captured, corralled, tamed, and domesticated, but it does not have to be delegalized, deprived of juridical capacity to enter into legal community with others and to perform actions with recognized legal effects. Indeed, it would be absurd for the law of persons to contain a series of pronouncements declaring that an animal cannot sue or be sued, or incur obligations, or enter a contract, or make a valid will, or acquire and sell property. All this is superfluous because a nonrational animal is incapable of doing these things. Nor can an animal commit a legal wrong by failing to observe the law (*Digest*, 9.1.3), so it is unnecessary to release the animal's owner from the requirement that force can lawfully be exercised over the animal only if the animal is first incriminated. By nature, a nonrational animal is incapable of submitting its actions to the governance of law or entering into reciprocal legal relations of obligations with others, and therefore there is no need for the law of persons to cancel any supposed legal identity as a person.

The crux is, then, the nature of the creature to be controlled. The type of control that can be imposed on any creature cannot be dissociated from its nature. Because a nonrational animal is incapable of being ruled by law, one need not deprive it of juridical personality, that is, exclude it from legal community with others, as a condition of achieving control over it. But a human being can be ruled by law, and consequently, to control a human as usable property, he must be legally disestablished. The type of domination integral to slavery cannot be disassociated from the consideration that a slave is a human with a distinct nature capable of being governed by law and so incapable of being used as property unless deprived of his natural capacity to enjoy legal community with others.

From within the perspective of Roman law, slavery thus appears as the establishment by law of a distinctively antilegal method of ruling a human being. This conception of slavery suggests one possible interpretation of the famous pronouncements on liberty, slavery, and *jus naturale* mentioned in the first section of this chapter, in particular, the various statements pronouncing that all humans are free under *jus naturale* and that slavery, which exists *jus gentium*, is contrary to nature.

The obvious initial difficulty facing any attempt to recover the meaning of these statements is that both *libertas* and *jus naturale* had several strikingly different senses in both the juridical and the extra-juridical literature. This diversity opens these so-called natural law statements to different interpretations. Thus, the presence of two distinct definitions of *libertas* in the *Digest*—as a status concept and as a negative act concept—was emphasized earlier in this chapter. It follows that both definitions would have to be considered in any comprehensive examination of the pronouncements about *jus naturale* and *libertas*. But if *libertas* is taken to be a status concept in these pronouncements, so that the *libertas/servi* antithesis is understood to refer to two opposed methods of ruling a human being, then the contention that all humans are free under *jus naturale* may in turn be understood to mean that rule by law is natural to a creature with a human nature, and slavery is thus contrary to nature because it requires the deliberate negation by law of the natural capacity to be governed by law. Thus, by nature, a human, but not a nonrational animal, is capable of legal community with all other humans as human. Accordingly, *jus naturale* can here be properly translated as "natural law," conceived as the universal legal community of all creatures capable of being ruled by law and consequently capable of entering into a relationship of law with all others apart from membership in the legal system of any particular community. Slavery exists *jus gentium*, in the legal systems of all the separate cities; liberty for all exists *jus naturale*, in the idea of a universal legal community in which all are recognized as juridical persons.

But putting aside issues about natural law, and returning to the principal concern of this chapter, the main point has to do with the distinct type of control constitutive of slavery. The crux is the two faces of law:

Law can be used to regulate the conduct of a human recognized as a juridical person, but it can also be used to deprive a human of juridical personality so that he can be ruled extra-legally as property.

The Original Issue Resolved

One purpose of this chapter has been to offer a distinctively premodern frame of reference in which to reconsider the meaning of the question What is liberty? Ancient Roman law provides such a framework because, far from presupposing a world in which all human beings were recognized as juridical persons, it regarded the denial of legal personality to some humans in and by society as a universal legal phenomenon. Slavery was *jus gentium*, "the law of all peoples." From this perspective, the surviving works of Roman jurisprudence depict a dualistic legal world with two opposed types of rule coexisting together as lawful in every society: rule by law over juridical persons and rule over slaves as property. Accordingly, two distinguishable conceptions of liberty received expression in Roman jurisprudence: one conceived in opposition to slavery, the second in opposition to law. There are two distinct concepts of liberty because human beings are susceptible to being ruled in two opposed ways.

From this standpoint, it is appropriate to return to Richard Flathman's *Philosophy and Politics of Freedom* and to the debate in contemporary philosophy over the two concepts of liberty. The initial point to be made here is obvious. Although two distinct concepts of liberty were articulated in ancient Roman law, neither one is a positive conception. Both are intelligible apart from (1) the political idea of citizen participation in making the laws by which juridical persons are governed and (2) the philosophically generated ideas that "only the good man is free" (Philo) and that "all who are not virtuous are...slaves" (Diogenes Laertius, "Life of Zeno," 7.31–32). Person, citizen, and virtuous agent are distinct identities. That they are distinct does not mean, however, that there are no interesting connections among the three identities, and indeed, it is certainly intriguing that the Stoics invoked the *libertas/servi* polarity as a component of their account of virtue and vice. This use of the imagery of slavery, even in an extra-legal sense, suggests the possibility that the genealogy of positive liberty needs to be considered in tandem with the dualistic legal world of antiquity, and not merely in opposition to negative liberty as the absence of external coercion.

The main argument of this chapter, however, is that the liberty "incompatible with slavery" (Flathman 1987, 18) and the negative notion of liberty as the absence of external coercion are distinct concepts. So in conclusion, I offer a few final remarks about the difference between them. On this score, it will prove illuminating to return to a key idea in Flathman's analysis.

In his analysis of the current philosophical debate over liberty, Flathman recognizes different versions of the negative concept of liberty, marked by different views of what counts as an external constraint on action. He therefore proceeds to distinguish between "pure negative liberty" and "impure negative liberty" (30). "Pure negative liberty" refers to the Hobbesian notion of liberty as the absence of external impediment to motion. On this view, the only constraint on action that counts as a negation of liberty is an exercise of physical compulsion that makes some action of another human being impossible (as when an individual is prevented from leaving a room by locked doors). For Flathman, this type of intervention picks out what he calls "the paradigm case of unfreedom" (31) because here the action of one human is extinguished by the action of another, in contrast to such "impure" interventions as threats, warnings, unwelcome offers, and bribes, which leave the targeted individual in a position to act otherwise even though he incurs the risk of suffering the consequences of choosing noncompliance.

The difficulty with this "paradigm case of unfreedom," at least so far as slavery is concerned, is that it does not capture the unfree situation of slavery in its totality (even though Flathman also recognizes slavery as a flagrant case of unfreedom). No doubt, a constituent element of slavery is a permanent vulnerability to being subjected to "external impediments to motion" that stop action from occurring. But this is not the whole story, and what is left out may be identified by focusing on the property aspect of slavery. Insofar as the slave is considered lawful property, whose body and behavior is available for use by an owner, then a core feature of the master-slave relation is not impeding the slave from any action but directing and inducing the slave to act as his master desires, so that he can be effectively used as property. The point here is obvious: The slave is a servant. The slave as servant is especially manifest in ancient Rome and Greece, where slaves served in all manner of jobs: as clerks, administrators, tutors, physicians, even police (see Bradley 1994, 58–64).

From this standpoint, the slave may be understood as in some sense "an instrument of action" (Aristotle, *Politics* I, 1254a), and the unfreedom of slavery cannot be assimilated to "the paradigm case of unfreedom," in which action is extinguished.

An alternative conceptualization of the unfree condition of slavery is thus required, and the obvious alternative is some version of "other-determination": The unfreedom of slavery is understood as a condition in which, although there is action in the sense of bodily movement, this action is somehow determined by the will of another. The language frequently associated with slavery encourages and reflects this alternative: The slave is said to have no will of his own, to be an object rather than a subject of action, to be a patient rather than an agent, to be heteronymous, to lack self-determination or autonomy, and so on. On this conception, then, action is not made impossible, but its determination is assigned to another human. More precisely, this approach distributes the component parts of a single human action between two human beings. One human being conceives and formulates the alternatives, deliberates among them, decides on some specific act to be performed, and makes known his decision, whereas the other human receives the decision and proceeds to do the chosen act. Perhaps the purest version of this conception of slavery is expressed in Aristotle's *Politics*, where he gives as an example of a so-called natural master-slave relation, the rule that the soul of a human being exercises over his own body (I, 1254b).

Here, in contrast to "the paradigm case of unfreedom," it is not action that is extinguished but a separate agent. What is misleading about this alternative way of thinking about slavery, or at any rate the legal institution of slavery, is that it collapses the distinction between two discrete, separately embodied human beings. To conceive the master-slave relation as a relation in which the component parts of a single human action are divided between two humans, so that one wills and the other automatically acts, is to call upon magic. Slavery seems to be a condition that evokes totalizing conceptions of power, but the image of the slave as a perfectly responsive instrument is fantasy. Insofar as master and slave are two separate human beings, and the slave is not physically prevented from acting but induced to serve, then the control situation must be one mediated by some sort of reasons for action offered on the one side and some sort of subjectivity on the other side.

The problem of conceptualizing the unfreedom of slavery requires, then, a specification of the control situation that eliminates neither action nor a separately embodied actor.

At this point, it is relevant to return to the preceding account of slavery in Roman law. The crux is the binary definition of the slave as a human situated in two relations: a relation to a master as property and a relation to the larger legal community as lacking legal standing because excluded from the legal community. The slave is a legal null and consequently cannot perform acts with legal effects and does not have to commit a legal wrong in order for the use of coercion against him to be lawful. He is thus unprotected by law from the arbitrary use of coercion, and accordingly he becomes capable of being physically used as property.

From this juridical perspective, neither model of unfreedom—that in which motion is made impossible by physical constraint or that in which action takes place but is somehow determined by the will of another human—fits the dependent condition of the slave. Both models miss the legal construction of slavery. The crucial consideration is that a human reduced to slavery suffers a legal death rather than a physical death. Delegalization deprives a human not of action or agency but, rather, of the legal protection of his body and the legal recognition of his will. It is this delegalization that places a slave in a desperate choice situation: If he chooses not to comply with the will of the master, he runs the risk of suffering painful consequences, while at the same time, his act of noncompliance remains unprotected by law and without legal effect. The control situation in which a slave is situated is thus two-tiered, involving (1) the use or threat of the use of force by the master, (2) within a legally recognized framework that exempts his use of force from subordination to law.

A straightforward example will display this desperate choice situation. Take as an example flight from the threat of violence unsubordinated to law. First consider the case of a juridical person accosted by a thief who threatens, "Your money or your life." The target of this unlawful threat has "pure negative liberty" in that words do not constitute "an external impediment to motion" that prevent him from acting in defiance of both alternatives, by, say, taking flight in an attempt to obtain the protection of the law from his assailant. Next consider the legal situation of a slave threatened, apart from any transgression of law, with violence if he does not comply with his master's desires. If he takes flight, not only is he unprotected by law, but anyone who attempts to assist him is in violation of law. This is the point of a fugitive slave law (as at *Digest*, 11.4). A slave has nowhere to turn within lawful society. His existence is liminal (an appropriately Roman term) in that he remains alive, existing within society as a separately embodied human, but he does not exist inside the legal community of that society. So if he flees, hoping for freedom, his flight cannot be into the legal community; it must be out of that community entirely. He has no legal community, and freedom for him must take the form of an exodus in which he not only escapes his oppressors but acquires a law of his own.

It is now possible to recognize that something is wrong from the outset with the employment of the distinction between pure and impure negative liberty as a framework for thinking about the liberty "incompatible with slavery." That distinction reflects the idea that there are distinct versions of negative liberty marked by different views of what counts as an external constraint on action, for example, physical compulsion, threats, warnings, intimidation, an offer that cannot be refused. This approach invites the theorist, attempting to conceptualize the unfreedom integral to slavery, to identify some specific type of constraint or externally imposed obstacle to action as that which renders the slave unfree, as though the slave is not free because he is subjected to ———, where the blank is to be filled in with the name of some type of constraint. Assuming, then, that the constraint in question is not "external impediment to motion," it follows that it must be some other specifiable act of interference ("domination" for Quentin Skinner [1998, 85, n. 58], who is expressly operating within this same approach derived from a famous paper by Gerald MacCallum [1991]). But this project of identifying the unfreedom of slavery with a distinctive type of constraint is misconceived, or so the preceding discussion of Roman law would suggest. The distinctive feature of the control situation existing between master and slave is that one human is placed by law above the law and the other human is placed by law outside the law, so that recourse to constraints of any imaginable type is released from subordination to law. The slave is not unfree because he is subjected to some peculiar type of constraint but because he has no legal protection from the arbitrary will of his master, however expressed.

The preceding remarks suggest one final point: Because the unfreedom of slavery does not consist in being subjected to some distinct type of constraint, so in turn the liberty integral to juridical personality is not the absence of some identifiable type of constraint. Liberty consists, as traditionally understood, of liberties, that is, of the entire range of institutions, laws, and rights by which the rule of law is expressed and upheld.

References

Amiranti, Luigi. 1981. "Sulla schiavitu in Roma antica." *Labeo* 27: 26–38.
Aristotle. 1988. *Politics*. Ed. Stephen Everson. Cambridge: Cambridge University Press.
Bradley, Keith. 1994. *Slavery and Society at Rome*. Cambridge: Cambridge University Press.
Brunt, P. A. 1988. "Libertas in the Republic." In *The Fall of the Roman Empire and Related Essays*. Oxford: Oxford University Press.
Caesar. 1917. *The Gallic Wars*. Trans. H. J. Edwards. Cambridge, Mass.: Harvard University Press.
Crifò, Giuliano. 1958. "Su alcuni aspetti della liberta in Roma." *Archivo Giuridico*, 3–72.
Crook, John. 1967. *Law and Life of Rome 90BC-AD212*. Ithaca, N.Y.: Cornell University Press.
Davis, David Brion. 1966. *The Problem of Slavery in Western Culture*. Ithaca, N.Y.: Cornell University Press.
Didier, Philippe. 1991. "Les diverses conceptions du droit naturel a l'oeuvre dans la jurisprudene Roma des 2 et 3 siecles." *Studia et Documenta Historiae et Juris* 47: 195–262.
The Digest of Justinian. 1985. Trans. Alan Watson, ed. Theodore Mommsen and Paul Krueger. Philadelphia: University of Pennsylvania Press.
Diogenes Laertius. 1925. *Lives of Eminent Philosophers*. Trans. R. O. Hicks. Cambridge, Mass.: Harvard University Press.
Dumont, J.-C. 1987. *Servus: Rome et l'esclavage sous la Republique*. Rome: Ecole française de Rome.
Finley, Moses. 1983. *Ancient Slavery and Modern Ideology*. Middlesex, Eng.: Penguin Books.
Flathman, Richard. 1987. *The Philosophy and Politics of Freedom*. Chicago: University of Chicago Press.
Frezza, Paolo. 1949. "Jus Gentium." *Revue internationale des droits de L'antique* 2: 259–308.
Garnsey, Peter. 1996. *Ideas of Slavery from Aristotle to Augustine*. Cambridge: Cambridge University Press.
Honore, A. M. 1961. "Ownership." In *Oxford Essays in Jurisprudence*, ed. A. G. Guest. Oxford: Oxford University Press.
The Institute of Gaius. 1988. Trans. W. M. Gordon and D. F. Robinson. Ithaca, N.Y.: Cornell University Press.
Justinian's Institutes. 1987. Trans. Peter Birks and Grant McLeod. Ithaca, N.Y.: Cornell University Press.
Kaser, Max. 1993. *Jus Gentium*. Cologne: Böhlau Verlag.

Kelsen, Hans. 1970. *Pure Theory of Law*. Trans. Max Knight. Berkeley and Los Angeles: University of California Press.
Levy-Bruhl, Henri. 1931. "Theorie de l'esclavage." Reprinted in *Slavery in Classical Antiquity: Views and Controversies*, ed. M. I. Finley. Cambridge: W. Heffer, 1960.
Livy. 1935. *Roman History*. 14 vols. Vol. 9, trans. Evan T. Sage. Cambridge, Mass.: Harvard University Press.
MacCallum, Gerald. 1991. "Negative and Positive Freedom." In *Liberty*, ed. David Miller. Oxford: Oxford University Press.
Ostwald, Martin. 1995. "Freedom and the Greeks." In *The Origins of Modern Freedom in the West*, ed. R. W. Davis. Stanford: Stanford University Press.
Patterson, Orlando. 1982. *Slavery and Social Death*. Cambridge, Mass.: Harvard University Press.
Pettit, Philip. 1997. *Republicanism: A Theory of Freedom and Government*. Oxford: Oxford University Press.
Philo. 1929. "Every Good Man Is Free." In *Works*, vol. 9, trans. F. H. Colson and G. W. Whitaker. Cambridge, Mass.: Harvard University Press.
Pitkin, Hanna F. 1988. "Are Freedom and Liberty Twins?" *Political Theory* 16: 523–52.
Robleda, O. 1976. *Il diritto degli schiava Nell' Antica Roma*. Rome: Pontificia Universita Gregoriana.
Skinner, Quentin. 1998. *Liberty before Liberalism*. Cambridge: Cambridge University Press.
Watson, Alan. 1985. *Roman Slave Law*. Baltimore: Johns Hopkins University Press.
Xenophon. 1994. *Cyropaedia*. In *Works*, vol. 6, trans. Walter Miller. Cambridge, Mass.: Harvard University Press.

CHAPTER EIGHT

Hobbes and the Principle of Publicity

Jeremy J. Waldron

Richard Flathman's book *Thomas Hobbes* has many virtues, not least that it presents a Hobbes concerned above all with the rational integrity of the case that is made for absolute or near-absolute sovereign authority.[1] "It is," says Hobbes in a passage that Flathman highlights as a celebration of individuality, "unreasonable ... to require of a man endued with Reason of his own, to follow the Reason of any other man."[2] Now, in context, this is an observation about the responsibilities of priests and teachers:

> [F]or there is none should know better than they, that power is preserved by the same Vertues by which it is acquired; that is to say, by Wisdome, Humility, Clearnesse of Doctrine, and sincerity of Conversation; and not by suppression of the Naturall Sciences, and of the Morality of Naturall Reason; nor by obscure Language; nor by Arrogating to themselves more Knowledge than they make appear; nor by Pious Frauds; nor by such other faults as in the pastors of God's Church are not only Faults, but also scandalls, apt to make men stumble one time or other upon the suppression of their Authority.[3]

But it applies equally to the prerogatives of the sovereign. It may have been true of the inhabitants of Hobbes's England that "not one perhaps of ten thousand knew what right any man had to command him."[4] But the answer was to *teach* them the basis of that right by guiding them, as active intellects, through reasoning supportive of political obligation that might as well have been *their* reasoning, rather than requiring them simply to submit passively to conclusions reached as a result of the reasoning of another.

In this chapter, I want to take further this theme of respect for individual intellect, so prominent in Richard Flathman's presentation of Hobbes. I would like to do so, too, in a way that advances Flathman's agenda of forcing a confrontation (though not necessarily a hostile confrontation) between Hobbes's thinking and ours, or in the words of Flathman's editor, "between Hobbes and the architects, critics, reformers, and everyday participants of modern liberal democracies."[5] The connection is as follows:

One of the most interesting positions constitutive of contemporary philosophical liberalism is a view about the relation between political order and truth. Liberals, particularly in the Enlightenment tradition, believe that political order can be sustained without myths or lies, without false consciousness, and without ideology (in the pejorative sense of that term).[6] Enlightenment liberals are committed to what John Rawls has called the "principle of publicity":[7] A condition of a society's being well-ordered is that "[t]he political order does not ... depend on historically accidental or established delusions, or other mistaken beliefs resting on the deceptive appearances of institutions that mislead us as to how they work."[8] I believe that Thomas Hobbes accepted a version of this principle and that philosophically it is a fact of the first importance about his theory of politics that he did so.

The principle of publicity can be applied wholesale or piecemeal. Its piecemeal application amounts to a requirement that particular laws always be accompanied by reasons that show exactly why the law is justified, that is, reasons that show what its purpose is and what assumptions, factual and moral, underlie it. Laws should be persuasive, not merely coercive.[9] Hobbes certainly accepted that: "It belongeth to the Office of a Legislator, . . . to make the reason Perspicuous, why the Law was made."[10] I want to concentrate, however, on the principle of publicity in its wholesale application, that is, as it applies not just to particular laws but to the whole apparatus of state authority. For it is undeniable that Hobbes also accepted the principle in its wholesale application. He thought it essential for subjects to understand the true grounds of sovereignty, authority, and political obligation and to submit themselves to sovereign authority for the right reasons, not just for any old reason and not just as the upshot of any old propaganda that the sovereign and his counselors concocted. He accepted this, and he regarded his own mission qua philosopher as a contribution to this particular aspect or incident of authority. But it is less clear *why* Hobbes accepted the principle of publicity. Why did he think it important in a well-ordered society for people to be undeceived about the nature and justification of their political arrangements?

The starting point of our exploration is Hobbes's insistence in chapter 30 of *Leviathan* that it is "against [the sovereign's] Duty to let the people be ignorant, or mis-informed of the grounds, and reasons of... [the sovereign's] essentiall Rights."[11] This insistence is found throughout Hobbes's political writings: It is in *The Elements of Law*[12] and also in *On the Citizen (De Cive)*.[13] In *Leviathan,* it is phrased as a responsibility not to let the people be ignorant. This seems to be an active duty on the part of the sovereign to inform his people of the truth, as well as a duty not to mislead them and a duty not to permit them to be misled by others.

In the earlier works, it is the third of these that is emphasized most heavily. There are, says Hobbes in *De Cive,* "certaine perverse doctrines" that "dispose the mindes of men to sedition" and that the sovereign must "root...out of the mindes of men."[14] (Later I shall consider the Hobbesian position that the sovereign must prohibit the teaching of such views.) It is remarkable, however, that in all three of these works, Hobbes was adamant that extirpating such errors from the minds of men could be accomplished only by the sovereign's positively shouldering the burden of seeing that his subjects are taught *the truth.* A ban on the dissemination of false subversive views is not enough. "[O]pinions which are gotten by education... cannot be taken away by force,"[15] said Hobbes. "It is therefore the duty of those who have the chief Authority; to root those out of the mindes of men, not by commanding, but by teaching; not by the terrour of penalties, but by the perspicuity of reasons."[16] Without such teaching, public order is always in danger. What is invoked here, of course, is Hobbes's conviction that social and political order cannot be maintained by force: "[T]he power of the mighty hath no foundation but in the opinion and belief of the people.... [I]f men know not their duty, what is there that can force them to obey the laws? An army, you will say. But what shall force the army?"[17] The grounds of the subjects' duties have, as Hobbes puts it, "the rather need to be diligently, and truly taught; because they cannot be maintained by... terrour of legal punishment."[18]

Of course, an authoritarian may recognize the need to supplement coercion with indoctrination without committing himself to the liberal principle of publicity. One can believe in the necessity of indoctrination without believing in the importance of teaching the truth. And there would appear to be room in Hobbes's philosophy, too, for a distinction of this kind. Hobbes believed that most people are inclined to accept, at least as a starting point, whatever they hear from their social superiors, and he believed that the latter would accept, again at least as a starting point, whatever they are taught in the universities by *their* superiors.[19] He uses a sort of "trickle-down" metaphor. The universities "are the Fountains of Civill, and Moral Doctrine, from whence the Preachers, and the Gentry, drawing such water as they find, use to sprinkle the same (both from the Pulpit, and in their Conversation) upon the People."[20] Places like Oxford and Cambridge are the fountains of political theory; the clergy and the gentry, who in their youth attend the universities, draw water from these fountains and sprinkle it abroad in their sermons, in their little homilies from the magistrates' benches, and in their general conversation. And if social hydraulics works as it ought, this holy water eventually trickles all over the common people, drenching them in civic doctrine. The division of labor in this process depends on a degree of deference between persons (or classes) that seems to have no necessary connection with verisimilitude:

> They whom necessity... keepeth attent on their trades, and labour; and they, on the other side, whom superfluity, or sloth carrieth after their sensual pleasures (which two sorts of men take up the greatest part of Mankind,) being diverted from deep meditation, which the learning of truth, not onely in the matter of Naturall Justice, but also of all other Sciences necessarily requireth, receive the Notions of their duty, chiefly from Divines in the Pulpit, and partly from such of their Neighbours, of familiar acquaintance, as having the Faculty of discoursing readily, and plausibly, seem wiser and better learned in cases of Law, and Conscience, than themselves. And the Divines, and such others as make shew of Learning, derive their knowledge from the Universities, and from the Schooles of Law, or from the Books, which by men eminent in those Schooles, and Universities, have been published.[21]

That Hobbes did not believe this process necessarily depended on the truth of what was taught, or (sticking with the aquatic metaphor) that he did not think the hydraulics depended on the purity of the waters, is shown by his concern about the effect of the falsehoods currently being taught by academics.[22] The time of his writing was only a hundred years or so after the English Reformation, and the universities were still drenched, if not in Roman Catholicism, then in the spirit or ghost of Roman Catholicism, which preached quite severe limits on the authority of the temporal state. It is no wonder, said Hobbes, if the current generation of scholars "yet retain a relish of that subtile liquor, wherever they were first seasoned, against the Civill Authority."[23] Moreover, the university teaching of philosophy was overwhelmingly dominated by the false and pernicious writings of Aristotle, so much so as to be almost unworthy of the name "philosophy"—"the nature whereof," said Hobbes, "depends not upon Authors." What was presently being taught, he said, should be called "Aristotelity," not philosophy![24] Still, false or not, the beliefs that were taught at Oxford and Cambridge were effective (their effect being to destabilize the social order). One might infer from this that if *true* doctrine were taught, it would be equally effective (this time in stabilizing the social order, if indeed that is what true doctrine does).[25] But why not as well infer that *any* doctrine taught in this way would be effective according to its lights, so that the sovereign should choose, as a basis for political indoctrination, whatever view would most enhance his authority or whatever view would best ensure the stability of the body politic, irrespective of its truth or falsity?

Suppose, for example, that the people are more likely to refrain from rebellion if they believe that kings are ordained by God by a sort of hereditary divine right. That view is false, according to Hobbes, at least so far as heredity is concerned.[26] But is it not possible that it might still be effective as a public ideology, that is, as material for indoctrination in the pulpit and the universities? After all, the history of ideas seems to show people accepting as self-evident truths—indeed, in Hobbes's view, people in England were *currently* accepting as self-evident truth—lies that were much more ludicrous and implausible than this. Or suppose the sovereign's power would be enhanced by a spirit of sacrificial patriotism, a spirit similar to that which sent millions of young men willingly to their deaths in Europe in 1914–18. On Hobbes's own view, there is no justification whatever for such patriotism.[27] But if university teachers could be persuaded that it was a well-founded demand of morality (and, again, professors have believed and taught much sillier things than this), and if they taught it to their pupils, who would then sprinkle it abroad among the general population from the pulpit, from the bench, and at their dinner tables, then surely the sovereign would have available to him a citizen army that was more powerful (because better motivated) than the armies available to sovereigns who were more fastidious about teaching only the truth about the reasonableness of patriotic sacrifice.

Why, in the face of these possibilities, does Hobbes insist that the sovereign has a duty to ensure that the people know the *truth* about their duties, as opposed to some plausible and politically more effective lie?

There are passages where Hobbes comes close to condoning such lies. The section of *The Elements of Law* from which I have been quoting begins thus: "Another thing necessary, is the rooting out from the consciences of men all those opinions which seem to justify, and give pretence of right to rebellious actions."[28] He follows this by offering as examples a whole list of opinions that we know he thinks are false, such as "that a man can do nothing lawfully against his private conscience; that they who have the sovereignty are subject to the civil laws."[29] But there are other opinions that we know Hobbes thinks are true that might also "seem to justify, and give pretence of right to rebellious actions," for example, the view that a man is at liberty to disobey a sovereign who commands him not to resist those that assault him.[30] And it is possible that the currency of (true) opinions like this has the effect of undermining the power of the sovereign.[31] So—again—if this is the sort of thing that truth amounts to, why would anyone interested in augmenting the power of the sovereign be committed to teaching only the truth? Hobbes *says* he wants to root out from the consciences of men all those opinions that legitimize rebellion. But to the extent that some of his own theorems might be regarded as a "Rebells catechism,"[32] he does not seem to be really committed to extirpating those opinions; quite the contrary.

Later I will examine the implications of Hobbes's considered position on this, summed up in the proposition that "Doctrine repugnant to Peace, can no more be True, than Peace and Concord can be against the Law of Nature."[33] But even if we take him at his word on this—that ultimately the truth does promote peace—what is striking, still, is his insistence that truth not be exaggerated for the sake of peace and stability. Though Hobbes is certainly committed to securing a belief in sovereign authority, he commits himself at the very beginning of *Leviathan* to argue also against "those that contend... for *too much* authority."[34] Consider his view that monarchy is the best political system. There is no doubt that Hobbes believed a society would be better off if most people in it thought (as he did) that this view was true.[35] And no doubt more of them could be persuaded to think this if well-known experts in logic were to go around saying that it was *demonstrably* true. But Hobbes is unwilling to put this spin on a desirable truth; he does not think that the proposition about monarchy *can* be demonstrated, and he does not try to conceal this from his readers.[36] Not only in his own mind but also publicly, Hobbes goes to fastidious lengths to distinguish between a proposition conducive to peace that he thinks he can support with demonstrative argument and a proposition conducive to peace that he thinks is true "but put with probability."[37] That's the mark of the Hobbesian commitment that interests me.

One further point: Richard Flathman notes that Hobbes, in addition to refusing falsely to exaggerate the basis of the sovereign's authority, also believes that the sovereign must "eschew various comforting but in his view delusive evasions of the true character of rule."[38] In the modern world, absolute rulers go to great lengths to drape themselves in the costumes of democracy, representation, and the rule of law. They believe it is to their advantage to do so, and they believe it enhances the security of their regime. They figure they are more likely to gain support from squeamish subjects (as well as meddling foreigners) if they understate their absolutism, falsely (even incoherently, in Hobbes's view) representing their sovereign power as divided, devolved, and limited by the laws they pass. In Hobbes's view, this too is a mistake: He thinks it would be a mistake for the sovereign not only actually to weaken his authority but also even to try to persuade his subjects or the world that it is weaker than it is (or ought to be). People must be taught *the truth* about absolutism, and that means the truth about its extent as well as the truth about its limits and its desirability. The sovereign should not, in Hobbes's account, let his state slip into the hands of spin doctors who will "let the people be... mis-informed of the grounds, and reasons of those [the sovereign's] essentiall Rights."[39]

Some say that Hobbes's commitment is not to *the truth* as such but simply to *his own theory:* It is the conceited regard of an opinionated writer for the dissemination of his own convictions. On a couple of occasions, Flathman comes close to this view by adopting the following phraseology to describe Hobbes's position:

> [T]he Sovereign must take control of "the universities" and see to it that they teach the truth and nothing but the truth (that is Hobbes's own doctrines!) on these subjects.... As with the natural philosopher, the Sovereign translates "his" (i.e., Hobbes's!) science into power by teaching it to others.[40]

I think Flathman's interpolations are unhelpful. Like any other serious thinker, Hobbes *thinks* that what he is writing is true; otherwise he would write something else. "I am a man that love my own opinions, and think all true I say."[41] But that does not mean he *equates* the predicates "true" and "held by me" or "held by Hobbes."[42]

Moreover, Hobbes by no means thought it obvious that *his view*—whether characterized as "the truth" or not—should be taught in the universities and publicized abroad. Admittedly, he does say in the "Review, and Conclusion" to *Leviathan,*

> [T]here is nothing in this whole Discourse,... as far as I can perceive, contrary either to the Word of God, or to good Manners, or tending to the disturbance of the Publique Tranquility. Therefore, I think it may be profitably printed, and more profitably taught in the Universities.[43]

And one is hardly overwhelmed by his "modesty" in chapter 30 of that book when he imagines an interlocutor asking, "[I]s it *you* will undertake to teach the Universities?" Hard question, responds Hobbes, and then he adds coyly, "it is not fit, not needful, for me to say either I *[sic]*, or No; for any man that sees what I am doing may easily perceive what I think."[44] Still, Hobbes was familiar enough with the ancient doctrine of *arcana imperii* (secrets of statecraft) to understand the theoretical option that the truth about politics should not be widely disseminated, that its circulation should be restricted "to insinuate itself with those whom the matter it containeth most nearly concerneth."[45] In the preface to *De Cive,* he mentions that

> [t]he wise men of remotest antiquity believed that this kind of teaching... should be given to posterity only in the pretty forms of poetry or in the shadowy outlines of Allegory, as if to prevent what one might call the high and holy mystery of government from being contaminated by the debates of private men.[46]

And the rest of the preface shows that he thought this belief at least worthy of an answer. Later, in *Leviathan,* Hobbes returned to the issue. He explicitly addressed—and, as he thought, answered—the objection that the truth about politics was too difficult for the common people to grasp.[47] All this is a way of emphasizing that Hobbes's commitment to the principle of publicity was not a simple a fortiori consequence of his dogmatism, his vanity, or his own affection for positions he had staked out. His commitment was an affirmative answer to an open question, and one that he was willing to support with argument.

(We know also—and we may suspect that *he* knew[48]—that nothing would have filled his contemporaries with greater horror than Hobbism being taught in the universities as the basis of civic education.[49] He did not tailor his views to appeal to his patrons—on the contrary, his stubborn pursuit of the truth about politics tended to alienate them[50]— and there is no indication that he thought the sovereign qua teacher should tailor *his* views to the predilections of his audience either.)

What, then, is the ground of this commitment in Hobbes? Why did he insist that it is against the sovereign's duty "to let the people be ignorant or mis-informed of the grounds, and reasons of those [the sovereign's] essentiall Rights"? Why did he put no faith in pure indoctrination, by which I mean indoctrination carried out without regard to truth, especially given the view (which we have already noted) that men tend to accept at least as a starting point whatever they hear from their social superiors? Why insist so stridently on something like the liberal principle of publicity in the face of the possibilities furnished by that sort of credulity?

The answer is that Hobbes appears to have believed, with some quite refreshing proto-Enlightenment optimism, that in the kind of politics he envisaged, civil doctrine would be so much at the mercy of individual reason that any attempt to base sovereign authority on something other than "the perspicuity of reasons"[51]—any attempt to base it on falsehood or myth or mystery—would leave political allegiance terribly vulnerable to the ability of actual individuals to figure things out for themselves and to spot a lie when they heard one. The detail of Hobbes's argument for this belief is worth spelling out, for two reasons. First, although the belief is important for the whole enterprise, the argument for it is implicit rather than enunciated in Hobbes's account of reason in politics. The second reason for spelling the argument out in detail is that it appears to contradict the premise of Hobbes's concern about false teaching in the universities: How could he profess concern about men's credulity and about the effectiveness of "Aristotelity"[52] if at the same time he believed people have the capacity to figure out when they are being lied to? I want to show that this contradiction is more apparent than real. The Hobbesian argument has three phases to it. There is, first, the assertion of a general philosophical connection between human reason and truth. Second, there is a special and compelling quality to that connection in areas, such as politics, where survival is at stake. And third—perhaps most important—it matters that the Hobbesian sovereign is going to have to make very unusual, unfamiliar, even extravagant claims for himself, claims that are bound to be treated skeptically in the first instance by those who hear them and that have no hope at all of long-term acceptance except on the basis of whatever rational, survival-oriented arguments may be produced to support them.

The natural desire of men is for truth (if they can possibly get it) rather than falsity, even falsity that has been (to use a phrase from the furniture trade) "antiqued" or "distressed" for effect: "[M]en are not generally so much inclined to the reverence of Antiquity, as to preferre Ancient Errors, before New and well proved Truth."[53] People certainly harbor all sorts of illusions about all sorts of things and often seem "obstinately bent to maintain them"[54] in a way that resists any demonstration of their falsity. And people do tend to take things on faith from those they regard as their betters. Hobbes is pulled in several different directions on this point. He actually has some faith in naive untutored reason: "[T]hey that have no Science, are in better, and nobler condition with their naturall Prudence; than men, that by mis-reasoning, or by trusting them that reason wrong, fall upon false and absurd generall rules."[55] Bookish men are often of a "fluttering" demeanor, "as birds that entring by the chimney, and finding themselves inclosed in a chamber, flutter at the false light of a glasse window, for want of wit to consider which way they came in."[56] On the other hand, we know that Hobbes thinks it inevitable that most men will take their lead in civic doctrine from their social superiors. And he also insists—as we shall see in the third phase of this argument—that natural reason cannot reach appropriate conclusions in politics unaided by experience organized expertly and transparently as a science. In general, although Hobbes is well aware of men's readiness to accept what others tell them, he insists that even here we are not talking about simple credulity. "The propositions which we receive for truth, we alwaies grant for some reasons of our owne."[57] We are not always gullible in our trust in others; rather, we trust them because we cannot see any reason why the other should want to deceive us.[58] Those, on the other hand, who can see such a reason do tend to fall back on their own prudential resources. So much is a matter of *basic* rationality.

Beyond that, politics engages certain special concerns. As Hobbes continually emphasizes, politics concerns matters of life and death. It is because the stakes are so high in this area of life, or as he puts it, "because the damage is so great, that a properly expounded doctrine of Duties is so useful."[59] Reasoning about politics is reasoning about the avoidance of war and death; it is a domain of reasoning in which individual persons have the strongest possible incentive to be as careful as they can. So even if the connection between reason and truth is tenuous in certain areas of speculation, there is intense survival-related pressure to make that connection as tight as possible in politics.[60] However much people may relish mystery, foolishness, and flattery, if they become aware that others are trying to fool them, flatter them, or mystify them about the prospect of some threat to their lives, they have an incentive—the strongest possible incentive, in Hobbes's account—to resist that foolishness and to pierce through to the truth if they can. Moreover, such resistance would be not only predictable but utterly respectable, according to Hobbes, because "every man by right of nature is judge himself of the necessity of the means, and of the greatness of the danger" so far as self-preservation is concerned,[61] and "every man, if he be in his wits,"[62] will properly resist anything that tends to destroy him.

I should emphasize that none of this changes for Hobbes when the source of the falsehood or mystification is a person in political authority. Hobbes insisted, notoriously, that "[t]he Obligation of Subjects to the Soveraign, is understood to last as long, and no longer, than the power lasteth, by which he is able to protect them."[63] Readers often ask who is to be the judge of this, the subject or the sovereign.[64] The answer is obvious and irresistibly dictated by the logic of Hobbes's theory. Ultimately, only the subject can be the judge, for the judgment is about his own survival.[65] To allocate such a judgment to the sovereign would be, at best, to beg the very question that was at stake, namely, is this man really entitled to be treated by me as a sovereign on the ground (and for Hobbes there is no other ground for political obligation) that submission to him would promote my survival in the long term?[66]

I have been arguing that people have greater reason to be diligent in seeking the truth where their survival interests are at stake and that this is why Hobbes's sovereign should not be in the business of misleading them about the grounds of his authority. In this matter—intimately related to the survival prospects of his subjects—there is too much risk that the sovereign's lies will be exposed or his spin rejected. Because of what is at stake—because individuals have the power to reason, and because of what individual reason is for—it would be foolish for a sovereign to risk telling lies to people about issues relevant to peace and survival. Against this, someone may cite Hobbes's well-known observation that if self-interest is involved, the search for truth tends to be distorted rather than enhanced. Hobbes observed that men dispute endlessly and often irrationally about shared standards of right and wrong, where their interests are at stake, but not about geometry

> because men care not, in that subject, what be truth, as a thing that crosses no man's ambition, profit, or lust. For I doubt not, but if it had been a thing contrary to any man's right of dominion, or to the interest of men that have dominion, that the three Angles of a Triangle should be equal to two Angles of a Square, that doctrine should have been, if not disputed, yet by the burning of all books of Geometry suppressed, as far as he whom it concerned was able.[67]

But the contrast here is between a case in which interest pits men against one another and a case in which their interests are not in competition, rather than a contrast between a case in which interests are involved and a case in which they are not. If you and I have a competing interest in a matter, then our *dialogue* about it will tend to be distorted by the cross-cutting effects of our opposed interests. Self-interest will certainly upset public reason (which, as we will see below, is one of the reasons Hobbes did not make the move from a principle of publicity to a principle of free speech). But it does not follow that self-interest itself distorts a man's reasoning about his own security or survival. Quentin Skinner, I think, misses this distinction in his book *Reason and Rhetoric in the Philosophy of Hobbes* when he attributes to Hobbes the view that there is an opposition between reason and interest that surfaces, for example, in representative assemblies.[68] In the passage that Skinner cites,

Hobbes is certainly saying that individual interests distort the public orientation of reasoning in such assemblies, but it by no means follows that individual interest necessarily distorts individual reasoning. Indeed, one has to think entirely to the contrary if there is to be any connection at all between Hobbesian reason and Hobbesian psychology.

The third phase of Hobbes's argument concerns the peculiar nature of the arguments (about life and death) that are involved in connecting survival and sovereign authority. In his argument for sovereign authority, Hobbes does not take himself to be reminding people of something they know implicitly already. Nor does he think his political theory is straightforwardly susceptible to natural reason or intuition.[69] He is well aware that the positions for which he is arguing will appear uncongenial—"To most men this sovereignty and absolute power seems so harsh that they hate the very name of it"[70]—and that his arguments for those positions may be (as we would say) counterintuitive. Rebuttals based on the unfamiliarity or uncongeniality of the reasoning are going to have to be firmly resisted:

> [A]n argument from the Practise of men that have not sifted to the bottom, and with exact reason weighed the causes, and nature of Common-wealths, and suffer daily those miseries, that proceed from the ignorance thereof, is invalid. For though in all places of the world men should lay the foundation of their houses on the sand, it could not thence be inferred, that so it ought to be. The skill of making and maintaining Commonwealths consisteth in certain Rules, as doth Arithmetique and Geometry; not (as Tennis-play) on Practise only: which Rules, neither poor men have the leisure, nor men that have had the leisure, have hitherto had the curiosity, or the method to find out.[71]

Thus, if Hobbes's arguments do not work as arguments, then the positions will be lost; there is nothing else to support them.[72] Hobbes knew, then, that his task was difficult and that if the reasoning the sovereign deployed were to be exposed as a sham, there would be nowhere else to turn for support for his positions.[73] When I say that Hobbes acknowledges that his conclusions are uncongenial to most people, I do not mean that he thinks they go against people's self-interest. Hobbes is not (as Skinner seems to think) contrasting reason with interest here.[74] Instead, the argument is about short-term interests versus interests that are so long term that nothing but good political science will enable men to grasp them:

For all men are by nature provided of notable multiplying glasses (that is their Passions and Selfe–love) through which every little payment appeareth a great grievance, but are destitute of those prospective glasses, (namely Morall and Civill Science,) to see a farre off the miseries that hang over them, and cannot without such payments be avoided.[75]

Because the issue is between immediately apparent interest, on the one hand, and difficult and counterintuitive propositions about long-term interest, on the other, nothing but impeccable argumentation (set out in a way that is proof against assaults mounted in the name of short-term reasoning) will do, so far as the intellectual basis of Hobbesian sovereignty is concerned. Hobbes has no choice, then, but to present the argument for his position as science; and because the certain sign of science is, for him, the ability to "demonstrate the truth thereof perspicuously to another,"[76] he has no choice but to present his theory in a way that respects the intellects of his audience. The motto from St. Paul that ends *De Cive*—"Let every man be fully persuaded in his owne mind"[77]—sums up the inescapable spirit of Hobbesian civil doctrine.

How, finally, do we reconcile all this with Hobbes's own concerns about men's credulity and irrationality? Two points are important. First, the fact that Hobbes believes (and rightly) that there is nothing except reason for him to rely on does not mean that he is particularly confident reason will work. On the contrary, as Skinner has pointed out, Hobbes was constantly exercised by concern about how much reason could achieve unassisted by anything except the laying out of a demonstrative argument, and *Leviathan,* in contrast to some of his earlier work, "embodies a new and far more pessimistic sense of what the powers of unaided reason can hope to achieve."[78] The great merit of Skinner's book is that it presents Hobbes's torment about the use of rhetoric to supplement argument in aid of truth in circumstances where he had become convinced there was nowhere else to turn.

For, second, although Hobbes thought that the teaching of false political theories had an effect, it was not the sort of effect he was looking for. He acknowledged that the writings of Aristotle and of the radical Catholic natural lawyers were very effective in destabilizing existing institutions. But they were incapable of producing the sort of long-term, settled support for sovereign authority that Hobbes indicated was required. Their effectiveness was in the production of wild, unstable beliefs and the sort of "fluttering" mentality I mentioned earlier.[79] Hobbes knew that political arrangements of the type he thought were needed could not possibly be supported in this way. They required settled and resolute support, not the kind of intellectual support that would be vulnerable to every whim of philosophical fashion. Men are constantly in danger of being driven away from the burdens and sacrifices of citizenship and of losing sight of the real but long-term interests that such burdens and sacrifices serve. If the sacrifices are supported by nothing better than lies or mythology, then there is no guarantee whatsoever that they will not be subverted by the first piece of plausible nonsense that comes along arguing in the other direction. This point is connected to Hobbes's general picture of mental life unguided by any standards of intellectual discipline: "The secret thoughts of a man run over all things holy, prophane, clean, obscene, grave, and light, without shame, or blame."[80] Without the discipline of reason, political ideology is tremendously insecure, and the discipline of reason is incapable of mitigating this insecurity except as logic, that is, except in a way that is firmly oriented to the pursuit and preservation of truth. Again, I do not want to exaggerate the point.[81] There was no guarantee in Hobbes's system that truth and sound argument could in fact secure the sort of stable support that was needed. But Hobbes thought it *certain* that lies (of the sort that were currently being taught) would *not* conduce to stability. And so, he maintained, the prudent sovereign had no choice but to experiment with the teaching of the truth.

Our conclusion so far is that Hobbes thought telling people the truth about the basis of authority and obligation would be in the sovereign's best interest—that is, "not onely his Duty, but his Benefit also, and Security."[82] Now I want to ask whether this is purely a matter of strategy for Hobbes, or whether there is also an element of respect. Is there a sense in his philosophy that persons as rational agents are *entitled* to be told the truth about matters like these? Hobbes certainly never puts it quite like that. But it is worth noticing a number of ways in which his mainly strategic argument approaches the character of an argument based on respect.

Consider first the sovereign who does decide to risk a lie to his subjects, about the basis of his legitimacy, for example, or about the sacrifices he is entitled to ask of them. There is no guarantee that such a sovereign will be found out.[83] But he *is* taking a chance. By lying to the people, the sovereign is putting himself in a position akin to that of "the Foole" in chapter 15 of *Leviathan:* He would have to rely on people's gullibility, on their error, "which errours a man cannot reasonably reckon upon as the means of his security."[84] In other words, such a sovereign relies as much as "the Foole" does on insulting his subjects' intelligence on a matter where it is important that they know the truth (because there is no other reliable basis on which they can figure out what they owe to the sovereign).

Moreover, the foolish sovereign is not entitled to defend his lies by saying that they are being put about in a good cause. If they are accepted at face value by his subjects (and that presumably is the acceptance he seeks), the tendency of such lies will be to promote more (or perhaps less)[85] obedience than is in fact required. To the extent of that excess (or shortfall), they are lies in a bad cause, not a good cause. Any appearance to the contrary stems from the careless assumption that Hobbes is anxious to secure any old submission to the sovereign, rather than the exact type or degree of submission that it is in fact safe and appropriate for a subject to provide.

A second point is that even if the argument *is* strategic—the sovereign is better off if his people are taught the truth—it is strategic in relation to the interests of the entire political community, not just in relation to the interests of the individual or individuals who happen to occupy the office of sovereign. As Hobbes puts it, "[the] grounds upon which one person has a right to govern, and the rest an obligation to obey... are necessary to be taught the people, who without them cannot live in peace *among themselves.*"[86] The sovereign, after all, is constituted by the people, and each of his acts is imputable to the people. The lies that, in the formulation I have been using, we imagine him telling the people are really lies they tell themselves. Such lies would, therefore, be wrong or inappropriate, because they are ways in which people might systematically mislead themselves and each other about issues of life and death, issues that are extraordinarily complex and that in fact require—for safety's sake—the most careful and fastidious reasoning.

Third, we should not neglect the importance for Hobbes of respect for science as such, for scientific standards, and thus indirectly for the intellects to which scientific standards pay tribute. In *The Rhetoric of Leviathan,* David Johnston has observed Hobbes's enthusiasm for the idea of a society enlightened by science and permeated by the practical and technological achievements that science would make possible.[87] Certainly, Hobbes did not think such a society would be possible without the establishment of peace and sovereign authority, and it is worth remembering that in the famous passage about life in the state of nature—"nasty, brutish, and short"—he listed navigation, engineering, and geography as prominent casualties of war.[88] But he also did not think such a society possible except among a people more deeply imbued with the ideas and values of science and intellectual rigor.[89] An enlightened society would have to be a society freed from mythology, fantasy, and superstitious religion. Before what Hobbes referred to as "the Night of our naturall Ignorance"[90] could be enlightened with science, it would have to be freed from the kingdom of darkness that populated the night with ghosts and goblins and phantoms. And that emancipation could not take place if the very political power that guaranteed the peace (in which alone science and enlightenment could flourish) was itself supported by myths and lies of various sorts.

The same point can be put another way. One can imagine an intellectually respectable argument yielding the conclusion that the sovereign must be prepared to support his state with lies; that is, one could imagine a rationally compelling argument for a noble lie or for *arcana imperii*. There is nothing in such an argument inherently insulting to reason; it would be a sort of "Government House" intellectualism, along the lines of the passage in the *De Cive* cited earlier.[91] However, such an argument could hardly be sustained if one of its premises was the need to establish sovereign authority in order to secure peace as a condition of general open-ended enlightenment in society; for then the overall aim of the enterprise would be at war with the means employed to pursue it. One would be seeking peace in order to foster the growth of the very intellectual inquisitiveness that would undermine the lies that supported the sovereign as guarantor of peace.

One last point in this connection: I have said almost nothing about the importance of Hobbes's contractarianism for his subscription to the principle of publicity. Hobbes, we must remember, is at bottom a theorist of government by consent, and even if he has some curious ideas about the relation between consent and duress—"Covenants entred into by fear... are obligatory"[92]—he certainly cannot give up the connection between consent and understanding without serious damage to the overall structure of his theory.[93] In Hobbes's politics as much as in Rawls's, everyone is deemed to know about the system of government and the principles underlying it all that he would know if their acceptance were the result of an agreement.[94] It would be wrong, however, to regard this as an independent Hobbesian argument for the commitment to publicity. The contractarian structure, with this implication, is appropriate for modeling a politics already committed to the principle of publicity. If there is no such commitment, we should choose a different model-theoretic structure, such as "the impartial spectator" of classical utilitarianism.[95] Still, Hobbes's contractarianism is important because it makes clear how many strands of his political theory come together in his version of the principle of publicity, how much he would have to give up if he abandoned it, and how far it is to be understood as a principle in terms of which we deal with one another, rather than as a mere stratagem for a distinct political class.

For us today, it is very difficult to separate a commitment to truth from a principle of free speech or, at the very least, from what Immanuel Kant referred to as "freedom of the pen."[96] So we are naturally inclined to see Hobbes's rejection of freedom of speech as tantamount to his rejection of a commitment to truth.[97] Though (as we have seen) Hobbes doubted that self-serving *lies* put about by the sovereign would survive the scrutiny of his subjects' prudential reasoning, that does not mean he believed that the mass of individual subjects would eventually arrive at the truth about politics if left to their own and each other's devices in a free marketplace of ideas. For one thing, the processes by which the "marketplace of ideas" would work, so far as political truth was concerned, might well involve civil war as the best approximation to a winnowing process. And for another thing, there was no reason, Hobbes thought, to suppose that truth would win out even *eventually* if people had no guidance but their own gullibility limited by their own experience. Flathman is right to notice in Hobbes a "consuming fear of the disruptive and destructive power of ideas and doctrines, beliefs and opinions"[98] and to observe that even if Hobbes thought it counterproductive for the sovereign to probe a man's "inward thought, and beleef,"[99] he nevertheless regarded the teaching, publishing, and dissemination of doctrines as outward actions whose supervision was crucial to the well-being of the commonwealth. According to Hobbes, anyone who purports to teach in effect purports to govern,[100] so if a teacher is not licensed by the sovereign, he is a potential competitor, and the reason for governing him, Hobbes adds, is not that the would-be teacher is the sovereign's subject but that the people he purports to teach are.[101]

So there is no question for Hobbes of any entitlement to academic freedom or freedom of the press. The government has a right to regulate and restrict what is taught in the universities and to eradicate all beliefs that lead subjects to disobedience, replacing them with beliefs that are supportive of subjects' civil duties.[102] "[A]ppointing Teachers, and examining what Doctrines are conformable, or contrary to the Defence, Peace, and Good of the people" is one of the essential rights—indeed, one of the essential duties—associated with the office of sovereign.[103] If the sovereign fails to do so, the commonwealth is weakened and insecure. Equally debilitating would be a license for people to publish what they liked in political philosophy. So far as the contemporary canon was concerned, Hobbes was adamant: "I cannot imagine, how any thing can be more prejudiciall to a Monarchy, than the allowing of such books to be publikley read, without present applying such correctives of discreet Masters, as are fit to take away their Venime."[104]

I have already mentioned that the subject always retains the right to judge for himself whether a putative sovereign is in fact furnishing the protection he purports to furnish.[105] It is worth noticing the uneasy relation in which this stands to Hobbes's views about freedom of opinion. Summing up his position on freedom of opinion, Hobbes says,

> [T]he Right of Judging what Doctrines are fit for Peace, and to be taught the Subjects, is in all Common-wealths inseparably annexed . . . to the Sovereign Power. . . . For it is evident . . . that men's actions are derived from the opinions they have of the Good, or Evill, which from those actions redound unto themselves; and consequently, men that are once possessed of an opinion, that their obedience to the Sovereign Power will bee more hurtfull to them, than their disobedience, will disobey the Laws, and thereby overthrow the Common-wealth, and introduce confusion and Civill war; for the avoiding whereof, all Civill Government was ordained.[106]

This looks as though Hobbes is saying that it is important that the sovereign rather than the subject be the judge of whether obedience to the sovereign power is hurtful to the subject. In fact, that is not quite what he is saying. According to this passage, if there is to be *any purveying of opinion* on a matter so crucial to political obligation, it is to be done only by the sovereign or those authorized by him. Still, in the last analysis it is up to the subject to judge whether submission is hurtful to himself or not. Indeed, it is precisely because this is something for the subject to judge that Hobbes is so insistent that the sovereign cannot afford to be nonchalant about the *dissemination* of political opinions.

So—as I said at the start of this section—it is hard *for us* to drive a wedge between an entitlement to act on one's own judgment (concerning the sovereign's authority) and an entitlement to voice and disseminate one's judgment. We are accustomed to think that if an individual is entitled to act on an opinion, he must surely be entitled to express it to others. But Hobbes's denial of that is no more inconsistent than are his suggestions that my allegiance may be at an end before your allegiance is, or that a subject may have the right to resist a sovereign who is rightfully using force against him.[107] In all these cases, the rights and duties in question are based, in an intensely individualistic way, on the self-interest of the person concerned, and the apparent disparity between them is due simply to Hobbes's refusal to engage in any spurious reconciliation of conflicts of such individual interests under the heading of something like the general good.

If publicity does not entail freedom of speech, still less does it entail any principle of a right to political participation.[108] Just as Hobbes denies there is any more liberty in a democracy than in a monarchy,[109] so he would presumably also deny there is any more transparency. Another way of putting this, using some ideas from the end of the previous section, is that one can model the principle of publicity in a Hobbesian monarchy or oligarchy using the underlying contractarian structure.[110] It is certainly important for people to know what system of government they are under, and Hobbes is constantly at pains to ensure that people are under no illusions that what pretends to be a democracy may actually be an aristocracy of orators.[111] So publicity, although it does not require day-to-day participation, may still be relevant to the understanding in society of such participation as there is.

To finish, I want to consider two or three passages in Hobbes's writings that might be read in a way that refutes the argument I have been developing in this chapter. I have presented Hobbes as committed to a version of the liberal principle of publicity; I have presented him as an opponent of the strategy of supporting authority with myths and lies; I have presented him as a principled supporter of the idea of truth in politics. But the passages I want to consider offer some support for alternative readings. They suggest (1) that Hobbes is a Machiavellian about truth, (2) that Hobbes is a pragmatist about truth, or (3) that Hobbes is a conventionalist about truth. There is some merit to each of these interpretations, but I will show that none of them undermines the central contention of my analysis.

1. To say that Hobbes is a Machiavellian about truth is to imply that he thinks and recommends that the sovereign should regard truth as subordinate to some other more basic goal, like peace or stability, and as something to be manipulated if need be in pursuit of that more basic goal.[112] A Machiavellian sovereign might be prepared to lie to other sovereigns, or he might be prepared to lie to his own subjects. I know of nothing in Hobbes's work to exclude the former possibility, but it is the latter that I want to focus on. In an otherwise compelling essay entitled "Truth and Politics," Hannah Arendt groups Hobbes among the thinkers who believe that lies told to the people about the basis of political authority might actually serve the needs of authority. She says, for example, that Hobbes thought "lying can very well serve to establish or safeguard the conditions for the search after truth,"[113] explaining in a note that she has in mind a passage from one of the later chapters of *Leviathan*:

> Hobbes explains that "disobedience may lawfully be punished in them, that against the laws teach even true philosophy." For is not "leisure the mother of philosophy; and Commonwealth the mother of peace and leisure"? And does it not follow that the Commonwealth will act in the interest of philosophy when it suppresses a truth which undermines peace?[114]

Indeed, the passage she refers to is even worse than that, for Hobbes talks explicitly about "the suppression of True Philosophy" as something that might be necessary.[115] It is not easy to reconcile the deliberate suppression of truth with the principle of publicity. Still, we have to be more careful than Arendt was with such passages. The deliberate suppression of truth is not the same as the deliberate dissemination of a falsehood, particularly when the only reason given for the legitimate suppression of "True Philosophy" is the possibility of its being taught "by such men, as neither by lawfull authority, nor sufficient study, are competent Judges of the truth."[116] An analogy may help. In our society, the prescription and dispensing of controlled drugs for medical purposes is permitted only to licensed physicians and pharmacists, because amateurs are capable of doing great harm without specialized pharmaceutical knowledge. Suppose the authorities come across an unlicensed individual dispensing morphine to a patient for whom (as things turn out) such a prescription is actually indicated. We might still favor the prosecution of the dispenser even though he got lucky on this occasion and dispensed the right drug (and in the right dosage, etc.) because our overall aim is to secure not just appropriate but *reliably* appropriate prescription of dangerous drugs. Similarly, if we think (as Hobbes did) that the dissemination of political doctrines is at least as much in need of control as the dissemination of dangerous drugs, we might countenance the prosecution of an unlicensed purveyor of ideas even if the ideas he was purveying on a given occasion happened to be true.

Flathman mentions another passage that is more alarming at first sight than it turns out to be on analysis. In an annotation to chapter 6 of *De Cive*, Hobbes suggests that certain principles, dogmas, and doctrines are capable of generating "dissensions, discords, reproaches, and by degrees war it self" quite independently of their truth or falsehood:

> [N]either doth this happen by reason of the falsehood of the Principle, but of the disposition of men, who seeming wise to themselves, will needs appear such to all others: But though such dissensions cannot be hindered from arising, yet may they be restrained by the exercise of the supreme power, that they prove no hindrance to the public peace.[117]

Once again, though this is hardly congenial to our ideals of free speech, it is not a license for the sovereign or anyone else to *lie* for the public good. It is simply a recognition that the truth of what someone says is no warrant of his political responsibility. Although there *is* a truth about what conduces to peace and although it is important that that truth be taught, it does not follow that the teaching of truth as such—*any* truth in *any* circumstances by *any* teacher—is always a prophylactic against discord or civil war.

2. The objection we have just considered has Hobbes subordinating truth to some other value. But what if he were to *identify* them? The general conclusion for which I have been arguing—Hobbes's commitment to something like a principle of publicity—would certainly be undermined (or at least it would lose most of its interest) if Hobbes turned

out to be a crude pragmatist about truth in politics. Consider this passage, for example:

> And though in matter of Doctrine, nothing ought to be regarded but the Truth; yet this is not repugnant to the regulating of the same by Peace [that is, by the sovereign who keeps the peace]. For Doctrine repugnant to Peace, can no more be True, than Peace and Concord can be against the Law of Nature.[118]

It is tempting to read "Doctrine repugnant to Peace [cannot] be True" as if it meant that "true" in politics just *is* whatever conduces to peace and that "false" is whatever disturbs the peace or is likely to result in war.

The temptation should be resisted. On a close reading of the passage just quoted, Hobbes is comparing the connection between truth and peace with the connection between peace and the law of nature. The latter connection is certainly basic in Hobbes's system; he talks about "the first, and Fundamentall Law of Nature; which is, to seek Peace, and follow it."[119] Nevertheless, he understands that law as a theorem, not a definition or an axiom. Here is Hobbes's definition of law of nature:

> A law of nature, *(Lex Naturalis,)* is a Precept, or general Rule, found out by Reason, by which a man is forbidden to do, that which is destructive of his life, or taketh away the means of preserving the same; and to omit, that, by which he thinketh it may be best preserved.[120]

Clearly the connection between that and peace, though close, is synthetic and contingent. (Following peace is conducive to a person's individual survival only on account of the fact of our rough equality and only on condition that others seek it too.)[121] So because Hobbes compares the peace-truth connection with another connection that he takes to be synthetic, we should resist any inference that he thinks peace and truth are linked definitionally.

3. I guess the appearance that Thomas Hobbes was prepared to play fast and loose with truth is made a little more plausible by his insistence that certain types of proposition that *we* (modern liberals) take very seriously—for example, propositions about justice—have only conventional truth values. Moreover, he believed that anyone who denied this—anyone who sought to make political capital out of the allegedly *intrinsic* truth or falsity of certain propositions about *justice*—was politically

as well as philosophically a menace. That can easily sound like a decision, for political reasons, to suppress the truth about justice or to eliminate all debate about what the true meaning of justice actually is.

I certainly do not mean to deny that Hobbes was a conventionalist about the meanings of "justice" (and "right," "good" and "evil," "property," "honesty," and "honor"). He *did* maintain that in a well-ordered society, these terms have the meaning, and only the meaning, that the sovereign assigns to them. But that is not an alternative to truth, in his account; that *is* the truth about these terms. Hobbes believed that dispassionate enlightened inquiry into what we would call metaethics establishes that almost all moral and ethical vocabulary is relative either to the appetites and aversions of individuals in the state of nature or to the stipulations and conventions of the sovereign in civil society. That is the truth in metaethics not because we want or need it to be the case but because that is what philosophical inquiry reveals to be the case.

Moreover—and this is very important—I take it Hobbes is saying that *that* is what the people are to be taught. Once the sovereign has stipulated a meaning for "justice," the people are not to be taught (the falsehood) that the sovereign's stipulation is the intrinsic meaning of the term. Instead, they are to be taught that it is a purely conventional meaning and that, on account of the truth in metaethics, *that* is the best one can expect. I think Robert Kraynack gets this exactly right when he attributes to Hobbes the views not only that people should accept certain propositions about justice, which the sovereign stipulates, but also that people should accept those propositions about justice *on the ground that the sovereign stipulates them:* "Although this sounds like an . . . absurd claim, it is in reality a denial of pretense and accords perfectly with the views of an enlightened people. For a fully enlightened people would insist that the sovereign be recognized as nothing more than an arbiter."[122] It may not be altogether accurate to go on to say (as Kraynack does) that "Hobbes's sovereign seeks the end of doctrinal warfare by disavowing all interest in the rightness or truth of doctrines . . . and by imposing arbitrary settlements for the sake of civil peace."[123] As I have emphasized, Hobbes's subjects are to be told that "justice" has no inherent meaning apart from the sovereign's stipulations, not only because that is convenient and peace promoting but also because it is true. And they are to be taught that it is true.

I think Skinner disputes this. He says, in a footnote to his book *Reason and Rhetoric in the Philosophy of Hobbes*, "it would seem that, within a Hobbesian polity, subjects would be merely informed rather than taught about the character of moral discourse."[124] That has to be a mistake. Subjects will not be able to understand the wrongness of disputing with the sovereign about the definition of "justice" unless they understand that the word has nothing but conventional content. They will not be able to understand why bickering about its "true meaning" is a threat to peace unless they grasp that the term *has* no true meaning except by virtue of a sovereign stipulation.

Admittedly, the fact that the sovereign stipulates that action X is unjust might make X evil for the subject in a sense that is not just an echo of the sovereign's stipulation. For suppose the subject knows that the stipulation means the sovereign will punish X as a capital offense. Then that makes X evil for the subject, in the natural sense of repugnant to the subject's desires and appetites.[125] As Alan Ryan puts it, "[t]he Sovereign's ability to punish us for transgressing his rules makes situations good and bad in ways they were not before, but not in any sense in which they were not before."[126] Even so, the subject's apprehension of this complex situation will be distorted unless he understands the role of sovereign stipulation in determining what now counts as injustice (and what, consequently, it is dangerous to do). If the content of his belief is "Doing X is evil because of the danger of angering the sovereign even though X is or may well be *intrinsically* just," then his sense of political obligation will be nuanced in a way that is not only inaccurate but, in certain circumstances, dangerous to himself or others. It is better, surely, for him to hold the correct belief—which is that it is wrong to do X, first, because the sovereign has stipulated that X is unjust (and there is no question of X's being intrinsically just or unjust apart from such stipulation), and second, because it is dangerous to anger the sovereign.

Only if the stipulation is understood in this way by the subject can it plausibly be represented as an action of the sovereign in the fullest Hobbesian sense, that is, as a stipulation performed by the subjects themselves through the sovereign's action as representative. The representation idea[127]—crucial to the model-theoretic structure of Hobbes's contractarianism—cannot work here if the sovereign's stipulation of a meaning for justice is opaque to the subject's understanding. If the sovereign is the people's representative set up by agreement, then ideally they *own* his actions, which means they take responsibility for them *and understand them* just as if they were their own. Now, as I said earlier,[128] that is not itself an argument for publicity concerning stipulations, for there is no independent reason for saying that the contract-representation model must be able to work. Nevertheless its application here shows once again how central the publicity principle is to Hobbes's philosophy.

Thus, people are not only to be taught the sovereign's conventions; they are to be taught that they *are* conventions. Hobbes's skepticism about intrinsic moral meanings is itself to be taught as orthodoxy, along with the problems that it gives rise to and the conventional stipulations that follow in its wake. To the extent that the people are under a misapprehension about any of this, the sovereign will be failing in his duty and exposing himself foolishly to various forms of subversion that might be predicated on these misunderstandings. Beyond that, and in the spirit of the remarks on Hobbes's contractarianism with which we ended the section asking whether Hobbes felt any respect for subjects, the subjects' being under any misapprehension about metaethics is also a threat to their overall enlightenment and an obstacle to any attempt to unify their understanding of morals and politics with their understanding of science and logic generally.

All this makes Hobbes a rather more modern thinker than he is often presented as being, and in my view it makes him a *liberal* thinker, if not in his political conclusions, then certainly in his respect for individuals as reasoning beings. It surely makes him modern in the sense that his own determination to analyze politics and get to the bottom of human affairs is intended to resonate, all the way down, with the reasoning capacities of the ordinary individuals who are the subject matter of his inquiry: "For the Civill Authority being more visible, and standing in the clearer light of naturall reason, cannot choose but draw to it in all times a very considerable part of the people."[129] I have tried, in this chapter, not to exaggerate Hobbes's optimism about all this. He did take a rather chastened view, one that veered in his later years toward melancholy, if not despair.[130] Still, with Flathman, I find something enormously heartening in the eagerness with which Hobbes sought to reflect his own intellectual enterprise in *De Cive* and *Leviathan* in the understanding and enlightenment that he thought any good society should encourage in its members, and in his dogged refusal to abandon that enterprise when the truths that he discovered ceased to be familiar, safe, and respectable.

Notes

1. Richard E. Flathman, *Thomas Hobbes: Skepticism, Individuality, and Chastened Politics* (Newbury Park, Calif.: Sage, 1993), 6.
2. Ibid., 154, quoting Thomas Hobbes, *Leviathan*, ed. Richard Tuck (Cambridge: Cambridge University Press, 1988), chap. 47, p. 480; hereafter referred to as *Leviathan*.
3. *Leviathan*, chap. 47, p. 480.
4. Thomas Hobbes, *Behemoth, or The Long Parliament*, ed. Stephen Holmes (Chicago: University of Chicago Press, 1990), 4; hereafter referred to as *Behemoth*.
5. Morton Schoolman, "Series Editor's Introduction," in Flathman, *Thomas Hobbes*, x.
6. See Jeremy J. Waldron, "Theoretical Foundations of Liberalism," in my *Liberal Rights: Collected Papers 1981–91* (Cambridge: Cambridge University Press, 1993), esp. 43–61.
7. See John Rawls, *A Theory of Justice* (Cambridge, Mass.: Harvard University Press, 1971), 133, 454, 547–48, 582.
8. John Rawls, *Political Liberalism* (New York: Columbia University Press, 1993), 68. In a footnote, Rawls glosses this as follows: "[I]n a free society that all correctly recognize as just there is no need for the illusions and delusions of ideology for society to work properly and for citizens to accept it willingly. In this sense a well-ordered society may lack ideological, or false, consciousness" (*Political Liberalism*, 68–69).
9. For the idea that this is a distinct mode of legislating, see Plato, *The Laws*, trans. Trevor J. Saunders (Harmondsworth, Eng.: Penguin Books, 1970), bk. 4.
10. *Leviathan*, chap. 30, p. 240.
11. *Leviathan*, chap. 30, pp. 231–32.
12. Thomas Hobbes, *The Elements of Law: Human Nature and De Corpore Politico*, ed. J. C. A. Gaskin (Oxford: Oxford University Press, 1994), 176–77 (part 2, chap. 28, section 8); hereafter referred to as *Elements*.
13. Thomas Hobbes, *On the Citizen*, ed. Richard Tuck and Michael Silverthorne (New York: Cambridge University Press, 1998), 146–47 (chap. 13, section 9); hereafter referred to as *Citizen*.
14. Hobbes, *De Cive: The English Version*, ed. Howard Warrender (Oxford: Oxford University press, 1983), chap. 13, p. 160. (This is a contemporary translation from the Latin of the work whose modern translation is cited in note 13. This translation is hereafter referred to as *De Cive*.)
15. *Elements*, chap. 28, p. 176.
16. *De Cive*, chap. 13, p. 160.
17. *Behemoth*, 16, 58.
18. *Leviathan*, chap. 30, p. 232. See also Flathman, *Thomas Hobbes*, 143.
19. What follows is drawn in part from Jeremy J. Waldron, "Hobbes on Truth and Civil Doctrine," in *Philosophers on Education*, ed. Amelie Rorty (London: Routledge, 1998).
20. *Leviathan*, 491 ("A Review, and Conclusion").
21. *Leviathan*, chap. 30, pp. 236–37. See also *Behemoth*, 39, 54.
22. See *Behemoth*, 56–57. At 58, Hobbes observes that "[t]he core of rebellion, as you have seen by this, and read of other rebellions, are the Universities."
23. *Leviathan*, chap. 30, p. 237.

24. *Leviathan,* chap. 46, p. 462. (Hobbes is an early critic of the idea of a philosophical canon.)

25. Cf. *Elements,* chap. 28, pp. 176–77.

26. See *Leviathan,* 486 ("A Review, and Conclusion"). See also *Citizen,* chap. 10, pp. 117–18.

27. *Leviathan,* chap. 21, pp. 151–52. (Cf. Flathman, *Thomas Hobbes,* 131, 143, where Hobbes is described as "[c]onvinced that an 'enchanted' allegiance had long since ceased to be a possibility, and totally opposed to an 'enthusiastic' or 'patriotic' one.")

28. *Elements,* chap. 28, p. 176.

29. Ibid.

30. *Leviathan,* chap. 21, p. 151.

31. For the argument, see Jean Hampton, *Hobbes and the Social Contract Tradition* (Cambridge: Cambridge University Press, 1986), 197–207.

32. Bishop John Bramhall, *The Catching of Leviathan, or The Great Whale* (London: John Crooke, 1658), 515, cited by Hampton, *Hobbes and the Social Contract Tradition,* 199.

33. *Leviathan,* chap. 18, pp. 124–25.

34. Flathman, *Thomas Hobbes,* 97, quoting *Leviathan,* 3 (emphasis added). See also Quentin Skinner, "Hobbes and the Purely Artificial Person of the State," *Journal of Political Philosophy* 7 (1999): 24.

35. *Citizen,* chap. 10, p. 117.

36. *Citizen,* 14 ("Preface to the Readers").

37. Ibid.

38. Flathman, *Thomas Hobbes,* 99.

39. *Leviathan,* chap. 30, p. 232.

40. Flathman, *Thomas Hobbes,* 144, 145 (interpolations in the original).

41. *Leviathan,* 3 ("Dedication to Francis Godolphin").

42. When he is trying to find out whether some proposition is true or not, his method is not to ascertain—for example, by introspection—whether it is held by Hobbes!

43. *Leviathan,* 490–91 ("A Review, and Conclusion").

44. *Leviathan,* chap. 30, p. 237. See also the rather disarming (disingenuous?) modesty at *Leviathan,* chap. 30, pp. 232–33.

45. *Citizen,* 7 ("Preface to the Readers"). For the tradition of *arcana imperii,* see Peter S. Donaldson, *Machiavelli and Mystery of State* (Cambridge: Cambridge University Press, 1988). See also Quentin Skinner, *Reason and Rhetoric in the Philosophy of Hobbes* (Cambridge: Cambridge University Press, 1996), 426–37, for some observations on the significance of the fact that *De Cive* was published originally in Latin.

46. *Citizen,* 7 ("Preface to the Reader").

47. See *Leviathan,* chap. 30, p. 233, for a remarkable discussion.

48. See *Leviathan,* 491 ("A Review, and Conclusion") for an acknowledgment that "in the Revolution of States, there can be no very good Constellation for Truths of this nature to be born under." Hobbes certainly must have known that Oxford University had *Leviathan* burned in the Bodleian quadrangle; see Ryan, "Hobbes, Toleration, and the Inner Life," in *The Nature of Political Theory,* ed. David Miller and Larry Siedentop (Oxford: Clarendon Press, 1983), 203.

49. See Samuel Mintz, *The Hunting of Leviathan: Seventeenth-Century Reac-

tions to the Materialism and Moral Philosophy of Thomas Hobbes (Cambridge: Cambridge University Press, 1962).

50. Flathman points out that Hobbes "was hated by the established clergy for his materialism and reputed atheism and the more so for his argument that the Sovereign must control the clergy and religious doctrines and practices; the lawyers and judges despised him for his rejection of custom in general and common law and constitutionalism in particular; the parliamentarians regarded him as their enemy because he attacked both rule by assembly and mixed or divided government; his contractarianism and rejection of the divine right theory of kingship made him persona non grata among the courtiers and for a time with the king." (*Thomas Hobbes,* 97–98. These were not just matters of academic reputation. In the seventeenth century, issues like these were life and death for a political philosopher, and Hobbes was not exaggerating when he asked, concerning the rare individual who knew the truth about government, "[H]ow can he teach it safely, when it is against the interest of those that are in possession of the power to hurt him?" (*Behemoth,* 39).

51. *De Cive,* chap. 13, section 9, p. 160.
52. See note 24 and accompanying text.
53. *Leviathan,* 490 ("A Review, and Conclusion").
54. *Leviathan,* chap. 7, p. 48.
55. *Leviathan,* chap. 5, p. 36.
56. *Leviathan,* chap. 4, p. 28. Hobbes goes on to insist that ignorance is not the opposite of knowledge but, rather, a sort of middle "between true Science, and erroneous doctrine."
57. *De Cive,* chap. 18, p. 253.
58. *De Cive,* chap. 18, p. 254.
59. *Citizen,* 8 ("Preface to the Reader").
60. One might give this a naturalistic gloss: My individual reason is a capacity that exists naturally—a later age would say that it has *evolved*—in order to enable me to assess, as accurately as possible, propositions about the exigencies of my survival.
61. *Elements,* chap. 14, p. 79. See also *De Cive,* chap. 1, p. 27; *Leviathan,* chap. 14, p. 91.
62. *De Cive,* chap. 18, p. 264.
63. *Leviathan,* chap. 21, p. 153.
64. See Bishop Bramhall's question, quoted in Hampton, *Hobbes and the Social Contract Tradition,* 202.
65. Hobbes is adamant that this right is inalienable (*Leviathan,* ch. 21, p. 153) and, indeed, that the determination of what conduces to a person's survival cannot be asymmetrically distributed at all (*De Cive,* chap. 1, pp. 27–28). See also Flathman, *Thomas Hobbes,* 119–20.
66. I do not think this contradicts Hobbes's often-expressed doctrine that it is not for subjects to debate and dispute the sovereign's commands (see, e.g., *Leviathan,* chap. 29, p. 223). That doctrine has to do with attempts by the subject to second-guess the sovereign's judgment of the common good qua judgment of the common good. If subjects start doing that, then there can be no authority at all. Still, it is only on the basis of the subject's judgment about (his own) survival that anyone can be regarded (by the subject) as a Hobbesian authority on the common good or any-

thing else. Without that judgment or if such judgment is based on grounds that are patently incredible, there is nothing reliable for the authority to appeal to and no way it can get a grip on the subject's submission. Hampton may be right that the idea of subjects making their own judgments about the connection between authority and survival wreaks havoc with Hobbes's absolutism in just the way absolutism would be undermined by subjects making their own judgments about the common good. She may be right that an individual's entitlement to dispute the basis of the sovereign's authority (so far as the individual's own self-interest is concerned) is politically and pragmatically indistinguishable from his disputing the merits (so far as the commonwealth is concerned) of the sovereign's actions and edicts (see Hampton, *Hobbes and the Social Contract Condition*, 197–207; see also Flathman, *Thomas Hobbes*, 157, n. 10). Or she may be wrong about this. Either way, the position is fundamental in Hobbes's theory, and Hobbes must accept whatever follows from it so far as his absolutism is concerned.

67. *Leviathan*, chap. 11, p. 74. See also Hobbes's announced intention (at the end of *Leviathan*) to return to the less controversial speculations about "Bodies Naturall"; *Leviathan*, 491 ("A Review, and Conclusion").

68. See Skinner, *Reason and Rhetoric*, 349; *Leviathan*, chap. 25, p. 181.

69. Says Hobbes in *Behemoth*, "You may perhaps think that a man has need of nothing else to know the duty he owes to his governor, and what right he has to order him, but a good natural wit; but it is otherwise. For it is a science, and built upon sure and clear principles, and to be learned by deep and careful study, or from masters that have deeply studied it" (158–59; see also *Behemoth*, 144: "Common people know nothing by their own meditation; they must therefore be taught the grounds of their duty, and the reasons why calamities ever follow disobedience to their lawful sovereigns").

70. *Citizen*, chap. 6, section 17, p. 87. See also *Leviathan*, chap. 18, pp. 128–29.

71. *Leviathan*, chap. 20, p. 145.

72. Actually, that is not quite true: Hobbes observes disarmingly that even if his positions are not supported by reason, "yet I am sure they are Principles from Authority of Scripture; as I shall make it appear, when I shall come to speak of the Kingdome of God" (*Leviathan*, chap. 30, p. 233; the reference forward is to *Leviathan*, chap. 40, pp. 322–31). But since his theology is at least as controversial as his political theory, this does not add much.

73. Tom Sorell, in *Hobbes* (London: Routledge, 1986), chap. 10, has made much of Hobbes's conviction that a good political philosophy can appeal to the unaided reason of the ordinary person. If by "unaided reason," Sorell means reason before the teachers of "Aristotelity" get to it, then that is worth emphasizing. But I think it is a mistake to place too much reliance on an early passage in Hobbes to the effect that the task of political philosophy is to "put men in mind of what they know already, or may know by their own experience" (Sorrell, *Hobbes*, 143. The quotation is from *Elements*, 21).

74. See note 68 and accompanying text.

75. *Leviathan*, chap. 18, p. 129.

76. *Leviathan*, chap. 5, p. 37; see also Skinner, *Reason and Rhetoric*, 336.

77. *De Cive*, chap. 18, p. 265, quoting Rom. 14:5.

78. Skinner, *Reason and Rhetoric*, 347. See especially *Leviathan*, 483–84 ("A Review, and Conclusion").

79. See note 56 and accompanying text.

80. *Leviathan*, chap. 8, p. 52.

81. But Hobbes himself sometimes did, as in this passage from *Behemoth*: "I despair of any lasting peace amongst ourselves, till the Universities here shall bend and direct their studies to the setting of it.... For I make no doubt, but that solid reason, backed with the authority of so many learned men, will more prevail for the keeping of us in peace within ourselves, than any victory can do over the rebels" (56).

82. *Leviathan*, chap. 30, p. 233.

83. "For such is the ignorance and aptitude to error generally of all men, but especially of them that have not much knowledge of natural causes, and of the nature and interests of men, as by innumerable and easy tricks to be abused" (*Leviathan*, chap. 37, p. 304).

84. *Leviathan*, chap. 15, p. 102. (But see Flathman, *Thomas Hobbes*, 62–64, for a slightly different analysis of the implications here of Hobbes's response to "the Foole.")

85. See note 34 and accompanying text.

86. *Behemoth*, 160 (emphasis added).

87. David Johnston, *The Rhetoric of Leviathan: Thomas Hobbes and the Politics of Cultural Transformation* (Princeton: Princeton University Press, 1986), 122–33.

88. *Leviathan*, chap. 13, p. 89.

89. See Johnston, *Rhetoric of Leviathan*, 126–28.

90. *Leviathan*, chap. 44, p. 418.

91. See *Citizen*, 7 ("Preface to the Readers"). See also note 45 and accompanying text. For "Government House" theorizing, referring to rule-utilitarian theories that impose simple rules on the natives and limit the awareness of their utilitarian underpinnings (and exceptions) to the colonial rulers, see Bernard Williams, *Ethics and the Limits of Philosophy* (Cambridge, Mass.: Harvard University Press, 1985), 108–10.

92. *Leviathan*, chap. 14, p. 97.

93. I am grateful to Jeff Gordon for this point.

94. Rawls, *A Theory of Justice*, 133.

95. Ibid., 177–92.

96. Immanuel Kant, "On the Common Saying: 'This May Be True in Theory, but It Does Not Apply in Practice,'" in *Kant: Political Writings*, ed. Hans Reiss (Cambridge: Cambridge University Press, 1991), 84–85.

97. Indeed, Kant subtitled this part of his essay "Against Hobbes" (ibid., 73).

98. Flathman, *Thomas Hobbes*, 144. See also, Flathman, *Reflections of a Would-Be Anarchist: Ideals and Institutions of Liberalism* (Minneapolis: University of Minnesota Press, 1998), 35, for Hobbes's apprehensions about pluralism.

99. *Leviathan*, chap. 40, p. 323. See also *Leviathan*, chap. 8, p. 52, as well as chap. 42, p. 360: "[I]nternal faith is in its own nature invisible, and consequently exempted from all human jurisdiction," and the section on "the secret thoughts of a man."

100. *Leviathan*, chap. 36, p. 297.

101. *Leviathan*, chap. 42, p. 373: "And the reason hereof, is not because they that Teach, but because they that are to learn, are his Subjects."

102. Flathman, *Thomas Hobbes*, 147.

103. *Leviathan*, chap. 30, pp. 231–38. See also *Leviathan*, chap. 18, pp. 124–25.

104. *Leviathan*, chap. 29, p. 226.

105. See notes 63–66 and accompanying text.
106. *Leviathan,* chap. 42, p. 372.
107. See *Leviathan,* chap. 21, p. 152.
108. See Flathman, *Thomas Hobbes,* 135–42.
109. *Leviathan,* chap. 21, pp. 149–50.
110. But see also the very subtle discussion in *Elements:* "The first in order of time of these three sorts [of government] is democracy, and it must be so of necessity, because an aristocracy and a monarchy, require nomination of persons agreed upon; which agreement in a great multitude of men must consist in the consent of the major part; and where the votes of the major part involve the votes of the rest, there is actually a democracy" (118–19 [part 2, chap. 21, section 1]).
111. See Flathman, *Thomas Hobbes,* 156.
112. Cf. Niccolò Machiavelli, *The Prince,* ed. Quentin Skinner and Russell Price (Cambridge: Cambridge University Press, 1988), chaps. 15, 18. (It is a separate question, which I shall not discuss here, what Hobbes—or any other Machiavellian—might think about the truth value of the proposition that a value such as peace is more important than truth; see Leo Strauss, *The Political Philosophy of Hobbes: Its Basis and Its Genesis,* trans. Else M. Sinclair [Chicago: University of Chicago Press, 1932], chap. 8.)
113. Hannah Arendt, "Truth and Politics" in her collection *Between Past and Future* (Harmondsworth, Eng.: Penguin Books, 1977), 229.
114. Ibid., pp. 297–98. For the Hobbes citation, see *Leviathan,* chap. 46, p. 474.
115. *Leviathan,* chap. 46, p. 473.
116. Ibid.
117. *De Cive,* chap. 6, p. 96 (cf. Flathman, *Thomas Hobbes,* 144).
118. *Leviathan,* chap. 18, pp. 124–25.
119. *Leviathan,* chap. 14, p. 92.
120. *Leviathan,* chap. 14, p. 91.
121. *Leviathan,* chap. 13, p. 87; chap. 14, p. 92; chap. 15, p. 110.
122. Robert P. Kraynack, *History and Modernity in the Thought of Thomas Hobbes* (Ithaca, N.Y.: Cornell University Press, 1990), 171.
123. Ibid.
124. Skinner, *Reason and Rhetoric,* 320 n. 156.
125. *Leviathan,* chap. 6, p. 39.
126. Ryan, "Hobbes, Toleration, and the Inner Life," 212. Hence, Ryan is unsure about what the sovereign ought to teach the subjects concerning his stipulations: "It is not difficult to see how we [the subjects] have to admit that what the sovereign declares for justice and injustice are justice and injustice. What is less obvious is how we are to take the claim that we are to take for good and evil what the sovereign declares for such" (211).
127. *Leviathan,* chap. 16. See also Skinner, "Hobbes and the Purely Artificial Person of the State."
128. See notes 94–95 and accompanying text.
129. *Leviathan,* chap. 29, p. 227.
130. Flathman, *Thomas Hobbes,* 167.

CHAPTER NINE

Flathman's Hobbes

Richard Tuck

My students at Harvard treasure a story that Richard Flathman told about himself when he came to give a paper to a political theory seminar. He said that many times in departmental meetings he has been outvoted on some issue, and like a good colleague, he has agreed to go along with the result. Other members of the department have often tried to persuade him after the meeting that he had been wrong in his original position. "I tell them, you have my consent; do you want my soul as well?" This story is treasured because it captures so well the essence not simply of Flathman's personality but also of his political theory: What all his books have been about, to a greater or lesser extent, has been the preservation of people's souls from capture by their fellow citizens. His most interesting targets have not been the obvious and familiar threats to individual liberty, which all modern right-thinking people can more or less agree on (and most of which ceased long ago to be much of a threat to the communities where right-thinking people tend to live). Instead, his targets have been liberals themselves, or at least, the liberal traditions represented by what he has called "virtue liberals," such as Immanuel Kant, Jean-Jacques Rousseau ("who in my judgement is no liberal at all"),[1] John Stuart Mill, and John Rawls, and by a certain kind of rights theorist who is, at bottom, principally concerned with using rights to secure a civil order; John Locke is his prime example of this.

Against these writers, with their visions of communities united in the pursuit of widely disseminated and reasonable common goals, Flathman has pleaded for "willful liberalism," in which individuals are permitted and encouraged to make themselves, not to be made by the civic order. As he has admitted,

> [W]illful liberalism has affinities with libertarianism and especially with various strains in romanticism. The notion of liberation from state and other forms of power is reminiscent of libertarianism and even of individualistic anarchism, and the notions of self-making, self-enactment, and self-fashioning have manifest affinities with major tendencies in romanticism and expressivism.[2]

But nevertheless, he has been careful to distinguish between this brand of liberalism and at least the dreary Anglo-American free-market version of libertarianism, and more surprisingly, between it and romanticism; Flathman is suspicious of the historically ungrounded character of much romantic thought. Subtly, he insists that "the free spirit remains deeply, albeit never complacently or even comfortably, situated in a tradition, culture, and society."[3] His heroes are Michel Montaigne, Friedrich Nietzsche, Ludwig Wittgenstein, and Thomas Hobbes.

It was a remarkable insight on Flathman's part that Hobbes belongs in this company. Most twentieth-century interpretations of Hobbes have viewed him as the preeminently illiberal thinker, the theorist of "the counter-revolution" (in Quentin Skinner's evocative phrase),[4] whose political ideas treat all men as slaves—a word that Hobbes insisted in *De Cive* meant the same as "citizens."[5] Instead, Flathman seized on two profound features of Hobbes's work: The first was its general attack on moral realism, that is, Hobbes's repeated claim that there are no objective moral facts and that fundamentally everyone is his own judge of what is right for him. This skepticism is the central theme of Flathman's 1993 book, *Thomas Hobbes: Skepticism, Individuality, and Chastened Politics.*[6] The second feature, just as important as the first for Flathman, was the fact that Hobbes's *actual* politics were (in his striking term) "chastened." All readers of Hobbes have been aware (though not always vividly enough) that Hobbes was a moral skeptic, but they have usually associated that skepticism precisely with Hobbes's political illiberalism: Because nothing is true, there is no value worth defending against an effective sovereign. According to one traditional view, it was to defend a liberal point of view that could encompass the defense of such things as religious freedom that philosophers such as Locke moved toward a form of moral realism, in which those values had a proper purchase upon the citizens. Flathman is among the very few readers of Hobbes who have given full weight to the fact that Hobbes's actual political prescriptions always stressed the freedom that the subject of a Hobbesian sovereign should enjoy, and he has repeatedly drawn our attention to passages in Hobbes such as the notable plea for religious toleration in part 4 of *Leviathan*:

> And so we are reduced to the Independency of the Primitive Christians to follow Paul, or Cephas, or Apollos, every man as he liketh best: Which, if it be without contention, and without measuring the Doctrine of Christ, by our affection to the Person of his Minister, (the fault which the Apostle reprehended in the Corinthians,) is perhaps the best: First, because there ought to be no Power over the Consciences of men, but of the Word it selfe, working Faith in every one, not always according to the purpose of them that Plant and Water, but of God himself, that giveth the Increase: and secondly, because it is unreasonable in them, who teach there is such danger in every little Errour, to require of a man endued with Reason of his own, to follow the Reason of any other man, or of the most voices of many other men; Which is little better, then to venture his Salvation at crosse and pile.[7]

For Flathman, Hobbes (along with Nietzsche) is the principal philosopher to have wrestled with the problem of how to talk about civil life against a background of intense hostility to common or communally imposed values. Hobbes's men, Flathman has always argued, maintain their moral independence and distinctiveness in civil society, and the sovereign has to bend to their individuality, not destroy it. He has summarized his view at the end of *Thomas Hobbes* (I have numbered his propositions in order to refer back to them more easily):

> [1.] It is for me to decide whether to enter and whether and when to leave political society.
> [2.] The sovereign may do almost anything, has the power to do relatively little.
> [3.] Of the actions that the Sovereign may and can take, prudence/morality teaches her to take very few.
> [4.] Of the laws and commands the Sovereign does issue, I must and have the right to interpret and assess each of them for myself.
> [5.] When I judge that a command of the Sovereign entails an obligation for me, I am at liberty to refuse to discharge it.
> [6.] My various and fluctuating identities and identifications are with myself and those with whom I conduct my personal affairs, not with the Sovereign or the political society.[8]

The most dangerous regimes are those that seek to infiltrate values into men's minds, using the techniques of persuasion. Flathman sympathizes with Hobbes's apparent hostility to democracy, at least democracy understood as deliberative, in which each citizen tries to persuade his fellows of the correctness of his own view; indeed, successful persuasion is viewed with something close to horror by both Flathman and Hobbes, for it is through other people's oratorical arts that our individuality is most quickly stifled.

There is absolutely no doubt that Flathman is right about this aspect of Hobbes and that he is right, too, in sensing that this feature lay somewhere near the center of Hobbes's intellectual and emotional gravity. One of my favorite examples of Hobbes's views in this area is a little-known passage from one of his later works. Hobbes had recommended *Leviathan* as a textbook for teaching philosophy in the universities and was immediately rebuked by various Oxford theologians. He replied briskly,

> How would you have exclaimed, if, instead of recommending my *Leviathan* to be taught in the Universities, I had recommended the erecting of a new and lay-university, wherein lay-men should have the reading of physics, mathematics, moral philosophy, and politics, as the clergy have now the sole teaching of divinity? Yet the thing would be profitable, and tend much to the polishing of man's nature, without much public charge. There will need but one house, and the endowment of a few professors. And to make some learn the better, it would do very well that none should come thither sent by their parents, as to a trade to get their living by, but that it should be a place for such ingenuous men, as being free to dispose of their own time, love truth for itself.[9]

This vision of a university that is not a trade school, nor one in which one sect has an exclusive right to teach, but one in which men who are "free to dispose of their own time" pursue their own inquiries, tells us everything about the real character of Hobbes's theory, and about why Flathman admires him.

But the connection between Hobbes's horror of persuasion and his political ideas is more complex than Flathman, I believe, has fully acknowledged. Though there can be no question but that propositions 1 to 3 above are correct, propositions 4 and 5 must strike any reader of Hobbes as very implausible representations of his thought, and proposition 6 seems at least to run counter to another of Hobbes's fundamental fears, his terror of what Rousseau was later to call "partial associations." As far as our judging the sovereign's pronouncements is concerned, Hobbes tells us again and again that the key difference between the state of nature and civil society is precisely that in a state of nature, all persons do indeed have the right to make their own judgments about how to live their lives, whereas in civil society, they have to a great extent renounced that right:

> I observe the *Diseases* of a Common-wealth, that proceed from the poyson of seditious doctrines; whereof one is, *That every private man is Judge of Good and Evil actions.* This is true in the condition of meer Nature, where there are no Civill Lawes; and also under Civill Government, in such cases as are not determined by the Law. But otherwise, it is manifest, that the measure of Good and Evil actions, is the Civill Law; and the Judge the Legislator, who is always the Representative of the Common-wealth. From this false doctrine, men are disposed to debate with themselves, and dispute the commands of the Common-wealth; and afterwards to obey, or disobey them, as in their private judgements they shall think fit. Whereby the Common-wealth is distracted and *Weakened.*
>
> Another doctrine repugnant to Civill Society, is, that *whatsoever a man does against his Conscience, is Sinne;* and it dependeth on the presumption of making himselfe judge of Good and Evil. For a mans Conscience, and his Judgement is the same thing; and as the Judgement, so also the Conscience may be erroneous. Therefore, though he that is subject to no Civill Law, sinneth in all he does against his Conscience, because he has no other rule to follow but his own reason; yet it is not so with him that lives in a Common-wealth; because the Law is the publique Conscience, by which he hath already undertaken to be guided. Otherwise in such diversity, as there is of private Consciences, which are but private opinions, the Common-wealth must needs be distracted, and no man dare to obey the Soveraign Power, farther than it shall seem good in his own eyes.[10]

Flathman of course recognizes this renunciation, but he bases his argument on the passages where Hobbes apparently concedes to a subject the license to refuse to follow the sovereign's commands in very far-reaching cases: "[A] son, for example, 'will rather die than live infamous and hated of all the world' because he obeyed the command to execute one of his parents."[11] The son's own preservation is not at stake, and yet he can choose to disobey. This does indeed seem to be a powerful counterexample to Hobbes's general claim that (outside of direct and non-controversial threats to our own lives) we have no right to reclaim our own judgment vis-à-vis the sovereign's commands. Other notable cases in which subjects apparently retain their own judgment are the decision that each citizen takes about whether to fight at the sovereign's command[12] and the right of a believer to choose martyrdom for his religion.[13]

None of these examples makes Flathman's point, however, and the first suggests an interestingly different interpretation of Hobbes's general theory. This claim, that a son is free to choose death rather than dishonor, appears first in *De Cive*, and Hobbes did not directly repeat it in *Leviathan*.[14] But he returned to the issue in *Behemoth*, where he addressed it in some detail. *Behemoth* is a set of dialogues between a pupil *(B)* and a teacher *(A)* about the causes and legitimacy of the English Civil War. In the first dialogue, *B* asked,

> Is there nothing wherein a lawful King's command may be disobeyed? What if he should command me with my own hands to execute my father, in case he should be condemned to die by the law?
>
> A. This is a case that need not be put. We never have read nor heard of any King or tyrant so inhuman as to command it. If any did, we are to consider whether that command were one of his laws. For by disobeying Kings, we mean the disobeying of his laws, those his laws that were made before they were applied to any particular person; for the King, though as a father of children, and a master of domestic servants command many things which bind those children and servants yet he commands the people in general never but by a precedent law, and as a politic, not a natural person. And if such a command as you speak of were contrived into a general law (which never was, nor never will be), you were bound to obey it, unless you depart the kingdom after the publication of the law, and before the condemnation of your father.[15]

This remark appears to pick up a passage in *Leviathan* that has often been ignored: Chapter 30, "Of the *Office* of the Sovereign Representative," begins by attributing to the sovereign "the procuration of *the safety of the people*," and explains that

> this is intended should be done, not by care applyed to Individualls, further than their protection from injuries, when they shall complain; but by a generall Providence, contained in publique Instruction, both of Doctrine, and Example; and in the making, and executing of good Lawes, to which individuall persons may apply their own cases.[16]

This in turn seems to be related to passages in both *De Cive* and *The Elements of Law*.[17] So Hobbes's view, particularly on mature reflection, appears to have been that indeed citizens have no right to call into question the commands of the sovereign, but that this is true only if the commands are law-like in form, and in particular, only if they are couched *generally*, without reference to specific people. Surprisingly, in this respect (and as we shall see presently, in many other respects), Hobbes closely resembled Rousseau, who famously said in *The Social Contract* that "law considers subjects *en masse* and actions in the abstract, and never a particular person or action" and that "as the law unites universality of will with universality of object, what a man, whoever he be, commands of his own motion cannot be a law; and even what the Sovereign commands with regard to a particular matter is no nearer being a law, but is a decree, an act, not of sovereignty, but of magistracy."[18]

As for the other cases in which citizens apparently retain their own judgment, one—the freedom people apparently have not to go to war—is straightforward.[19] As Hobbes said in his remarks about conscience quoted above, the sovereign stands in for the citizen in making judgments about what conduces to the citizen's safety. In a state of nature, it is possible for a man to conclude that he is safest attacking another man; this, after all, is what turns the state of nature into a state of war. Similarly, once a civil society has been created, it is possible for its sovereign to conclude that a citizen will be safest attacking an enemy, and the citizen must follow that judgment just as he would have followed his own judgment in nature. Hobbes allows the citizen to nominate another to take his place in going to war, because a replacement would meet the requirements of the sovereign without questioning the sovereign's judgment that fighting should take place, and Hobbes accepts that if the citizen does not send a replacement, he is committed to fight up to the point at which he would have fought in nature, which might or might not be short of his own death, depending on the level of his courage (which Hobbes never regarded as irrational: "Courage may be virtue, when the daring is extreme, if the cause be good").[20] Either way, the citizen is not going against his sovereign's judgment, understood as the equivalent of the judgment the citizen would himself have made.

The case of martyrdom is more difficult, partly because of its relationship to Hobbes's general ideas about religion. Because Hobbes believed that Christianity is not like other beliefs, it was logically possible for a citizen to commit himself to Christianity against the commands of a non-Christian sovereign, though in no other respect (including, for gentiles, no other *religious* respect) could he question his sovereign's laws. If the sovereign was himself Christian, however, he then represented the citizen's Christianity in his judgments, just as he represented the citizen's beliefs about the laws of nature in the secular matters with which the laws of nature were concerned. This led to what is a well-recognized change in Hobbes's thought between *De Cive* and *Leviathan:* When Hobbes wrote *De Cive,* he believed that to be a Christian was necessarily to defer to the church on doctrinal matters, whereas by the time of *Leviathan,* he had come to believe that no Christian had ever been required to acknowledge the interpretative authority of the church.[21] Consequently, in *De Cive* he asserted that the sovereign representative must interpret Scripture "by means of duly ordained *Ecclesiastics*," but in *Leviathan* he claimed that the sovereign representative could authoritatively make up his own mind about interpretation. In either case, the sovereign represented his subjects, and they were therefore bound by his decision. This was not true of a non-Christian sovereign, so it was only in that situation that a citizen could refuse to obey—though he did not *have* to disobey. He could do as Naaman the Syrian did and conceal his true belief. But if Christians chose not to hide their faith, then, Hobbes observed sardonically, "[T]hey ought to expect their reward in Heaven, and not complain of their Lawfull Soveraign; much lesse make warre upon him. For he that is not glad of any just occasion of Martyrdome, has not the faith he professeth, but pretends it onely, to set some colour upon his own contumacy."[22]

If, then, we leave the difficult issue of Christianity on one side, it seems that Hobbes consistently argued that citizens are *not* entitled to interpret the laws of the sovereign for themselves. Does this mean that Flathman was wrong in enlisting Hobbes as a major supporter for his own appealing brand of liberalism? I do not think so, if we emphasize precisely what Flathman has always emphasized, the *willful* character of Hobbes's politics. Hobbes was indeed centrally concerned with the question of how people can live together if they are all involved in self-fashioning and if there are no external common standards, but his answer was that the association is itself willful: It is the bearer of what it is not anachronistic to call the "general will." In the remainder of this chapter, I will outline what I take Hobbes's theory of the general will to be, including its marked resemblance to Rousseau's ideas, and I will try to answer the question of whether these theories can be called liberal.

The first point to stress is that despite his frequent attacks on the practices of deliberative democracies, Hobbes was not at all antagonistic to a version of democracy. In all his works, he insisted that democracy was historically and conceptually the fundamental form of association and the form in which the general character of government was most clearly seen. (An example of this latter point would be his argument that a king must possess full legislative power because of the ridiculousness of supposing, by analogy, "the people of Rome to have had the absolute sovereignty of the Roman state, and to have chosen them a council by the name of the senate, and that to this senate they had given the supreme power of making laws, reserving nevertheless to themselves, in direct and express terms, the whole right and title of the sovereignty.")[23] Only a democracy could weld individual wills into a general will:

> When men have met to erect a commonwealth, they are, almost by the very fact that they have met, a *Democracy*. From the fact that they have gathered voluntarily, they are understood to be bound by the decisions made by agreement of the majority. And that is a *Democracy*, as long as the convention lasts, or is set to reconvene at certain times and places. For a convention whose will is the will of all the citizens has *sovereign power*. And because it is assumed that each man in this convention has the right to vote, it follows that it is a *Democracy*....
>
> *Democracy* is not constituted by agreements which individuals make with the *People*, but by mutual agreements of individuals with other individuals. The first part of the statement is evident from the fact that in every agreement the persons making the agreement must exist before the agreement itself. But prior to the formation of a commonwealth a *People* does not exist, since it was not then a person but a number of individual persons. Hence no agreement could be made between the *people* and a *citizen*. But after a commonwealth has been formed, any agreement by a citizen with the *People* is without effect, because the *People* absorbs into its own will the will of the citizen (to whom it is supposed to be obligated); it can therefore release itself at its own discretion; and consequently is in fact free of obligation.[24]

This quotation is from *De Cive*, which is the most blatantly democratic of all Hobbes's works (and which was to be the work studied most closely on the Continent in the eighteenth century), but even in *Leviathan*, the same theory is assumed. As Hobbes said at the beginning of chapter 18,

> A *Common-wealth* is said to be *Instituted*, when a *Multitude* of men do Agree, and *Covenant, every one, with every one,* that to whatsoever *Man*, or *Assembly of Men*, shall be given by the major part, the *Right* to *Present*

the Person of them all, (that is to say, to be their *Representative;*) every one, as well he that *Voted for it,* as he that *Voted against it,* shall *Authorise* all the Actions and Judgements, of that Man, or Assembly of men, in the same manner, as if they were his own.[25]

So the principle of *majoritarianism* turns out to be central to Hobbes's political thought: The agreement to form a civil society is simply an agreement to abide by the majority vote of the company. There is nothing here that is not also in Rousseau:

> This act of association creates a corporate and collective body, composed of as many members as the assembly contains voters, and receiving from this act its unity, its common identity, its life, and its will. This public person, so formed by the union of all other persons, formerly took the name of *city,* and now takes that of *Republic* or *body politic.*[26]

And

> [t]here is but one law which, from its nature, needs unanimous consent. This is the social compact; for civil association is the most voluntary of all acts. Every man being born free and his own master, no one, under any pretext whatsoever, can make any man subject without his consent.... Apart from this primitive contract, the vote of the majority always binds all the rest. This follows from the contract itself.[27]

The democracy that both Hobbes and Rousseau seem to have had in mind was what one might term a plebiscitary democracy, in which a measure is voted on but not discussed. Rousseau was hostile to communication among the citizens of his republic[28] and remarked in *Economie Politique* that "Athens was not in fact a Democracy, but a very tyrannical Aristocracy, governed by philosophers and orators."[29] Precisely similar sentiments are of course found in Hobbes.[30] Rousseau was aware that the Roman Republic had been a democracy of the plebiscitary kind, in which the *comitia* were not deliberative assemblies but simply mechanisms for registering votes; this was a principal reason why Rome played such a major part, and Greece such a small part, in the exposition of his theory. Hobbes, rather curiously, did not make this distinction, despite his deep knowledge of Roman history; rather, he consistently treated both Athens and Rome as examples of deliberative democracies. But he did at one point acknowledge that if a democracy could avoid deliberation, it might be free from the strictures that he generally leveled at the institution:

> These disadvantages found in the deliberations of large assemblies prove that *Monarchy* is better than *Democracy* in so far as in *Democracy* questions of great importance are more often passed to such assemblies for discussion than in a *Monarchy*; it cannot easily be otherwise. There is no reason why anyone would not prefer to spend his time on his *private business* rather than on *public affairs,* except that he sees scope for his eloquence, to acquire a reputation for intelligence and good sense, and to return home and enjoy the triumph for his great achievements with friends, parents and wife. The whole pleasure which *Marcus Coriolanus* drew from his deeds in war was seeing that his mother was pleased with the praise he received. But if in a *Democracy* the *people* chose to concentrate deliberations about war and peace and legislation in the hands of just one man or a very small number of men, and were happy to appoint magistrates and public ministers, i.e. to have authority without executive power, then it must be admitted that *Democracy* and *Monarchy* would be equal in this matter.[31]

It is clear from Hobbes's discussion of the superiority of monarchy over democracy in chapter 10 of *De Cive* that monarchy's superiority lay precisely in the fact that the transition from a democracy to a monarchy was a means of suppressing deliberation while preserving the moral legitimacy of democratic government.

I think that to some extent, Hobbes was wrestling with a problem posed by Aristotle. In book 4 of the *Politics,* Aristotle had argued that the special danger of a democracy was that it might behave as a single person, and that this was most likely if orators were allowed free reign:

> [One kind of democracy] is that in which not the law, but the multitude, have the supreme power, and supersede the law by their decrees. This is a state of affairs brought about by the demagogues. For in democracies which are subject to the law the best citizens hold the first place, and there are no demagogues; but where the laws are not supreme, there demagogues spring up. For the people becomes a monarch, and is many in one; and the many have the power in their hand, not as individuals, but collectively.... This sort of democracy, which is now a monarchy, and no longer under the control of law, seeks to exercise monarchical sway, and grows into a despot; the flatterer is held in honour; this sort of democracy is to other democracies what tyranny is to other forms of monarchy.[32]

For Hobbes, as he repeatedly said, the essence of political association was that "the people becomes a monarch" (in *De Cive* he also turned it around and said, arrestingly, that "the *King* is the *People*").[33] It was crucial that "the many" should have the power in their hands "not as individuals, but collectively"; anything else was, as he said in *The Elements of Law*, not "A union" but merely "A concord."[34] This was the source of his deep hostility to conventional accounts of mixed government; he recognized their Aristotelian roots in passages such as this, in which Aristotle expresses his desire for fractured and distributed political institutions to ward off democratic tyranny, and they received the full force of his general anti-Aristotelianism. But Hobbes seems nevertheless to have conceded the force of Aristotle's thought that a monarchical democracy was peculiarly vulnerable to corruption by demagogues, and the consequence was his advocacy of any form of government that preserved the democratic union while protecting it from orators.

In particular, Hobbes feared the tendency of orators to create parties or factions and to break down the democracy into partial associations. This is the theme of a powerful section in chapter 10 of *De Cive*, which (again) was clearly an inspiration for Rousseau (the last two sentences even seem to foreshadow Rousseau's characteristic prose).

> The third reason why deliberation in a large assembly is unprofitable is that it is a source of *factions* in the commonwealth, and factions are the source of sedition and civil war. For when well-matched orators confront each other with conflicting proposals and adversarial speeches, the defeated speaker resents the victorious speaker and with him all those who accepted his point of view, as if they had despised his own advice and good sense; he makes every effort to ensure that his opponent's policy works out badly for the country; for so he sees that his opponent will lose his glory and he will recover his. Besides, when the votes are sufficiently close for the defeated to have hopes of winning a majority at a subsequent meeting if a few men swing round to their way of thinking, their leaders get them all together, and they hold a private discussion on how to revoke the measure that has just been passed. They resolve among themselves to attend the next meeting in large numbers and to be there first; they arrange what each should say and in what order, so that the question may be brought up again, and the decision that was made when their opponents were there in strength may be reversed when they fail to show. This sort of effort and hard work, which they use to *fashion* a people, is usually called *faction*. When a faction is short of votes but superior or not much inferior in strength, then they try to get by arms what they could not get by eloquence and intrigue; and a civil war is born. But this, one will say, does not happen necessarily or often. One may also say that Orators are not necessarily greedy for glory, nor do great orators often disagree with each other on important issues.[35]

This response to defeat in a democratic assembly and this attempt to "fashion" other people are precisely what Flathman too has always feared about deliberative democracy, in which the participants are supposed to believe in the objective rightness of their cause and in the folly of their opponents.

For Rousseau, these were compelling arguments, but they were balanced by another argument that he found equally compelling *against* Hobbes. As Rousseau repeatedly said, modern monarchies could not seriously be proposed as solutions to the problems of the Hobbesian state of nature, for their most obvious characteristic was that they were engaged in endless and vicious war with one another. Modern armies have "committed more murders in a single day's fighting, and more violent outrages in the sack of a single town, than were committed in the state of nature during whole ages over the whole earth."[36] Since reading the Abbé de Saint-Pierre (Rousseau's mature political thought grew out of his critique of Saint-Pierre), he had been very conscious of the fact that princes make war in this fashion because their personal interests were not at stake.[37] Therefore, only the continuation of a Hobbesian democracy, rather than its self-annihilation, could genuinely secure its citizens from the threat of the state of nature, because only in a democracy would the sovereign's interest in this respect be identical to that of the citizens. Rousseau was not as confident as Kant was later to be (thinking along the same lines) that democratic republics would not make war, but he was aware that they are generally more pacific than modern monarchies. But of course, an argument of this kind against Hobbes does not in any way call into question Hobbes's fundamental political ideas: In its general shape it would presumably have been congenial to Hobbes, and it acutely locates one of the principal weaknesses in Hobbes's thought, namely, his refusal to consider the implications of international relations for his theory.[38]

If, then, Hobbes and Rousseau share a fundamental idea that the only way in which free, self-fashioning agents can live a political life together is through a plebiscitary democracy or its derivative, are they also both guilty of the kind of subversion of human freedom with which Rousseau, at least, is often charged; that is, do they both suppose that the citizens must be molded to fit into this civil society? And do they both believe that the general will can become completely detached from the citizens' own wills ("positive" rather than "negative" liberty)?

The natural response to the first question is that it would be strange for either of them to be committed to the illiberal theory that is often attributed to Rousseau, given that for each of them the point of a plebiscitary democracy is precisely that it protects the citizen from the "fashioning" that faction entails. Insofar as the citizens are to be molded, on either writer's account, it is in order to maintain a political order in which partial association and oratory are not permitted to intrude and dislocate the self-fashioning of the citizens. There is, of course, something of a paradox here, but it is a familiar one in all brands of liberalism: Individual freedom can only be maintained by a political order with the power to break social forces that threaten it, but that power is itself a threat to certain freedoms. This paradox is eminently recognizable in Hobbes's account of religious toleration, in which religious freedom is maintained only under the rule of a Leviathan powerful enough to withstand the blandishments of pope or bishop.

The second question is the more important, and it goes to the heart of the matter: On the face of it, in both Hobbes and Rousseau, that detachment of the general will is precisely what can happen. In Hobbes, this detachment is illustrated by a monarch whose will is the general will of the society yet who pays no attention to the wills of the individual citizens; in Rousseau, it is reflected in his remarks introducing the theme of the Legislator: "[T]he individuals see the good they reject; the public wills the good it does not see. All stand equally in need of guidance. The former must be compelled to bring their wills into conformity with their reason; the latter must be taught to know what it wills."[39] And it appears in his observations on voting:

> When in the popular assembly a law is proposed, what the people is asked is not exactly whether it approves or rejects the proposal, but whether it is in conformity with the general will, which is their will. Each man, in giving his vote, states his opinion on that point; and the general will is found by counting votes. When therefore the opinion that is contrary to my own prevails, this proves neither more nor less than that I was mistaken, and that what I thought to be the general will was not so. If my particular opinion had carried the day I should have achieved the opposite of what was my will; and it is in that case that I should not have been free.[40]

But we must not allow ourselves to be misled by Rousseau's rhetoric. In the former of these two passages, he is dealing not with the question of legitimacy but (so to speak) with the question of reasons of state: A *legitimate* act is one performed by the democratic sovereign, but it may not be a *wise* act. Just as in Hobbes, there is in Rousseau a space for deliberation on the part of the sovereign about what will actually redound to the benefit of the society, despite the fact that if the sovereign makes what turns out to be a mistake, his authority is not thereby called into question. The Legislator in *The Social Contract* is thought of as a being who possesses this kind of practical political knowledge about the formation and preservation of republics, but his political authority (if he has any) comes not from his knowledge but from the fact that he is an agent of the general will.[41]

In the latter of the two passages, Rousseau is also putting a familiar thought in a deliberately unfamiliar form: Every democrat has been puzzled about the status of his vote, given that he is already committed to respect the majority's wishes. Why express an opinion? There is, of course, no easy answer to this question, but Rousseau's way of putting the matter is not ridiculous, if the act of voting is thought of as contributing to the formation of a general will expressed by the will of the majority. It does not at all follow that when I vote, I must in some way neglect my own interests or that my wishes can be "wrong" in some deeper sense. The trick that a plebiscitary democracy performs is precisely to take particular interests and weld them together mechanically into a common interest, *simply* by counting heads—the commonality of the interest is given merely by the initial agreement of everyone that the will of the society shall be determined through that mechanism and that it will be decisive for each participant.

This, I take it, is what Rousseau meant in the famous passage from book 3 of *The Social Contract*:

> There is often a great deal of difference between the will of all and the general will; the latter considers only the common interest, while the former takes private interest into account, and is no more than a sum of particular wills: but take away from these same wills the pluses and minuses that cancel one another, and the general will remains as the sum of the differences.
>
> If, when the people, being furnished with adequate information, held its deliberations, the citizens had no communication one with another, the grand total of the small differences would always give the general will, and the decision would always be good. But when intrigues arise, and

partial associations are formed at the expense of the great association, the will of each of these associations becomes general in relation to its members, while it remains particular in relation to the State: it may then be said that there are no longer as many votes as there are men, but only as many as there are associations. The differences become less numerous and give a less general result.[42]

In Hobbes, of course, the self-dissolution of the democracy does mean that the will of the sovereign has no relationship to the particular wills of the citizens, other than at a very basic level, and it is clear that in this respect Hobbes is not particularly liberal. But if Rousseau's criticism of Hobbes's superstructure is right (and as we have seen, there is a great deal of plausibility to it), then within the general framework of a Hobbesian theory we can defend the continuation of a nondeliberative democracy; and in *De Cive*, we must remember, Hobbes himself proffered that thought. In that situation, Hobbes's sovereign becomes precisely the Rousseauian sovereign, and if Rousseau (understood along the lines sketched above) is a liberal, then so is Hobbes.

What we find in both Hobbes and Rousseau is an attempt to solve the problem of political association in the absence of both truth and persuasion. As citizens, we are not to believe that our sovereign is right, but we are to consider his rulings as decisive for us in our common life. We can only hold these two things in focus by seeing the sovereign as in some sense our continued creation, and the principle of majority voting as the fundamental mechanism by which men who disagree can shelve their disagreements in the interest of some degree of common activity. Majority voting in a plebiscitary setting is special because it has no necessary link to deliberation or persuasion: Questions of the truth or falsehood of the principles upon which people are voting do not affect the result. Though this argument does not—indeed, it is precisely its point that it does not—permit us to continue our disputes after the vote, it does not presume that the vote determines the truth of the matter nor, correspondingly, that a belief about the truth should stand in the way of our accepting the result of the vote.[43] In some ways, this is a very sophisticated psychological trick, reminiscent of the self-manipulation and suspension of belief practiced both in Antiquity and in the Renaissance, and it may well be that a trick of this kind is required of anyone who is going to participate fully in a democracy. But when Flathman said that he gave his consent when the vote went against him, but he did not give his soul, he was revealing that he is indeed the most authentic Hobbesian of our time.

Notes

1. Richard Flathman, *Reflections of a Would-Be Anarchist* (Minneapolis: University of Minnesota Press, 1998), 9.
2. Ibid, 14.
3. Ibid., 14.
4. See Quentin Skinner, "The State," in *Political Innovation and Conceptual Change*, ed. Terence Ball, James Farr, and Russell L. Hanson (New York: Cambridge University Press, 1989), 121–22.
5. Thomas Hobbes, *On the Citizen*, ed. Richard Tuck and Michael Silverthorne (New York: Cambridge University Press, 1998), 111 (chap. 9, section 9).
6. Richard E. Flathman, *Thomas Hobbes: Skepticism, Individuality, and Chastened Politics* (Newbury Park, Calif.: Sage, 1993); hereafter *Thomas Hobbes*.
7. Thomas Hobbes, *Leviathan*, ed. Richard Tuck (Cambridge: Cambridge University Press, 1996), 479–80 (385 in the 1988 edition).
8. *Thomas Hobbes*, 155.
9. Thomas Hobbes, *English Works*, vol. 7, ed. W. Molesworth (London: J. Bohn, 1845), 345 (*Six Lessons to the Professors of the Mathematics*, lesson 6).
10. *Leviathan*, 223 (168–169, 1988 edition). Hobbes put the same point extremely clearly in *The Elements of Law:* "For the conscience being nothing else but a man's settled judgement and opinion, when he hath once transferred his right of judging to another, that which shall be commanded, is no less his judgement, than the judgement of that other; so that in obedience to laws, a man doth still according to his conscience, but not his private conscience"; *The Elements of Law Natural and Politic,* 2nd ed., ed. M. M. Goldsmith (London: Frank Cass, 1969), part 2, chapter 6, section 12, p. 157; hereafter *Elements*.
11. Quoted in *Thomas Hobbes*, 77. Flathman is quoting here from *De Cive*, chap. 6, section 13.
12. *Leviathan*, 151–52 (112, 1988 edition).
13. *Leviathan*, 344–46, 414 (272–73, 330–31, 1988 edition).
14. The closest he comes to it is to reject as invalid "the Accusation of those, by whose Condemnation a man falls into misery; as of a Father, Wife, or Benefactor. For the Testimony of such an Accuser, if it be not willingly given, is praesumed to be corrupted by Nature; and therefore not to be received" (*Leviathan*, 98 [70, 1988 edition]).
15. Thomas Hobbes, *Behemoth, or The Long Parliament*, ed. Stephen Holmes (Chicago: University of Chicago Press, 1990), 51; hereafter *Behemoth*.
16. *Leviathan*, 231 (175, 1988 edition).
17. I am thinking of the discussion of law in *De Cive* in which Hobbes breaks law down into two aspects, "the part which forbids wrongs to be done and the part which punishes those who do them. The first of these, which is called *distributive,* is *prohibitive,* and is addressed to all men; the second, which is called *vindicative* or *penal,* is imperative, and is addressed only to the public ministers" (chap. 14, section 7,

p. 158; see also *Elements*, part 2, chap. 10, section 6, p. 187). These seem to Hobbes to have exhausted the types of law, and distributive law is always treated by him as general in form; see particularly *Leviathan*, 197 (148, 1988 edition).

18. Jean-Jacques Rousseau, *The Social Contract and Discourses*, trans. and ed. G. D. H. Cole, rev. J. H. Brumfitt and John C. Hall (London: J. M. Dent, 1973), 192 (chap. 2, section 6); see his *Oeuvres Politiques*, ed. Jean Roussel (Paris: Classiques Garnier, 1989), 274–75.

19. See *Leviathan*, 151–52 (112, 1988 edition).

20. *Elements* part 1, chap. 17, section 14, p. 94.

21. Compare *De Cive*, chap. 17, section 28, with *Leviathan*, 355–56 (281, 1988 edition): "When a difficulty arose, the Apostles and Elders of the Church assembled themselves together, and determined what should be preached, and taught, and how they should Interpret the Scriptures to the People; but took not from the People the liberty to read, and Interpret them to themselves."

22. *Leviathan*, 414 (331, 1988 edition).

23. *Elements*, part 2, chap. 8, section 7, p. 173.

24. *De Cive*, chap. 7, sections 5–7, pp. 94–95.

25. *Leviathan*, 121 (88, 1988 edition).

26. *The Social Contract*, 175; *Oeuvres Politiques*, 259 (book 1, chap. 5).

27. *The Social Contract*, 249–50; *Oeuvres Politiques*, 330–31 (book 4, chap. 2).

28. *The Social Contract*, 185; *Oeuvres Politiques*, 268 (book 2, chap. 3).

29. *The Social Contract*, 122; *Oeuvres Politiques*, 124.

30. For example, *De Cive*, chap. 10, section 7.

31. *De Cive*, chap. 10, section 15, pp. 124–25.

32. Aristotle, *Politics*, ed. Stephen Everson (Cambridge: Cambridge University Press, 1988), book 4, 1292a, p. 89.

33. *De Cive*, chap. 12, section 8, p. 137.

34. *Elements*, part 2, chap. 8, section 7, p. 173.

35. *De Cive*, chap. 10, section 12, pp. 123–24.

36. *The Social Contract*, 90; *Oeuvres Politiques*, 65.

37. See, for example, *Oeuvres Politiques*, 185–88.

38. The one place where Hobbes does address the issue is in chapter 13 of *Leviathan*: "Athough there had never been any time, wherein particular men were in a condition of warre one against another; yet in all times, Kings, and Persons of Soveraigne authority, because of their Independency, are in continuall jealousies, and in the state and posture of Gladiators.... But because they uphold thereby, the Industry of their Subjects; there does not follow from it, that misery, which accompanies the Liberty of particular men" (*Leviathan*, p. 90 [63, 1988 edition]).

39. *The Social Contract*, 193; *Oeuvres Politiques*, 276 (book 2, chap. 6).

40. *The Social Contract*, 250; *Oeuvres Politiques*, 331 (book 4, chap. 2).

41. "The decemvirs themselves never claimed the right to pass any law merely on their own authority. 'Nothing we propose to you,' they said to the people, 'can pass into law without your consent. Romans, be yourselves the authors of the laws which are to make you happy.' He, therefore, who draws up the laws has, or should have, no right of legislation, and the people cannot, even if it wishes, deprive itself of this incommunicable right, because, according to the fundamental compact, only the general will can bind the individuals" (*The Social Contract*, 195; *Oeuvres Politiques*, 278 [book 2, chap. 7]).

42. *The Social Contract*, 185; *Oeuvres Politiques*, 267–68 (book 2, chap. 3). I presume that the arithmetical language is an attempt to capture the idea of vote counting and majoritarianism; it may be vague because Rousseau recognized the role of qualified majorities in various electoral situations; see his observations at the end of book 4, chap. 2 (*The Social Contract*, 251; *Oeuvres Politiques*, 331–32).

43. If, that is, we wish to stay members of the association. Both Rousseau (*The Social Contract*, 250; *Oeuvres Politiques*, 331 [book 4, chap. 2]) and Hobbes (*Behemoth*, 51) presuppose that we can drop out of the association if we cannot stand the measures the sovereign passes.

CHAPTER TEN

Liberalism's Leap of Faith

Anne Norton

Before my most recent reading of Flathman, I had been inclined to (Flathman might say "tempted by") the view that a respectable institutional liberalism (a liberalism one could live with, if not within) could be understood through Martin Heidegger's image of the bridge.[1] One might take this bridge, as I do, as an architectural icon for that liberalism that lets things be. The bridge is the answer Heidegger finds to the question "What is a built thing?" Building gathers together; building marks out boundaries. "The construction, the building, is a force for unity and the composition of differences in an order. The bridge *gathers* the earth as landscape around the stream." It governs. "It guides and attends the stream through the meadows." For Heidegger, the bridge calls that which it bridges into being: "The banks emerge as banks only as the bridge crosses the stream."[2]

This image, I think, captures the defining attributes of a familiar liberalism: that which emerges from the work of most liberal theorists and most students of the history of liberalism, most liberal citizens and most liberal political discourse. Liberalism is acknowledged as a construction, but pride of analytic and historical place is given to its role as constructor, to the constitutional character of liberal institutions. This construction of liberalism connects the varied enterprises of "bringing the state back in," the new institutionalist school in U.S. political development, and constitutional theorists in the United States and the new Europe. These varied schools are united by a common privileging of institutions. For all of them, institutions do more than merely govern. Institutions constitute, forming liberal practices and liberal citizens. They make not only rules but practices, not only regulations but habits and expectations. They create the categories in which citizens understand themselves. They inculcate norms of civility and mark the modes and parameters of transgression. They do not rule citizens; they make them.

This understanding of liberalism might seem to mute the citizen's capacity for agency, choice, consent, and responsibility with which an institutionalist liberalism is wont to distinguish itself from its more authoritarian competitors. Yet the image of the bridge also accommodates the persistent understanding of liberalism as "letting things be," an understanding that provides common footing to liberal theorists—particularly of the pragmatic stripe—libertarians, and laissez-faire economists. Here the image captures liberalism's sense of itself as government governed. In this understanding, the deliberately minimalist institutions of government operate to ease and facilitate, to remove obstacles and provide a favorable context for civil and commercial activity.

Given this capacity to capture the constitutive oppositions of an institutionalist (or at least institutionalized) liberalism, one should not be surprised that the image of the bridge has been repeatedly employed as an evocation of progress, unity, and overcoming, recently and notably in the rhetoric of the 1996 presidential campaign in the United States. Heidegger's image is expansive enough to accommodate laissez-faire economists, communitarians, libertarians, new institutionalists, constitutional theorists, and Bill Clinton. It is not quite big enough for Flathman. The current of liberalism that Flathman carries has a different valence and a different direction.

The metaphor that best captures Flathman's liberalism is not that of the bridge but that of what moves beneath the bridge: "Even where the bridge covers the stream, it holds its flow up to the sky by taking it for a moment under the vaulted gateway and then setting it free once more." In Flathman's account, one sees the bridge called into being by the stream. The stream—which liberal constructions initially appear to evade or overcome—remains beneath the bridge, untouched.

Under the liberalism of stated rights, established institutions, and limited government runs the current of another liberalism. This liberalism, the liberalism of our occasional practice and our enduring history, has shifting currents, rapids, and shallows. The force that at one moment winds quietly and benignly through the country can gather itself into a powerful, unrestrained torrent, sweeping everything before it. This is Flathman's willful liberalism. It is a force of change and movement, gathering momentum as it flows, never exhausted, never closed. One is borne and moved by it. It travels inexorably toward an indeterminate end. This is a liberalism more in accord with the tumultuous, destructive, fertile, and inventive liberalism of history and of our experience.

Liberalism in history—practiced, embodied liberalism—is a profoundly destructive force.[3] It tears down established churches, dismantles relations of persons and property, transforms serfs to subjects, and subjects to citizens. This liberalism—liberalism as Nemesis, liberalism as Shiva Nataraja—cuts off heads and eats its young. The forces of popular passion unleashed by the removal of authoritarian constraints can readily overpower even the most durable and established institutional constructs. The stream washes over the bridge, knocking people off and carrying them away. Sometimes the bridge itself is taken down. This is the liberalism of the American and French Revolutions, the liberalism of Shays's Rebellion and of the Reign of Terror. The liberalism of established institutions and limited government has its origins here, in the repudiation of limits and establishment.

This liberalism, the liberalism of our history, is more fecund, more daring, and more dangerous than the institutional liberalism to which it gives rise. Flathman gives us insight into the source of that daring and dangerous fecundity—what William Blake called "that generous fire."[4]

In their assault on the old order, liberal revolutions were animated by the will that things should be otherwise. As Edmund Burke wrote, "All the decent drapery of life is to be torn off. All the superadded ideas, furnished from the wardrobe of a moral imagination ... to cover the defects of our naked, shivering nature and to raise it to dignity in our own estimation, are to be exploded."[5] Liberal revolutionaries willed the establishment of orders that were more just, more egalitarian, more free than those they set themselves against. They willed the new. They willed it blindly.

The orders and institutions that liberal revolutionaries envisioned and established were unprecedented. Their success, their effects, their evolution were all uncertain. The will to make a new world entailed the risks of accident and error. The refusal to regard history as the necessary limit of ambition, to accept that what had been was the limit of what could be, opened minds to theory and opened practice to experiment.

Liberalism's allegiance to theory and experiment, the unbounded ambition to make a new world order, was willful, admirable, and dangerous.

Those revolutionaries, with "their laps full of seed, their hands full of generous fire"[6] find, if not houseroom, at least a room to haunt, in Flathman's geistliche philosophy. This is a liberalism mindful of the dangerous passions and suppressed memories that haunt liberalism. Here the Promethean forces that destroyed and then remade the world command reverence. Some remember their power with fear; others, with hope. That difference should serve as a warning that the passions that still run beneath the constraints of liberalism may not remain quiet. Whether we acknowledge them or not, they are our own.

Flathman's reading reminds us that the liberal refusal of the past, the willful refusal to be bound by rationality, is an instance of the modern hunger for novelty. Modernity, as Jürgen Habermas writes, "is the epoch that lives for the future, that opens itself up to the novelty of the future."[7] In this epoch, as Reinhart Koselleck writes, "expectations have distanced themselves evermore from all previous experience."[8] Liberalism has been the creature and the creator of this modernity. Flathman's conception of a willful (all-too-willful?) liberalism confronts us with the moral and historical consequences of this modern, liberal passion for the new.

Liberalism is willful, Flathman writes, and will is always, inevitably, aporetic. In the passion for novelty, the certainties of Enlightenment rationalism lapse. The known novelty is an invitation to explore the unknown, a gate into regions where reason cannot reach. Liberalism desires not the boundary but what lies beyond it. In that desire, will triumphs over rationality. Modernity's willing leap into an aporetic future is *amor fati*, not rational choice.

In this understanding of liberalism, elements of Enlightenment rationalism are alien and suspect, and the enterprise in its entirety is put in question. Rationality commands. The enlightened are obliged to subject their separate wills to a single command, to surrender will and singularity to a common, uniform, and unforgiving standard. The dictates of reason permit no deviation. Liberalism does. Here, whether one finds oneself swept away by the world historical passions liberalism unleashes or removed to a safe distance, one can choose to obey the dictates of reason or to disregard them. Liberalism can accommodate calm adherence to ancient custom, the relentless quest for novelty, quietism, and restlessness—and these all within the same subject. Passions and appetites; desires, hopes, and fears; defiance and refusal—all contend on equal terms with the commands of reason. Singular liberals shape themselves—and shape themselves differently—in relation to these contending forces. They know what reason would conceal: that rationality is no certain guide in an uncertain future. The turmoil of liberal history, though it provides no map through the present, at least marks its hazardous indeterminacy.

The recollection of liberalism's willful history enables us to see similarly destructive and passionate ideals underwriting (perhaps undermining) the ameliorative institutions of contemporary liberalism. Liberalism knows that it wishes—wills—things to be otherwise. It wills the new: a justice, a freedom, a form of life that has not been seen before, that is unknown. Yet liberals cannot know whether the worlds they create experimentally will be more just, more egalitarian, or more free than those they left behind. They are willing to risk the loss of peace, of security, and of what freedom and justice there is on the chance that the world they make will surpass the world of their inheritance.

This great gamble, this willful faith, changes not only the politics of nations but the ethics of individuals. At such moments, in these acts of brave and blind ambition, willful liberals craft their own, un-Christian, passions. They will, they accept, and they will suffer fates they cannot foresee.

They are infidels, these liberal revolutionaries, unwilling to keep faith with the past, unfaithful to established religions as well as to established law. Yet liberal revolutions and liberal revolutionaries have been animated by their own scandalous and heretical faiths. They have placed their faith not in God but in themselves. They have faith that they will be able to contend with (if not to conquer) the unknown. They have faith in their ability to shape the new world orders they intend to bring into being. They have faith, as Flathman reminds us, that their regulative institutions can serve their revolutionary ideals. They place their faith not in reason but in will.

There are other heresies to be found in this all-too-human faith. Flathman's willful liberals refuse the fences and negations of a more conservative and more reasonable liberalism for their own daring constructions. They refuse the known, the predictable, and the calculable for the unknown, the experimental, and the speculative. In doing so, not only do they abandon memory, practice, and institutions, but they also abandon themselves.

For the individual, the willingness to become what one is requires that one be willing to become other than what one is. The desire to make oneself in accordance with one's will is a refusal of the present self for a future self that exceeds it. This future self, surpassing the first, is beyond its comprehension, almost beyond its grasp.

Flathman's willful liberals may be freed from the boundaries of their inherited constitutions. They are not, however, undisciplined. On the contrary, these singular individuals find themselves subject to several disciplinary regimes. "The discipline strong voluntarists favor" Flathman writes, "must begin with quite rigorously impositional social and cultural training." This training "engenders fluency in the various 'languages' that have evolved into modes of experience or traditions of thought and sensibility."[9]

In this account, Flathman demonstrates an observant understanding of the subject. The subtle work of the ideological state apparatus—training, discipline, acculturation—is decisive. These, like all acts of authority, effect more and less than they will. They fail in certain of their aims, and they achieve effects they did not aim for. The subject is the work of these institutions, but like all work, it surpasses its author. The customs, traditions, institutions, disciplines, regimes, and projects that order citizens and subjects do not determine them. The subjects so created can affirm, amend, or reject themselves.

It may be, as Michel Foucault suggested, that our common project as singular individuals is "perhaps not to discover who we are but to refuse who we are." That refusal acquires significance only after it has been given content. The will to become other than one is thus entails the refusal—or more properly, the refusal, acceptance, and amendment—of a complex of languages, traditions, customs, practices, ideals, values, beliefs, and experiences. The richer that array, the more thorough the individual's engagement with and knowledge of the forces that fashioned the inherited self, the more important (and the more impressive) the refusal of that self will be. Self-overcoming is, in this account, a public process, a critical engagement with inherited traditions and extant discourses. Only through a critical engagement with this inherited constitution can the singular individual learn, in Nietzsche's words, "how to become what one is." Much has been written on the demands, difficulties, and discipline of this undertaking. For Flathman's willful liberal, this is an undertaking indeed, for in it one buries the deceased self.

The demanding ascesis that crafts the singular self is not the final discipline the willful liberal will confront. In a liberalism of institutions as well as ideals, singular individuals will be obliged to accord themselves to laws, customs, regulations, and practices alien (and often hostile) to their ideals. Liberals may say "I desire, I wish, I want to, I pursue, I think," but they should be very hesitant to say either "you must" or "we are." Liberals must accommodate themselves to liberalism.

Singular individuals *may* accommodate themselves to liberalism. But, most important, liberalism *must* accommodate itself to them. Flathman writes, "[L]iberalism as I envision it is committed to the ideal of individuality and hence self-enactment as a formal but not substantive end and to the widest possible freedom of action as a necessary but not sufficient condition of effective pursuit of this ideal."[10] The partially achieved contentlessness and neutrality of liberal institutions is the precondition for liberalism's incalculable achievement.

Liberalism, in Flathman's vision, is not wholly without content because for Flathman, liberalism is not exhausted by its civil practices or institutional apparatus. Liberalism is realized in the practices of singular individuals who are neither entirely nor always liberal. This is the point at which most liberals, and most liberalisms, lose their nerve. The efforts of more orthodox liberals to find common ground, common ends, or an original position betray an anxious rejection of the possibilities of individuality. In stark contrast, Flathman argues that willful liberalism entails "receptivity to the idea that quite radical diversities, incommensurabilities, and so forth ... are to be welcomed, not feared."[11] Patrick Neal writes elsewhere in this volume that "in some ways, such an individuality is the madwoman in the attic for contemporary rationalist liberalism.... Flathman is at the door to the attic, loudly demanding that liberalism recognize its own."[12]

Flathman's demand is, I think, far more radical. It is not merely that Flathman wishes liberalism to recognize the presence of the alien, the inassimilable, the embarrassing, and the awkward in the individualities it must accommodate. Nor is it simply a matter of releasing the madwoman. However dangerous she is, she is up there with Abraham, Samuel

Taylor Coleridge, Muhammed, Vincent van Gogh, and a host of other visionaries. Nor, finally, is it a matter of recognizing that he—or I or you—could be the madwoman. Flathman's conviction that radical diversities are to be welcomed follows, instead, from the recognition that there are goods that are radically opposed, even at war with one another. One might come to this recognition through a seemingly contradictory regard for the value of the lives and practices of e. e. cummings and Abraham Lincoln, Emma Goldman and H. L. Mencken, or any set of singular individuals whose beliefs and practices were fundamentally opposed. Because liberalism is, in substance, the work of individuals radically different in kind and opaque to one another, the content of liberalism is infinitely various, in constant flux, and incalculable.

This fitting of one oddly shaped stone with another does not diminish those from whom liberal institutions and liberal nations are built. They remain whole. Liberalism is built, like a stone house, of strong and coherent wholes. Like a stone house, it is built not around but of those disparate elements, unyielding in their difference, unaltered in their combination. Seen in the long shadow of this building, the project of the communitarians—grounded on a pervasive sameness, composed of like elements whose likeness is only increased in their combination—seems like the plan for a house built not only on but of sand.

"Thou Shalt Have No Other Gods before Thee"

In the beginning of *Willful Liberalism*, after the dedication and the table of contents, before the substance of the work, Flathman has placed—without attribution—a shocking epigram: "Thou shalt have no other gods before thee." Flathman thus announces, quietly and discreetly, the heroic blasphemy that will animate the work. We—we liberals, or perhaps, we willful ones—are to serve no higher god than ourselves. We are to remain unyielding in our differences, the stones with which liberalism builds.

For Flathman, willful liberalism insists, with Friedrich Nietzsche, that "whatever kind of bizarre ideal one may follow... [o]ne should have it in order to distinguish oneself, not to level oneself."[13] This is very distant, then, from the self-abnegation and surrender, service and sacrifice sought in the religious traditions of Christianity, Judaism, Islam, and (for that matter) Hinduism and Buddhism. One does not serve God or the gods, nor does one sacrifice or surrender oneself. Rather, as Flathman affirms, with Nietzsche, the ideal is one "of a spirit who plays naively—that is, not deliberately, but from overflowing power and abundance—with all that was hitherto called holy, good, untouchable, divine."[14]

Flathman is not the first theorist (Jean-Jacques Rousseau comes readily to mind) to broach the question of our divinity. Blasphemy is an old and honored tradition in political theory. It is a rare philosopher who can be found in the canon but not on the Index of one or another religion. Flathman's account has the distinction, however, of drawing our attention to an often-neglected attribute of the divine. Deities—the gods of ancients and animists, of Jews, Gentiles, Muslims, and Hindus—share an incalculability. They are inscrutable, unpredictable, arbitrary, and capricious. Their willfulness secures them from calculability.

The incalculability of Flathman's human gods places them in an ethical order perhaps not beyond good and evil but at least beyond responsibility. Responsibility is an ethic (and a politics) of certainties: certainty that reason can trace agency, that intentions can be discerned by reason, and that will has foresight. It is an ethic alien to the changing, the uncertain, and the divine.

Flathman's willful liberals are not zealots (even in the cause of their own divinity), but they have their own virtues and their own mode of excommunication. Indeed, that formula of excommunication serves as a recurring coda in *Willful Liberalism* and *Reflections of a Would-Be Anarchist:* "My ideal is *mine:* 'This is what *I* am, this is what *I* want:—*you* can go to hell."[15]

This extraordinary and liberating formula is a challenge and a corrective (perhaps I should merely say "a supplement to") more common liberalisms. "This is what *I* am, this is what *I* want" counters the tendency to self-mortification evident in the more pious virtue liberalisms, in communitarianism, and in the concern with care. The addendum "*you* can go to hell" decisively disavows the tendency toward evangelism (martial and pacific), paternalism, and simple meddling that have dogged liberalism's history. This posture dispenses with the privileging of pity and of the victim and with the endemic impulse to confess.[16] Rather than holding others responsible, it refuses to take responsibility for them, leaving them to themselves. Rather than obliging us to be our brother's keeper, it reminds us of the wisdom and the propriety of indifference.

The respectful indifference of Flathman's willful liberal offers a powerful and attractive alternative to the politics of recognition. In the wake of decolonization and desegregation, liberal citizens and liberal theorists confronted persistent inequalities: structures of deference and hierarchy that did not fade away with the dismantling of formal political institutions. Liberal citizens marked by the signs of race and gender or burdened by social resentment of their ethnicity, religious practices, or sexual orientation began to demand more from one another. Political inclusion and legal equality came to be recognized as insufficient guarantors of the social equality these subaltern citizens sought. They demanded public recognition on their own terms, not as individuals but as members of social and political categories.

Here Flathman gives a different, more quotidian, and more useful content to his concurrence with Jacques Derrida that "l'autre est tout autre" (the other is entirely other).[17] Self-respect is manifest in the refusal of unchosen and indiscriminate alliances. Respect for others is manifest in the refusal of pretended knowledge of another's emotions, intellect, will, taste, or needs and in the willingness to let one another be.

Flathman does not oblige us to decide whether "l'autre est tout autre" in any or every sense. He does provide us with guidance for acting ethically toward several difficult categories of others. Relations of equality are not required. Singular individuals may oblige themselves to be responsible for those who cannot be responsible—wholly or in some respect—for themselves. The danger of paternalism, always present in discussions of responsibility, is offset by the singular individual's imperative to autonomy, passion for privacy, and inclination to solitude. The merits of this approach are several. It can accommodate at least certain of those others who are wholly other. It recognizes relative and momentary relations of need and power and obliges those advantaged in such relations to assume the attendant responsibilities: the healthy for the infirm, the educated for the untaught, the competent for the incompetent, the sane for the insane. Perhaps more important, the assumption of superiority in any respect carries with it the obligation of responsibility. The inclination of the singular individual—which I read as "Obey? Oh no!" and "Govern? No, indeed!"—tends to offer a range of action from "taking responsibility for" to "letting be" in Heidegger's term, or "taking things lightly" in Richard Rorty's. This ethical continuum imposes no obligation on the object, neither deference nor obedience; not even tractability can be required.

The ethical standard for the singular individual is, like the prisoner's instruction to Cyrus, "Do what is due to yourself."

Perhaps more importantly, and less evidently, Flathman's liberal is also very much at variance with the appetitive, interested individual of rational choice. This construct, as influential perhaps in popular discourse as it has been in the academy, presumes a concurrence of appetites and interests that renders individuals calculably transparent to one another. These individuals, like those participants in the politics of recognition, are turned wholly outward. They (often quite literally) cannot afford to be indifferent to one another. Flathman's liberal, of course, is a being of more particular interests and more eccentric appetites (and more "bizarre" ideals) than the rational actor. Moreover, this very singular being is not fundamentally rational at all. Will and desire have primacy over reason and calculation in these beings, though their passions include (as Nietzsche and many of his readers have reminded us) the desire for knowledge and the will to temper and refine oneself.

The Delphic imperative "Know yourself" is a powerful restraint in this philosophy. When one is so instructed, one finds oneself doubly cautioned: knowing that one does not know and knowing that even that powerful, cautionary insight is limited to oneself. Indifference and irresponsibility appear from this position to be not the evasion of ethics but occasional ethical requirements. In practice, indifference may be mandated by one's own lack of knowledge or by one's recognition of the ethical potential of a form of life alien or hostile to one's own.[18] In practice, irresponsibility may be mandated either by respect for another's autonomy or by the desire to relieve another's burden and spare oneself embarrassment. "Did you already know this?" Nietzsche asks. "A wrong shared is half right. And he who is able to bear it should take the wrong upon himself."[19] The ludic, playful element in irresponsibility is here as well. "And if you are cursed I do not like it that you want to bless. Rather join a little in the cursing."[20]

It is this Zarathustrian counsel, I think, that prompts Flathman to remind us that whether we curse or bless the peculiar liberalism he articulates, in the end, these are his ideals, and if we do not like them, we can go to hell.

Notes

1. Martin Heidegger, "Building Dwelling Thinking," in *Poetry, Language, Thought* (1971), trans. Albert Hofstadter (New York: Harper and Row, 1971), 152.
2. Ibid.
3. Perhaps the best formal account of this aspect of liberalism is in Karen Orren's *Belated Feudalism* (Cambridge: Cambridge University Press, 1991).
4. William Blake, "The Book of Los" (1795), in *The Poems of William Blake*, ed. W. H. Stevenson, text by David Erdman (London: Longman, 1972), 278.
5. Edmund Burke, *Reflections on the Revolution in France* (1790) (London: Methuen, 1905), 69.
6. Blake, "The Book of Los," 278.
7. Jürgen Habermas, "Modernity's Consciousness of Time and Its Need for Self-Reassurance," in *The Philosophical Discourse of Modernity: Twelve Lectures,* trans. Frederick Lawrence (Cambridge: MIT Press, 1987), 5.
8. Reinhart Koselleck, *Futures Past,* trans. Keith Tribe (Cambridge: MIT Press, 1985), 276.
9. Richard Flathman, *Reflections of a Would-Be Anarchist: Ideals and Institutions of Liberalism* (Minneapolis: University of Minnesota Press, 1998), 34; hereafter *Reflections*.
10. Ibid., 58.
11. Richard Flathman, *Willful Liberalism: Voluntarism and Individuality in Theory and Practice* (Ithaca, N.Y.: Cornell University Press, 1992), 217; hereafter *Willful Liberalism*.
12. Patrick Neal, "The Voice of Richard Flathman in the Conversation of Liberalism," chapter 1 in this volume.
13. *Willful Liberalism,* 176, quoting Nietzsche's *Will to Power,* para. 349.
14. *Willful Liberalism,* 176, quoting Nietzsche's *Will to Power,* para. 349.
15. *Willful Liberalism,* 177, 190, quoting Nietzsche's *Will to Power,* para. 349. In *Reflections,* a more recent work, the passage appears first as an elaboration of the "radically individualized" perfectionism of what Flathman revealingly calls "willful or virtuosity liberalism." Flathman differentiates this from the perfectionism of the evangelist and the drill instructor, questions whether it can be socially or politically cultivated, and, again discreetly (this time in a footnote), identifies it as divine. Later in *Reflections,* Flathman cites the passage again, connecting it on this occasion to Hobbes. Hobbes's philosophy, Flathman writes, "extended to all of humankind" the power Hobbes recognized in philosophers, who "had always the liberty, and sometimes they both had and will have the necessity, of taking to themselves such names as they please for the signifying of their meaning" (*Reflections,* 55, 168 n. 3).
16. Andrew Ross's account of the trial and execution of Julius and Ethel Rosenberg furnishes a telling account of the insistence on public confession—on utterance; Ross, *No Respect* (New York: Routledge, 1989). The more prosaic and quotidian insistence on eliciting confessions (of one's sexuality, one's politics, one's familial relations, etc.) should be familiar to all of us.
17. Jacques Derrida, *The Gift of Death,* trans. David Wills (Chicago: University of Chicago Press, 1995).
18. Recognition of the ethical propriety of indifference would do much to quiet

the often-puerile and occasionally dangerous debates over such practices as female circumcision and veiling.

19. Friedrich Nietzsche, *Thus Spoke Zarathustra*, trans. Walter Kaufmann (Harmondsworth, Eng.: Penguin Books, 1978), 68.

20. Ibid.

CHAPTER ELEVEN

Mouths, Bodies, and the State

Jane Bennett and William E. Connolly

Linguistic Skepticism and Positive Onto-Stories

Richard Flathman is a skeptic and a would-be anarchist. His skepticism is lodged, first and foremost, in the indeterminate character of language. He doubts that definitive meaning inheres in utterances and that rules have sufficient power to secure the regularities they seek. Flathman's anarchism is a political affirmation of this linguistic condition. The attraction of anarchy—like the value of linguistic indeterminacy—is that it provides space for individuals as individuals and for new idiolects to form. Anarchy finds its limit in the need to maintain some social regularities, to apply some disciplines to selves, and to enforce laws against those who would otherwise act as predators:

> If action occurs exclusively or primarily through or in language..., and if in the absence of rules language has no meaning, it would be difficult to exaggerate the importance of rules and rule-governedness in human affairs. Rules and rule following are mainstays in that they introduce into human affairs not only observable regularity but meaning or intelligibility, steadiness and mutual confidence.[1]

Flathman is thus a would-be anarchist: the "would-be" allows him to affirm selective disciplines, regularities, normalities, and punishments, while the anarchism inoculates him against "the too ready, the insufficiently skeptical and cautious, acceptance of the institution of government" (*Reflections*, 83).

We admire Flathman's thinking and learn much from it. But we do not endorse all of its priorities and inflections. It is not that we accept the ideals of community and unity he resists or all the disciplinary practices he opposes or the transcendental models of morality he unravels. We stand with him and in his debt on these matters. But we find ourselves moved by a nonteleological onto-story within which we locate the indeterminacy of language and the insufficiency of rules. Our (unavoidably speculative) picture of nature, or onto-story, accentuates the somatic as much as the linguistic, and we emphasize the play of differential intensities inside rules, meaning, and regularity as much as we emphasize the indeterminacy of language. Moreover, we draw upon this imaginary to articulate an ethic in which arts of the self and micropolitics play a significant role. Eventually, these considerations carry us toward a multivalent politics in which the state plays an active role. We are uncertain how far we differ from Flathman on the ontological register. But because there are discernible differences between him and us at each of the other points, it is possible that they are anchored partly in that dimension.

Flathman argues that rules are both less determinate than regularians think and less dangerous than their critics often contend. If the former is the case, then "fears concerning what ruling, rules, and rule following can do *to* us are also exaggerated" (*Reflections*, 50). The way we would put that point is to say that although linguistic articulation is shot through with indeterminacy, certain features of the bodied character of human beings ensures both regularity *and* the undoing or renovation of regularity. We are led to these questions: *Why* are rules indeterminate? Is this simply a feature of language? Or is it also a trait of the world in which linguistic practices are set? We now enter the terrain that Ludwig Wittgenstein, who inspires much of Flathman's interpretation, touches through limit terms such as "facts of nature" and "form of life." We agree with Flathman and Wittgenstein that one cannot say a lot about these conditions. But our imagination of this vague background may still differ from their imagination of it.

Friedrich Nietzsche suggests that both the quest for clarity in language and the barriers to its achievement arose in part from the animal need to draw crude distinctions crucial to survival—distinctions between, say, edible and poisonous plants and between benign and dangerous animals. To accomplish this, it was necessary to treat as "equal" things that shared a few affinities but differed in numerous other respects:

> Innumerable beings who made inferences in a way different from ours perished.... Those, for example, who did not know how to find often enough what is "equal" as regards both nourishment and hostile animals—those, in other words, who subsumed things too slowly and cautiously—were favored with a lesser probability of survival than those who guessed immediately upon encountering similar instances that they must be equal. The dominant tendency, however, *to treat as equal what is merely similar*—an illogical tendency, for nothing is really equal—is what first created any basis for logic.[2]

These linguistic equalizations enter into habits, organic functions, perceptions, and institutional regimes. They become corporealized as well as socially coded. But they are never completely stabilized. The similarities-rendered-equal and the differences-rendered-similar periodically manifest themselves as rebel forces within habits, organic functions, and so on. These energetic disturbances both enable creativity in thinking and help propel interventions for reform of the rules. Our point is that the process of stabilization and destabilization of rules is lodged not only in language but also in other complex somatic or cultural relays. And the energy for resistance and change is somatic.

At this point, Flathman might say, "But these other zones—habits, organic functions, etc.—are also structured like a language"; to which we reply, "Yes, but to variable degrees depending upon the zone in question, and in those zones where the kinship to language is more distant, the most effective form of intervention may not be a linguistic one." Sometimes self-conscious work on the meanings of a network of terms is most appropriate; at other times, techniques of the self that work on the corporeal composition of habit, belief, and sensibility are most appropriate. Most often, all are needed in conjunction.

This complexity may help explain one of the most important differences between Nietzsche and Wittgenstein when, to use the latter's term, "therapy" is needed. For whereas Wittgenstein concentrates on sharpening our sense of the complexity and ambiguity of language, Nietzsche joins those operations to arts of the self that reach into zones of (proto)-thought, feeling, perception, and sensation imperfectly structured like language. A six-month-old baby, for instance, can imitate something it saw yesterday even before it can speak or understand words. The amygdala—a small brain that stores thought-imbued intensities below the level of articulation and epistemological debate—exerts distinctive effects on subjective and intersubjective thinking, perceptions, judgment, actions, and articulations. It also communicates actively with other brains capable of more refined thought, perception, judgment, articulation, and action. That is why Michel Foucault, who follows Nietzsche on this score, found it necessary to supplement a symbolic-systems approach:

> It is not enough to say the subject is constituted in a symbolic system. It is not just in the play of symbols that the subject is constituted. It is constituted in real practices—historically analyzable practices. There is a technology of the constitution of the self which cuts across symbolic systems while using them.[3]

But what about the world engenders this condition in which "nothing is really equal"? Nietzsche, we want to say, treats the ambiguity and indeterminacy of language as one sign among others of fundamental dissonances and surpluses in the order of being. We call his interpretation of those signs an onto-story, not because it grounds human being in a set of transcendental moral commands or mechanical causes or final ends of history—Nietzsche resists these interpretations—but because it projects into the world anarchic energies that exceed, elide, and rebuff attempts to represent them, to explain their operations, to become attuned to a natural end adhering in them, or to discern moral certainties emanating from them. The categories of interpretation and explanation, although indispensable to life, are also too crude, coarse, and blunt to capture numerous forces that slide around them and slip through them. We thus draw selective sustenance from Nietzsche, adopting an "antimetaphysical metaphysic" in two senses of that phrase. First, we imagine a streak of mobility and the capacity for surprise in a world that exceeds our categories of interpretation and is governed by no final purpose. Second, we offer this fabulous projection as a contestable reading to be placed into competition with other fantastic imaginaries. Because we suspect it is impossible to be entirely agnostic on these matters—because we find it implausible to be postmetaphysical in the way some find Martin Heidegger, Wittgenstein, Hannah Arendt, Richard Rorty, and Jürgen Habermas to be—we try to articulate the primary picture, or positive onto-story, that inspires us. We try to take our thinking to those numerous, fugitive points where it bumps into its own limits, even though we know our articulation will be incomplete.

We endorse the Nietzschean critique of teleological and voluntarist views of the world. We also accept his hunch—he sometimes calls it a "conjecture" or a "supposition," incorporating skepticism into interpretation without stopping interpretation from proceeding—that the ambiguous character of language signifies an element of disordered energy between the world and our capacities of interpretation. We think that Nietzsche overstates his case when he characterizes the world as "chaotic" at bottom. For numerous patterns and fortuitous regularities appear in those hybrid formations of nature and culture. Some patterns enchant us, some frustrate us, and some do both in ways that draw us to the sublime.

Our interpretation corresponds pretty closely to the view of philosopher of science John Dupré in *The Disorder of Things*.[4] Extrapolating from recent research in physics, genetics, biology, chemistry, and linguistics, he concludes that there is a profound element of disorder in and among the systems these disciplines study. He defines himself as "a promiscuous realist": realist in the sense that he thinks there is a fundamental way of the world that we can glimpse and chart to some degree; promiscuous in that he doubts there is a complete or final unity of things to be captured by the sciences as they advance. We are skeptical enough to contend that the way things appear to us is not necessarily the way they would appear to someone with a divine microscope. But more pertinently, our onto-story extends through skepticism in epistemology and linguistics to a fundamental conception of the world. For first, the regularities in the world are themselves inhabited by pressures and surpluses that make them differ from themselves in ways that sometimes accumulate to make those regularities quiver and shake and generate new assemblages. And second, these regularities often bump into other forces that modify them. A geological formation may result in an earthquake with all kinds of consequences for other things in the world; a mutation may then heighten the cognitive capacity of some animals or spawn a new disease; a state economy humming along smoothly may collapse from sudden climatic change or from the gradual disintegration of its political legitimacy; a new pattern of cultural pluralism may emerge out of an old set of dissonant regularities; and an established political regime may become a hollow shell as its participants retreat from the patterns of work, investment, and trust upon which it depends.[5]

What, more precisely, is the relation between the projections of our onto-story and a philosophy of epistemological skepticism? Both contend that things go on in the world that exceed our capacity to know them. But the Nietzschean onto-story adds a critical step. It suggests, in line with several religious traditions, that it is difficult or impossible to live without projecting a faith onto the world beyond one's current capacity to prove the projection. Such a faith may be either theistic or nontheistic (as is the Nietzschean faith of an energetic world without divine design). This onto-story suggests, moreover, that it is sometimes possible to "contest" alternative projections at this level. The idea of contestation advanced here thus involves two interwoven dimensions. One first debates the issues at the level of belief and argument ("Your faith involves the following paradox," or "What you say here is deeply at odds with what you say there," or "How do you square that projection with the experimental findings of science?"). And second, one contests a contending onto-faith through performative actions and tactics that open up new possibilities of thinking at the more visceral level of being, the level of protothoughts, predispositions to belief and action, and ethical sensibility situated below epistemological belief, knowledge, and explicit moral judgment.[6] Flathman and Wittgenstein approach this register when they speak of the way "training" can engender operational certainties below the level of epistemic doubt or debate. It is equally important to think sometimes about whether and how such operational certainties can be strengthened or altered.

In our experience of things, culture and nature are mixed together, and both are unfinished. There are "gaps" in nature, as Nietzsche says, and nature is woven into the somaticization of cultural processes. We can intervene in the culture of nature to some degree, and we can sometimes establish a degree of attunement to differences circulating through them. Ecologists have, for example, arranged an ensemble of bacteria, aquatic animals, and plants into a "living machine" that transforms human excreta into drinking water without using chlorine and without a sludge remainder.[7] But we neither master nature nor uncover a set of final ends inscribed in it. If we were to put this point in Flathman's terms, we would say that the indeterminacy of language precludes both our control over it and our enslavement to its rules. Nietzsche locates this point on an ontological register when he says,

> Cause and effect: such a duality probably never exists; in truth we are confronted by a continuum out of which we isolate a couple of pieces.... The suddenness with which many effects stand out misleads

us. Actually it is only sudden for us. In this moment of suddenness there is an infinite number of processes that elude us.[8]

"An infinite number of processes that elude us": Nietzsche suggests that the human net of cause and effect is too coarse to capture the small fish that swim through it and too fragile to cope with forces that occasionally accumulate to tear it apart. Nietzsche thus weaves a strand of ambiguity into the fabric of interpretation and a thread of surprise into explanatory schemes. To love the world is to love appearances despite the mobilities circulating through them and the absence of an intrinsic purpose installed above them. One tries to act with purposive effect in a world of fractious holism. And one cultivates an ethical perspective appropriate to this condition. Nietzsche thinks some pre-Platonic Greeks approached the combination needed: "Oh those Greeks! They knew how to live. What is required for that is to stop courageously at the surface, the fold, the skin, to adore appearance.... Those Greeks were superficial—out of profundity.[9]

Such an onto-story cannot be presented at length. The more you talk about it, the more the logic of presentation drifts toward one of the perspectives you resist. And yet it must be presented briefly, so that you will not be charged with failing to live up to a project that is not yours (e.g., "Nietzsche does not explain X"; "Dupré does not have a rigorous epistemology"; "Aha! You implicitly adopt a metaphysic even while you purport to be postmetaphysical"). Our strategy, then, is to compare our onto-story with others that differ from it and then try to embody it in our political interpretations, ethical orientations and the balances we adopt between interpretation and intervention. We do not, for instance, think that deep cultural explanations are always more useful than rough-and-ready ones because we do not think the cultural/natural world is susceptible to deep and complete explanation. The perspective we adopt suggests why language has so much porosity and indeterminacy; it suggests why social explanation is both needed to guide interventions and likely to encounter surprises that force theorists back to the drawing board, and it draws us to those fugitive places where thinking encounters the unthought, where social practice becomes incorporated into corporeal dispositions, and where corporeal dispositions encounter nests of recalcitrance and creativity.

From Significance to Sonority

Let us say something more about what comes into focus within the onto-picture we sketch. What kind of theorizing—about language, rule-following, and ethics—issues from it?

Such thinking finds it particularly hard to elide the trajectories, resistances, and insistences of bodies, human and otherwise. Perhaps this is because its nontheism provides little impetus to denaturalize experience. We do not imagine that the world turns toward us an entirely legible face. In such a world the corporeality of life not only stands before us but also finds expression through us. This is not to say that matter in motion cannot have levels of complexity or have beautiful, even spiritual, effects; it *is* to say that these effects are never external to the variable bodies that harbor them. We do not think Flathman would object to such a naturalistic energetics; it finds expression, for example, in his reading of Thomas Hobbes. But the way he talks does seem to inflect linguistics over somatics, rules over ethical comportments, and conduct over ethos. Consider, for example, his claim that rules are insufficient to the behaviors they enjoin.

Flathman warns against the tendency to "sublime rules" (*Reflections*, 67); that is, to impute an unwarranted efficacy to them. Rules cannot, he says, "themselves determine the conduct of those to whom they apply" (*Reflections*, 55). The gap between rules and conduct is presented as a problem of *signification*. Rules are made up of words, and the signification of words is inherently multiple and fluctuating. Drawing upon Hobbes to explain why this is so, he writes that "the marks that we invent and use, 'besides the signification of what we imagine of their nature, have a signification also of the nature, dispositions, and interest of the speaker'" (*Reflections*, 54). Hobbes could here be taken to say that the formation of a disposition involves a lot of work on several corporeal registers, shaping linguistic signification as well as gestures, skin texture, facial demeanor, tone of voice, heart rate, and so on. To alter a disposition, then, would be to alter several of these zones in relation to the others. Flathman, however, highlights the issue of "unintelligibility" and seems to suggest that bodies play a reduced role as linguistic complexity increases:

> As language develops, ... the minimal discipline and uniformity that perception and the passions impose on language diminish further.

> Although these... deficits in mutual intelligibility are to some extent made good by conventions, as language becomes more abstract... the likelihood of mutual misunderstanding increases apace. (*Reflections*, 54)

Rules are unreliable producers of conduct, Flathman suggests, because the language in which they are set generates misunderstanding within even the most closely knit linguistic community and because "perception and the passions," compared to language, move at a stolid pace.

For us, however, language is not only a matter of significations and failures of signification. It is also about sound, noise, and differential intensities or affects. Is there not, as Gilles Deleuze and Félix Guattari suggest, a "sonority" to language that cannot be ignored as long as humans are animals? Sonority: the aural effectivity that living, moving, snorting, weeping, laughing bodies possess. Sonority does not represent, for it does not operate via images or in the visual mode; it is, rather, a "block that opposes the visual memory."[10] Franz Kafka's stories are filled with enactments of such sonority:

> The receiver gave out a buzz of a kind that K. had never before heard on a telephone. It was like the hum of countless children's voices—but yet not a hum, the echo rather of voices singing at an infinite distance—blended by sheer impossibility into one high but resonant sound which vibrated on the ear as if it were trying to penetrate beyond mere hearing.[11]

This sonorous buzz is neither the form nor the content of expression; it is "pure and intense"; it is "always connected to its own abolition—a deterritorialized musical sound, a cry that escapes signification, composition, song, words."[12] To return to our earlier invocation of Nietzsche and the "illogical" but necessary tendency to "treat as equal what is merely similar": Sonority can often be heard as the babble of differences that have been equalized.

Sonority is a property of bodies-in-space. The sonority K. heard was the emission of an *assemblage* of bodies, some technological, some metallic, some electric, some microbiological, some human. Moreover, each of these bodies can by itself be sonorous. Take, for example, a particular, even "singular" human body: Its teeth grind and chatter, its lips smack and whistle, its tongue says "Ahh." Deleuze and Guattari go so far as to say that to use the mouth for speaking is to "deterritorialize" the mouth from its more primitive, sonorous function. Language use steals the mouth from sound, including those sounds that accompany eating:

[L]anguage always implies a deterritorialization of the mouth, the tongue, and the teeth. The mouth, the tongue, and the teeth find their primitive territoriality in food. In giving themselves over to the articulation of sounds, the mouth, tongue, and teeth deterritorialize. Thus, there is a certain disjunction between eating and speaking, and even more, despite all appearances, between eating and writing [because] ... writing goes further in transforming words into things capable of competing with food.... To speak, and above all to write, is to fast.[13]

"To speak is to fast": Language deterritorializes the mouth, tongue, and teeth; in language, sonority recedes in favor of signification (as well as signification's regular failure). Language steals the mouth from eating and sonority and tries to make it pronounce and mean; language bends the sense of taste into the sense of meaning. But some sonority manages to attach to language use nonetheless. There are cries, moos, meows, buzzes, mutterances, laughter, and so on *in words*. These disruptive sounds make possible a play on words, the spellbinding effect of stories told aloud, the enchanting power of chants:

> Children are well-skilled in the exercise of repeating a word ... in order to make it vibrate around itself.... Kafka tells how, as a child, he repeated one of his father's expressions in order to make it take flight on a line of non-sense: "end of the month, end of the month."[14]

Sonority can distract humans from the sense of what someone is saying and propel them to idiosyncratic associations and thoughts, that is, to engage in something like what Flathman calls an idiolect. Idiolects are "speech acts [that] ... make use, willfully ... of the argot of a social and cultural *sous-monde*" (*Reflections*, 28); they are polyglot, hybridizing ways of talking that disclose the singular character of those whose mouths employ them. The effects of sonority—and perhaps also the effects of idiolection—are only weakly captured by the terms "determinacy" or "indeterminacy."

What difference might augmentation of the "indeterminacy" of language with the "sonority" of language make to thinking about ethics, to thinking about what Flathman frames as the gap between rules and conduct? For one thing, it puts pressure on the theorizer—it nags her—to remember that ethics is about bodies-in-space. Flathman needs a little nagging, we think, for he confines the entities capable of closing the gap between rules and conduct to things like "beliefs," "interpretations," "judgments," the "acceptance, commitment, or subscription" to the rule—

each of which is minimally somatic in the sense that it originates or operates in the first instance in the space of reflection and self-consciousness. Compared to René Descartes, Flathman is a critic of mentalism. Compared to Nietzsche, Deleuze, and Kafka, he inclines toward it.

Flathman shies away from the *how* of belief, interpretation, judgment, acceptance, and so on. What are the bodily regimes; the social rituals; the individual and joint exercises; the litanies, habits, and routines; the institutional and technical organizations of body-space through which one or many might be induced to enact a rule in a particular way? Instead of exploring the gap between belief in an ethical code and the energy to enact it, Flathman explores the gap between "rule-following" and "the question" of a rule's rightness: "[T]he fact that something is an established rule may raise but cannot itself settle the question of whether the rule ought to be obeyed" (*Reflections*, 62). The inadequacy of "rules" to "conduct" is due, then, to the rules' indeterminate meaning (which undermines mutual intelligibility) and to the fact that rules, although discursive entities, do not include the voice of "Thou Must Obey."

We agree that rules are inherently ambiguous, and we agree they do not work without "commitment," "acceptance," "subscription," or a felt sense of "obligation." But these words may underplay the visceral element in the enactment of desires and ethical commitments. The latter require bodily movements in space, mobilizations of heat and energy, an overcoming of somatic inertia by means of movements of the face and limbs, a series of choreographed gestures, a distinctive assemblage of co-incidents.

Flathman at times moves toward this terrain, for example, in his citation of Hobbes and discussion of the passions and dispositions that enter into rules, in his reference to the "inculcation" of the beliefs that surround and inform the practices of rule-following (*Reflections*, 71), and in his claim that "if rules and rule following take us to or away from any destination they do so by the elbow not by the throat (*Reflections*, 50). We are struck, in particular, by the visceral quality of that last statement. In it, Flathman points to a somatic dimension of rule-ing, and he even gestures toward the bodily techniques through which ethics proceed, for good and ill. The ostensible point Flathman makes by means of this statement is that the power of rules is the polite and noncoercive kind of power rather than the crude and aggressive kind. But the statement also marks a point in Flathman's work where rule-following moves from a state of mind and problem of signification to a matter of elbows, throats, postures, comportments, and disciplines.

Why does Flathman not take on more robustly the bodily dimension of rule-following and the how of ethical conduct? In some theorists, the relative neglect of somatic ethos issues from an onto-story within which earthly life and animal behavior are denigrated. It is unlikely, however, that this is the reason in Flathman's case. Flathman's neglect seems to issue, rather, from an aesthetico-political aversion to the regularian personality and to the disciplinary and antisingularity society it would impose. Flathman clearly does not value the "supersensible" over the "sensible." But we wonder whether he sides more with Arendt on the automatism of nature and bodies or with Nietzsche on the dissonance, gaps, and lines of flight in them.

Flathman *likes* rules to be slippery so that people can elude the coercive traps set by them. From the perspective of a would-be anarchist, the gap between rules and conduct is not a sickness to be cured but a condition to be (mildly) treated. More important, it is an opportunity to be exploited, for the failure of rules to self-enact can be part of a project to

> diminish the incidence of rote, mechanical, mimetic, or otherwise submissive behaviors. To the extent that individuals and groups... recognize that interpreting and judging are necessary to rules and rule following, attentive and self-critical thinking and acting will be legitimated and otherwise encouraged. (*Reflections*, 56)

It is Flathman's aversion to moralizing that discourages a close or long consideration of the question of the *how* of ethics. To consider the sonorous element of language as part of its indeterminacy is to think about arts of the self and micropolitics and not just rules and rule-following. And it is to explore the relation between the shape of ethical dispositions and the tactics by which they become installed or modified. These tactics may make Flathman nervous because they could be used to foster uniformity. They sometimes make us nervous too, but we also believe them to be essential, *first, to the development of individuality, and second, to cultivation of responsiveness to the singularity of others.* Is it possible to prize the sonority and ambiguity of language, the diversity of interpretation and self-critical thinking, while also attending to the sensibilities—the organization of intensities and indifferences—that respond to those ambiguities? We think so.

Both Flathman and we place the question (of conduct/ethos) within the frame of a *system* or *network* of relations. For Flathman, that system is rules and rule-following; for us, it is ethos and the somatic, pedagogical, institutional, and imaginational technologies the system involves. We use the phrase "technologies of self" to include both disciplinary practices in the service of the state or cultural regime *and* those disciplines that constitute a more artistically crafted form of ascesis. If the system is first and foremost a system of bodies in space, then the possibility of sonority always exists, and moreover, *we should encourage it and engage in practices that let it be heard.* We look for "where the system is coming from and going to, how it becomes, and what element is going to play the role of heterogeneity, a saturating body that makes the whole assembly flow away and that breaks the symbolic structure, no less than it breaks hermeneutic interpretation, the ordinary association of ideas, and the imaginary archetype."[15]

From Adverbs to Techniques

We imagine the indeterminacy of language and the slippery grip that rules have upon conduct to be situated in a natural-social world that shares similar (non)attributes. Within such an onto-story—of a world of indistinct moral direction and slick natural paths—the assignment or choice of a locus of ethical action is a matter of great import. Flathman places his bets on the willful individual. This is a reasonable wager, especially given the reflective contextualizations with which he surrounds and supplements his "rule-follower":

> [T]here is much to agree with in ... the ... view that *all* rule following, regardless of the clarity and consistency of the rules in question, presupposes a setting of widely shared and seldom-examined concepts, beliefs, and dispositions, of capacities and skills acquired early in one's involvement in an activity and thereafter taken for granted. (*Reflections*, 90).

We would emphasize a plurality of sites of agency: The singular human, nonhuman animals, social movements, the state, nonstate corporate actors, and so on are all significant actors. But just as important as the site of moral agency is the issue of *how* it is to be prepared and maintained. As the passage just quoted suggests, Flathman's individual seems to be more or less fixed "early in one's involvement"; for us, the individual, though not double-jointed, is often a bit more limber, hence our ethical interest in the techniques of later-in-life change. Perhaps another reason for this differential interest is Flathman's intense sense of the extent to which "we are enigmas to one another" (*Reflections*, 91) and to ourselves. We suspect that Flathman too quickly reduces micropolitics to regularian impositions on selves who would otherwise be enigmas. We think that such techniques can also foster individuality, *and* that they can render us more responsive to the individuality of others. Following Foucault in his last works, we distinguish between disciplinary power and self-direction qua ascesis.

Flathman himself walks a little way down this slippery road. Following Michael Oakeshott, he admires a form of "the rule of law that, were it fully and durably realizable, would recommend a less suspicious or antagonistic stance toward this institution" (*Reflections*, 95). This ideal form is an "adverbial" kind of social discipline wherein rule-followers (also known as *cives*) "are associated with one another not by agreement in objective or purpose but exclusively by their subscription to ... rules that do not require them to do this or that but rather to do whatever they do in certain (civil) ways or manners" (*Reflections*, 95). This version of the rule of law aims not to authorize a particular set of ethical actions or pursuits or to determine "substantive satisfactions" (as Oakeshott calls them). Rather, the goal is to govern the performative style of "self-chosen actions" (Flathman's phrase), that is, to shape civil "personae" for rule-followers.

How are civil personae, or masks, formed? Flathman says little about the mechanism of such productions, but we might glean something from his vocabulary. We know that such a persona requires one to "subscribe" to the rule and to the adverbial practices enjoined by it, that is, "punctually, considerately, civilly, scientifically, legally, candidly, judicially, poetically, morally, etc." (*Reflections*, 97). "Subscription" seems to involve something like cool assent to an originally external rule, a kind of voluntary submission of will. Oakeshott says there is nothing of "enthusiasm" about it. Civil personae also adopt a particular "understanding" of conduct: The dimension of conduct to be focused upon is not its particular content but its procedural form. The emphasis is on the how, not the what, of conduct: Under ideal conditions, the "rule of law" is concerned solely with the (civil) *character of the enactment* of actions, actions whose substance comes from elsewhere. A third element in the production of civil personae is "discipline." The adverbial requirements of the rules are markers of the need to restrict the imagination of "substantive satisfactions" to those aims capable of being enacted in the proscribed manner or style:

> *Cives* must cultivate their human capacities to imagine desirable outcomes and to devise ways of pursuing them. At the same time, they must subject that imagination and those pursuits to the discipline of the considerations signaled by words such as *politely, temperately,* and *fastidiously; resolutely, candidly,* and *forthrightly; morally, legally,* and *civilly*.[16]

Nonetheless, although Flathman admires Oakeshott's strategy of "looking to qualities of character, understanding, and spirit rather than power-driven political mechanics to abate the difficulties inherent in political association" (*Reflections*, 99), he ultimately rejects it as unrealizable. Flathman then returns to the position that inspired his willful liberalism in the first place: a stance of iconoclastic dissidence and intense skepticism of political institutions. But when one sees that there are many adverbial relations that are *not* "civil," such as acting belligerently, cruelly, stingily, crudely, or violently, it becomes apparent that Flathman cannot avoid the dangerous terrain of moral judgments or even of ethical work on the self. He leaves the field of "character, understanding, and spirit" too soon. Perhaps greater attention to the how of critical civility might offer an alternative to a political minimalism. Such attention is needed, we suspect, even to support and sustain gadfly personae.

The Ambiguity of the State

Flathman is an enthusiast of the enigmatic individual and a nervous Nelly about the state. He pursues a "nervous combination of grudging acceptance and pervasive skepticism of government and politics" (*Reflections*, 79). We find this distribution of enthusiasm and grudgery to be skewed. By setting the liberating potential of individuality against the constraining effects of the state, Flathman underestimates how much existing state priorities support the conditions of individuality for some and limit the individuality of others. He also neglects, as the tag line "government and politics" suggests, the significant role that other institutional actors besides the individual and the state play in politics. As Flathman himself discloses in the case of so many other words, "politics" is a protean word and a protean set of activities. It involves direct state governance of individual conduct; social movements that pluralize or curtail the institutional possibilities of identity; micropolitical engagements that open up or close down a productive public ethos of diversity; corporate actions that shape consumption and employment options for the general population; state support or neglect for those facing unemployment, poverty, lack of child care, substandard housing, or homelessness; state regulation or subsidy of corporate policies; state support or neglect of such general infrastructural needs as education, roads, airports and rail lines, the quality of the environment, inclusive modes of consumption; and so on.

Seen in this broader perspective, Flathman's formula of enthusiasm and grudgery is likely to appeal most to individuals who prosper within the established priorities of the state and the corporate economy. To extend the social conditions of individuality to a wider segment of the populace is to balance selective skepticism toward the state against selective skepticism toward affluent modes of individualism that forget the special entitlements, subsidies, and supports upon which they rest. To broaden the scope of individuality today is to deploy the state positively to improve the general quality of public education, generalize health care, incorporate diversity into the military, increase corporate regulation, support job training, subsidize child care, finance welfare, and enhance environmental protection. Above all, success in any of these areas depends upon the catalyzing effect of social movements, which in turn require periodic outbursts of political enthusiasm.

Politics is as protean as individuality, and it is terribly important to the vibrancy and range of the latter. If a robust political culture were deflated significantly, many of the most admirable things in contemporary life, including the cultural infrastructure of individuality, would stagnate or contract. The experience of citizenship in the contemporary democratic state is, of course, asymmetrical, with the opportunities and benefits of participation varying significantly across lines of age, class, gender, ability, and race. Nonetheless, the most positive thing about the experience of citizenship remains its influence on the ethos of public and private life. The right to vote leaders in and out of office at a variety of levels of government renders our relations with bosses, teachers, corporate officials, welfare workers, police officers, university administrators, and government bureaucrats more critical and skeptical. These bouts of rambunctious independence, in turn, encourage the formation of social movements in the domains of gender, welfare, employment, gay and lesbian rights, union organization, welfare support, and environmental protection. Without such movements, the institutional space of individuality in schools, armies, corporations, unions, families, and public bureaucracies would wither. To the extent that the energies of multilayered citizenship become depleted, the possibilities of individuality itself are restricted and jeopardized. So the decline of citizenship—or the rise of cynicism—is not something an individualist should accept with equanimity. Selective skepticism toward the state is important, but in a pluralist and pluralizing culture, such skepticism must be matched by a vigorous practice of targeted, enthusiastic citizenship.

We agree with Flathman that the state is an ambiguous entity. But we inflect the terms of that ambiguity differently. The state does embody a standing temptation to normalize a variety of individuals. It also, however, functions as a target of social movements seeking to improve the prospects for plurality in one way or another, and if and when we are active and lucky, it enacts general policies in support of plurality. Creative pluralists seek to mobilize the state to foster conditions of cultural pluralism and individuality. It is true that state institutionalization too often "renders unfree, constant and predictable that which would otherwise be diverse, fluctuating and uncertain" (*Reflections*, 79). But it is important, for example, that the state regulate corporations that would otherwise be ruthless in their disciplinary practices. That sort of regulation, rather than squashing individuality and difference, can often protect and nourish them. Mandating the rights of gays to marry and to participate openly in the military is a form of state intervention that enhances pluralization. Similarly, as health maintenance organizations (HMOs) replace collective insurance schemes based on individual fees to doctors, it is pertinent to acknowledge how such a development both reduces per-capita medical costs and makes medical care available to more people. Rather than opposing the extension of HMOs in the interests of maintaining individual control over the choice of doctor (whatever the individual and collective financial cost), political pressure might be mobilized to give HMO patients greater leeway over doctor choice and to place the most crucial lifesaving medical services under the HMO umbrella. The state must get involved in these issues because it is already up to its neck in selective tax subsidies and supports for medical care.

Other state-centered movements are possible in employment, transportation, and environmental protection that support general welfare and individuality alike.

We know that our earlier invocation of Nietzsche sets us up to receive a Nietzschean rebuke about the state. Nietzsche's Zarathustra sees the state as "a new idol." The state "is the name of the coldest of all cold monsters. Coldly it tells lies too; and this lie crawls out of its mouth: 'I the state, am the people.'"[17] We, too, resist the quest of the state to identify itself as the people, but we often find it is the diverse energies of democratic citizenship that provide the best antidote to that tendency. We do endorse, with Zarathustra and Flathman, the need periodically to fly like an eagle above and beyond the state, to escape it for more artistic, more unlikely worlds. Such flights can expand and enrich the cultural imaginary, and they can also help induce generosity and joy— moods that, as Zarathustra also notes, are important supports for ethical life:

> Verily, I may have done this and that for sufferers; but always I seem to have done better when I learned to feel better joys. As long as there have been men, man has felt too little joy: that alone, my brothers, is our original sin. And learning better to feel joy, we best unlearn how to do harm to others and to contrive harm.[18]

Free spirits, especially today, are implicated in numerous and extensive patterns of interdependence. Even the eagles among us find themselves more and more managed, constrained, and enabled by state and corporate power. When one connects these temporal changes to Nietzsche's expectation of periodic surprises prepared below the level of cultural attention, it becomes clear how much a democratic state is needed to smooth out the worst effects of those collective surprises and to make something out of their positive possibilities. The state is dangerous precisely because it is indispensable. Its practices often deserve skepticism and criticism because the nourishment of plurality, civility, and individuality are so closely bound up with necessary bouts of political enthusiasm involving the state. There is no way to eliminate this fundamental ambiguity. The best thing is to juxtapose periodic flights with political engagements, to intersperse political skepticism with political enthusiasm. "Grudging acceptance" does not cut it.

Finally, it must be said that the politics of social movements must rise above the confines of the state as well as operate within it. When the U.S. state set out to investigate outer space, an unexpected cultural dividend was received. In 1968, *Apollo 8* sent back pictures of a vivid blue planet suspended in the middle of the solar system, a stunning, bright sphere unlike any other planet observable from the ground of the earth itself. This picture of the earth, taken from a site outside it, underlined how unique it is by comparison to other planets so far encountered. The others cannot even hold water, whereas the fine balance the earth maintains between evaporation and precipitation is sustained to a considerable degree by the behavior of *life* on the planet.[19] Today, states and corporations collide and collude to jeopardize the balances favorable to life. Neither a retreat to individualism nor absorption in state politics can suffice to counter these global tendencies. Nonstatist, cross-national movements, attentive to the global effects of local actions, are needed to put internal and external pressure on states, corporations, and individuals. In the late-modern time, the sites of citizen politics must be pluralized to compete with the range of global corporations. Of course, the obstacles are severe, and the chances of success are limited. Everyone knows that. But the stakes are also very high. The best chance to make up the deficits of politics comes from political mobilizations that reach the levels of agency through which the mess has been created.

Besides, it seems highly unlikely that the state will become the most dangerous idol in the United States of today or tomorrow. The "Judeo-Christian civilization," the purified nation, and the normal, disenchanted individual are more dangerous and more likely candidates for idolatry. The drive to restore the nation, for instance, is led by those who seek to weaken the capacity of the state to support general conditions of cultural diversity. We stand with Flathman against the nation, then, even while we demure from his singular grudge against the state. We contend—against nationalists and political minimalists alike—that cultivation of a positive ethos of political engagement between diverse constituencies provides the best basis for action below, at, and above the state in support of the social and economic conditions of cultural pluralism.

We are indebted to Richard Flathman for his supple philosophy of language, his appreciation of individuality, and his antinationalism, even as we resist the political minimalism in which those insights are set. Of course, we are not entirely sure how closely our readings of Flathman's reflective, sinuous prose correspond to the visceral intensities invested in it. We know for sure that Flathman's work challenges us to rethink things we thought we knew and to think for the first time about things we had previously left in the somatic stupor of the unthought.

Notes

1. Richard E. Flathman, *Reflections of a Would-Be Anarchist* (Minneapolis: University of Minnesota Press, 1997), 57; hereafter *Reflections*.

2. Friedrich Nietzsche, *The Gay Science*, trans. Walter Kaufmann (New York: Vintage Books, 1974), para. 111, p. 171.

3. Michel Foucault, "On the Genealogy of Ethics: An Overview of Work in Progress," in *The Foucault Reader*, ed. Paul Rabinow (New York: Pantheon, 1984), 369.

4. John Dupré, *The Disorder of Things: Metaphysical Foundations of the Disunity of Science* (Cambridge, Mass.: Harvard University Press, 1993).

5. Ilya Prigogine, the Nobel Prize–winning chemist, speaks of physical systems far from equilibrium that at key moments arrive at "bifurcation points," when a new formation appears. The outcomes of such forks, he says, exceed the powers of scientific prediction because of the very character of the "fluctuations" from which they emerge. The system "'chooses'... but nothing in the macroscopic equations justifies the preference for any one solution. This introduces an irreducible probabilistic element" (Ilya Prigogine and Isabelle Stengers, *Order out of Chaos: Man's New Dialogue with Nature* [New York: Bantam Books, 1984], 68).

6. The visceral register is the register of faith, and there is seldom or never a vacuum there. It consists of protothoughts and judgments too inarticulate and rough to be situated on the epistemic register. But its thought-imbued intensities nonetheless exert effects upon the epistemic level, affecting how one receives and inflects a porous argument (and all argument is porous), the degree one goes to in order to preserve a belief, the level of tolerance one has for paradox in one's beliefs, and so on. Contestation here is more performative and technical than argumentative. But most styles of argument and discourse move on the epistemic and performative registers simultaneously.

7. See Donella H. Meadows, *The Global Citizen* (Washington, D.C.: Island Press, 1991), 190–92; also on-line; available: http://www.livingmachines.com; 31 January 2002.

8. Nietzsche, *The Gay Science*, para. 112.

9. Ibid., preface, para. 4, p. 37.

10. Gilles Deleuze and Félix Guattari, *Kafka: Toward a Minor Literature* (Minneapolis: University of Minnesota Press, 1989), 5; hereafter *Kafka*.

11. Franz Kafka, *The Castle*, in *The Collected Novels of Franz Kafka* (New York: Penguin Books, 1988), 197–98.

12. Deleuze and Guattari, *Kafka*, 6.

13. Ibid., 20.

14. Ibid., p. 21.

15. Deleuze and Guattari, *Kafka*, 7.

16. Michael Oakeshott, *On History and Other Essays* (Totowa, N.J.: Barnes and Noble, 1983), 125.

17. Friedrich Nietzsche, *Thus Spoke Zarathustra*, trans. Walter Kaufmann (New York: Vintage Books, 1974), 48.

18. Nietzsche, *Zarathustra*, "On the Pitying," part 2, section 3.

19. Even when the planet was crystallizing into the earth, a "decisive reason why it was able to hold on to these volatile layers of melted comets was the emergence of living organisms which regulated crucial climatic conditions and kept them constant" (Tor Norretranders, *The User Illusion*, trans. Jonathan Syndenham [New York: Viking Press, 1998], 340).

Annotated Bibliography of Works by Richard Flathman

Books

The Public Interest: An Essay Concerning the Normative Discourse of Politics. New York: John Wiley and Sons, 1966.

    Against various skeptics, Flathman argues that the idea of the public interest has an important role in reasoned political discourse. Using ordinary language philosophy in order to open up shared ground for philosophy and political science, he maintains that we can arrive at well-founded judgments about the public interest in particular contexts, using systematic reasoning about purposes, rules, consequences, principles, and imperatives. Although emphasizing utilitarian standards of assessment in reasoning about the public interest, Flathman accepts moral pluralism as well as some appeal to political authority in cases where reasons give out in the face of competing values.

Political Obligation. New York: Atheneum, 1972.

    Flathman takes issue with theorists who argue that "obligatory" is part of the meaning of "law" and who charge that an attempt to justify obligation is therefore a sign of philosophical confusion. Instead, he argues that political obligation rests on a social practice that is binding because it is widely accepted and has good consequences. Flathman rejects the demand for a single ground of obligation and analyzes the various justifications of political obligation offered by Hobbes and Socrates. In order to create obligation, a state and society must embody values worthy of respect; citizens should have some share in determining legislation; emigration must be possible; and claims to obedience cannot rest on groundless assertions about the "contagious" effects of disobedience.

The Practice of Rights. Cambridge and New York: Cambridge University Press, 1976.

    Arguing against natural rights theorists, Flathman analyzes rights in terms of rule-governed social practices. Instead of a right to be free of interference, he presents a weaker "liberal principle," which claims that it is, prima facie, a good thing for people to be in a position to act upon and satisfy their interests, desires, objectives, and purposes. This principle stands in opposition to the claims of ascetics and perfectionists, who wish to argue that coercion is as "natural" or as warranted as liberty. Flathman criticizes libertarian or "private individualist" thinkers who celebrate private property rights, and he argues that the "civic individualism" of Aristotle, Rousseau, and Arendt shows that rights and community are compatible.

The Practice of Political Authority: Authority and the Authoritative. Chicago: University of Chicago Press, 1980.

Flathman argues in favor of formal-procedural theories of authority over substantive-purposive theories but then complicates the formal-procedural model of authority in several ways. He argues that a practice of authority depends upon a background of "authoritative" beliefs and values among those who recognize the authority of rules. Teleological or consequentialist considerations must also be taken into account in justifying authority. As far as possible, authority should enhance the freedom of agents, and there must be a place for civil disobedience in any practice of authority in order to allow the reevaluation and revision of rules.

The Philosophy and Politics of Freedom. Chicago: University of Chicago Press, 1987.

Outlining five types of freedom, Flathman argues for an idea of freedom as "situated" and "negative." Freedom of action involves an agent who is a participant in a shared, mutually meaningful language and set of social practices; the final arbiter of his or her socially influenced desires; and unhindered by obstacles put in place by other agents. "Positive," "autonomy," and "virtue-based" conceptions of freedom are rejected because they treat desires as brute forces or conflate freedom with other values. Flathman argues that in Western, liberal societies, freedom of action is valued in a deep, or "elemental," way. Thus, the burden of proof rests on those who would restrict freedom. In each case, such restrictions must be evaluated in terms of the interests and ends involved in particular social contexts.

Toward a Liberalism. Ithaca, New York: Cornell University Press, 1989.

This collection of essays develops common liberal themes from the study of several different issues, including the relationship between theory and practice, liberalism and authority, citizenship and authority, liberalism and the good of freedom, the need to moderate rights, and the justification of abortion rights. Drawing on Wittgenstein and Oakeshott, Flathman argues for a liberalism based on agreement in judgments about conceptions of the good and therefore against contemporary theorists such as Rawls and Ackerman, who wish for a more neutral kind of liberalism.

Willful Liberalism: Voluntarism and Individuality in Political Theory and Practice. Ithaca, New York: Cornell University Press, 1992.

Flathman draws on many writers not commonly thought of as liberal—such as Hobbes, William of Ockham, William James, Nietzsche, and Oakeshott—in order to develop a version of liberalism that stands in tension with current strands of liberal thought. Flathman's vision of a complementary relationship between individualism and social plurality entails a strong commitment to preserving the place of individuals situated in but never subsumed by their communities. His notion of "strong voluntarism" captures the privileged place of the "will" and willfulness as preeminently sources of self-control and self-command rather than as means of controlling or commanding others.

Thomas Hobbes: Skepticism, Individuality, and Chastened Politics. Newbury Park, Calif.: Sage Publications, 1993.

Flathman reads Hobbes's political philosophy as a valuable resource for a kind of liberalism that privileges opacity, unpredictability, self-making, and self-command, while always holding authority in suspicion. Hobbes's philosophy is interpreted as rooted in a deep skepticism and nominalism and as expressing a strongly individualist vision of human beings as authors of themselves and their worlds.

Reflections of a Would-Be Anarchist: Ideals and Institutions of Liberalism. Minneapolis: University of Minnesota Press, 1998.

Situating himself in a tradition of thinkers who focus on self-making and self-enactment—including Aristotle, Montaigne, Hobbes, and Nietzsche—Flathman begins by recognizing the appeal of anarchism while remaining committed to the necessity of institutions. In the essays that follow, these commitments inform his analysis and critique of rule-following, the rule of law, the police and policing, liberal versus civic, republican and democratic education, and the ways liberal polities sustain plurality and singularity.

Edited Volumes

Concepts in Social and Political Philosophy. Edited and with a contribution by Richard Flathman. New York: Macmillan, 1973.

H. L. Mencken. *The Philosophy of Friedrich Nietzsche.* Edited with a new introduction by Richard E. Flathman. New Brunswick, N.J.: Transaction Books, 1993.

Thomas Hobbes. *Leviathan: Authoritative Text, Backgrounds, Interpretations.* Edited with annotations and critical essays by Richard E. Flathman and David Johnston. New York: W. W. Norton and Company, 1997.

Articles

"Forms and Limits of Utilitarianism." *Ethics* 76 (July 1966): 309–17.

"Some Familiar but False Dichotomies Concerning 'Interests': A Comment on Benditt and Oppenheim." *Political Theory* 3, no. 3 (August 1975): 277–87.

"On the Alleged Impossibility of an Unqualified Disjustificatory Theory of Property Rights." In *Property* (Nomos 22), ed. J. R. Pennock and J. W. Chapman. New York: New York University Press, 1980.

"Rights, Needs, and Liberalism: A Comment on Bay." *Political Theory* 8, no. 3 (August 1980): 319–30.

"Liberalism and Authority." *Colorado College Studies,* 1981.

"Power, Authority, and Individual Rights in the Practice of Medicine." In *Responsibility in Health Care,* ed. George J. Agich. Dordrecht: Reidel, 1982.

"Rights, Utility, and Civil Disobedience," in *Ethics, Economics, and the Law* (Nomos 24), ed. J. R. Pennock and J. W. Chapman. New York: New York University Press, 1982.

"The Rights of Volunteers." In *Volunteerism in the Eighties*, ed. John D. Harman. Washington, D.C.: University Press of America, 1983.

"Egalitarian Blood and Skeptical Turnips." *Ethics* 93, no. 2 (January 1983): 357–66.

"Culture, Morality, and Rights." *Analyse und Kritik* 1, no. 1 (July 1984).

"Moderating Rights." *Social Philosophy and Policy* 1 (1984): 149–71.

"Liberalism and the Human Good of Freedom." In *Liberals on Liberalism*, ed. A. Damico. Totowa, N.J.: Rowman and Alanhead, 1986.

"Moderating Rights." In *Human Rights*, ed. Ellen Frankel Paul. Oxford: Blackwell, 1986.

"Convention, Contractarianism, and Freedom." *Ethics* 98, no. 1 (October 1987): 91–103.

"Absolutism, Individuality, and Politics: Hobbes and a Little Beyond." *History of European Ideas* 10, no. 5 (1989): 547–68.

"Liberalism." In *Encyclopedia of Ethics*, ed. Lawrence C. Becker. New York: Garland Publishers, 1992.

"Legitimacy." In *A Companion to Political Philosophy*, ed. Robert Goodin and Philip Petit. Oxford: Basil Blackwell, 1993.

"Liberalism and the Suspect Enterprise of Political Institutionalization: The Case of the Rule of Law." In *The Rule of Law* (Nomos 36), ed. Ian Shapiro. New York: New York University Press, 1994.

"Liberalism: From Unicity to Plurality and on to Singularity." *Social Research* 61, no. 3 (Fall 1994): 671.

"Hannah Arendt." In *The Cambridge Encyclopedia of Philosophy*, ed. Robert Audi. London: Cambridge University Press, 1995.

"Michael Oakeshott." In *The Cambridge Encyclopedia of Philosophy*, ed. Robert Audi. London: Cambridge University Press, 1995.

"Political Theory." In *The Cambridge Encyclopedia of Philosophy*, ed. Robert Audi. London: Cambridge University Press, 1995.

"Strains in and around Liberal Theory: An Overview from a Strong Voluntarist Perspective." In *The Liberal Political Tradition: Contemporary Reappraisals*, ed. James Meadowcraft. London: Edward Elgar, 1995.

"The Good or Goodnesses of Polity and Politics à la Liberalism: Plurality Rather Than Unicity, Singularity beyond Plurality." *Cardozo Journal of International and Comparative Law* 4, no. 2 (Fall 1995).

"Liberal versus Civic, Republican, Democratic, and Other Vocational Educations: Liberalism and Institutionalized Education." *Political Theory* 24, no. 1 (February 1996): 4–32.

"The Imagined and Wished for Imperium of Reason and Science: Russell's Empiricism and Its Relation to His and Our Ethics and Politics." *Philosophy of the Social Sciences* 26, no. 2 (June 1996): 162–80.

"Hobbes: Premier Theorist of Authority." *Hobbes Studies* 10 (1997): 3–22.

"Exchange with Stephen Macedo." *Political Theory* 26, no. 1 (February 1998): 81–84; 26, no. 3 (1998): 397–98.

"Fraternal, but Not Always Sisterly Twins: Negativity and Positivity in Liberal Theory." *Social Research* 66, no. 4 (Winter 1999): 1137–42.

"Wittgenstein and the Social Sciences: Critical Reflections Concerning Peter Winch's Interpretations and Appropriations of Wittgenstein's Thought." *History of the Human Sciences* 13, no. 2 (May 2000): 1–16.

"The Self against and for Itself: Montaigne and Sextus Empiricus on Freedom, Discipline, and Resistance." *The Monist* 83, no. 4 (October 2000): 491–529.

Book Reviews

Rational Decision (Nomos 7), by Carl J. Freidrich. *The American Political Science Review* 59, no. 2 (June 1965): 452–54.

Forms and Limits of Utilitarianism, by David Lyons. *Ethics* 76, no. 4 (July 1966): 309–17.

L'Obligation Politique, by Raymond Polin. *The American Political Science Review* 67, no. 2 (June 1973): 606–7.

Praxis and Action: Contemporary Philosophies of Human Activity, by Richard Bernstein. *The Journal of Politics* 35, no. 3 (August 1973): 747–53.

Wittgenstein and Justice, by Hanna Fenichel Pitkin. *The Journal of Politics* 35, no. 3 (August 1973): 747–53.

Anarchy and Cooperation, by M. Taylor. *Political Theory* 5, no. 2 (1977): 271–75.

The Shotgun behind the Door: Liberalism and the Problem of Political Obligation, by Philip Abbot. *The American Political Science Review* 72, no. 1 (March 1978): 211–12.

From Contract to Community: Political Theory at the Crossroads, by Fred R. Dallmayr. *The American Political Science Review* 73, no. 4 (December 1979): 1124–25.

Wittgenstein and Political Philosophy: A Reexamination of the Foundations of Social Science, by John W. Danford. *The Journal of Politics* 42, no. 1 (February 1980): 336–38.

A Matter of Principle, by Ronald Dworkin. *The American Political Science Review* 80, no. 2 (June 1986): 647–48.

Contingency, Irony, and Solidarity, by Richard Rorty. *Political Theory* 18, no. 2 (May 1990): 308.

Representations in American Politics, edited by Frederick M. Dolan and Thomas L. Dumm. *The American Political Science Review* 88, no. 4 (December 1994): 992–93.

Republic of Signs: Liberal Theory and American Popular Culture, by Anne Norton. *The American Political Science Review* 88, no. 4 (December 1994): 992–93.

Liberalism without Illusions: Essays on Liberal Theory and the Political Vision of Judith N. Shklar, by Bernard Yack. *The American Political Science Review* 90, no. 3 (September 1996): 642.

States of Injury: Power and Freedom in Late Modernity, by Wendy Brown. *Political Theory* 24, no. 4 (November 1996): 728–34.

Reason and Rhetoric in the Philosophy of Hobbes, by Quentin Skinner. *Ethics* 108, no. 4 (July 1998): 820–23.

Democracy's Discontent: America in Search of a Public Philosophy, by Michael Sandel. *The Philosophical Quarterly* 48, no. 193 (October 1998): 563–66.

Civic Virtues, by Richard Dagger. *Ethics* 109, no. 3 (April 1999): 659–61.

Sustaining Affirmation: The Strength of Weak Ontology in Political Theory, by Stephen K. White. *The Journal of Politics* 63, no. 4 (November 2001): 1302–3.

Contributors

Ronald Beiner is professor of political science at the University of Toronto. His books include *Political Judgment, Philosophy in a Time of Lost Spirit: Essays on Contemporary Theory, What's the Matter with Liberalism?* and the edited volumes *Hannah Arendt's Lectures on Kant's Political Philosophy, Theorizing Citizenship, Theorizing Nationalism, Kant and Political Philosophy: The Contemporary Legacy* (coedited with William James Booth), and *Canadian Political Philosophy: Contemporary Reflections* (coedited with Wayne Norman).

Jane Bennett teaches political theory at Goucher College. She is the author of *Thoreau's Nature* and *The Enchantment of Modern Life*.

William E. Connolly teaches political theory at The Johns Hopkins University, where he is professor and chair, and where his office is next to Richard Flathman's. His book *The Terms of Political Disclosure* (originally published in 1974) won the 1999 Lippincott Award for "a work of exceptional quality... still considered significant after a time span of fifteen years." Among his most recent publications are *The Ethos of Pluralization, Why I Am Not a Secularist,* and *Neuropolitics: Thinking, Culture, Speed,* all published by the University of Minnesota Press.

Peter Digeser is associate professor of political science at the University of California, Santa Barbara. His work has focused on the concept of power, the role of identity in liberal theory, and the place of ethics in international relations. He is the author of *Our Politics, Our Selves?* and *Political Forgiveness.*

Richard Friedman is a retired professor of political science at the State University of New York, Buffalo. His current research is in ancient Greek and Roman legal thought and contemporary political theory.

Nancy J. Hirschmann is associate professor of government at Cornell University. She is author of *Rethinking Obligation: A Feminist Method for Political Theory* and coeditor (with Christine Di Stefano) of *Revisioning the Political: Feminist Reconstructions of Traditional Concepts in Western Political Theory* and (with Ulrike Liebert) of *Women and Welfare: Theory and Practice in the United States and Europe.* She has been a fellow at the Bunting Institute of Radcliffe College, a National Endowment for the Humanities fellow at the Institute for Advanced Study in Princeton, and a recipient of an American Council of Learned Societies fellowship. She is currently finishing a book on the concept of freedom.

Bonnie Honig is professor of political science at Northwestern University and senior research fellow at the American Bar Foundation in Chicago. She is the author of *Democracy and the Foreigner* and *Political Theory and the Displacement of Politics,* as well as the editor of *Feminist Interpretations of Hannah Arendt.*

George Kateb teaches political theory at Princeton University. Among his books are *Hannah Arendt: Politics, Conscience, Evil; The Inner Ocean: Individualism and Democratic Culture;* and *Emerson and Self-Reliance.*

David R. Mapel is associate professor of political science at the University of Colorado, Boulder. He is author of *Social Justice Reconsidered* and coeditor (with Terry Nardin) of *Traditions of International Ethics* and of *International Society: Diverse Ethical Perspectives.* He has also published articles on the idea of civil association, political obligation, moral pluralism, and various ethical issues in international relations.

Patrick Neal is associate professor of political science at the University of Vermont. He is author of *Liberalism and Its Discontents* and other essays on liberal political thought.

Contributors

Anne Norton is professor of political science at the University of Pennsylvania. She is author of *Republic of Signs, Reflections on Political Identity*, and *Alternative Americas*.

Richard Tuck is professor of government at Harvard University. His books include *Natural Rights Theories, Hobbes*, and *Philosophy and Government, 1572–1651*. His current research concerns political thought and international law, tracing the history of thought about international politics through Grotius, Hobbes, Pufendorf, Locke, Vattel, and Kant. He is also engaged in work on the origins of twentieth-century economic thought.

Jeremy J. Waldron is Maurice and Hilda Friedman Professor of Law at Columbia University and director of Columbia's Center for Law and Philosophy. His publications include *The Right to Private Property, Nonsense upon Stilts, Liberal Rights, Law and Disagreement*, and *The Dignity of Legislation*, and he is author of numerous articles on liberalism, rights, social justice, democracy, cosmopolitanism, and the history of political philosophy.

Linda Zerilli is professor of political science at Northwestern University. She is author of *Signifying Woman: Culture and Chaos in Rousseau, Burke, and Mill* and the forthcoming *Feminism and the Abyss of Freedom*.

Index

Abraham, 237
Ackerman, Bruce, 3, 266
Amiranti, Luigi, 160
Anscombe, G. E. M., 40, 53
Arendt, Hannah, 52 n.3, 53–54 n.12, 116, 118, 125 n.13, 200, 247, 255, 266
Aristotle, 89, 164, 167, 175, 184, 189, 209 n.73, 222, 223, 266, 267

Bauman, Zygmunt, 11
Beiner, Ronald, xii, xiii, xv, 111–26
Belliotti, Raymond, 30
Benn, Stanley, 137
Bennett, Jane, xi, xiii, xv, 244–64
Berlin, Isaiah, xi, xii, 17, 18, 24, 56, 128–37, 153 n.31
Blake, William, 233
Bradley, Keith, 174
Brunt, P. A., 162, 163, 166
Burke, Edmund, 233
Buryeat, Myles, 52 n.3

Caesar, 165
Calvin, John, 21
Cavell, Stanley, 33, 36, 44–51
Clinton, Bill, 232
Coleridge, Samuel Taylor, 238
Conant, James, 49, 53 n.8, 54 n.17
Connolly, William, xi, xiii, xv, 244–64
Constant, Benjamin, 17

Cicero, 33
Cover, Robert, 15
cummings, e. e., 238
Cyrus, 241

Deleuze, Gilles, 252–53, 254
Derrida, Jacques, 240
Descartes, René, 36, 52 n.3, 254
Didier, Philippe, 156, 159
Digeser, Peter, xii, 56–85
Diogenes, Laertius, 173
Donaldson, Peter S., 207 n.45
Dumont, J.-C., 159
Dupré, John, 248
Dworkin, Ronald, xii, 3, 7, 33

Emerson, Ralph Waldo, x, 86, 87, 89, 92, 94–98, 104–7

Finley, Moses, 162
Florentinus, 162–66
Foucault, Michel, x, 114, 124 n.6, 134, 135, 236, 247, 257
Freud, Sigmund, 98
Friedman, Richard, xiii, 155–79
Frost, Robert, 99

Gaius, 157
Galston, William, 122
George, Robert P., 8

Gerenscer, Anthony Stephen, 83 n.2
Gilligan, Carol, 145
Goffman, Erving, xi, 118
Goldman, Emma, 238
Green, T. H., 7, 33, 56
Guattari, Félix, 252–53
Gutmann, Amy, 33, 122

Habermas, Jürgen, ix, xii, 56, 121, 122, 234, 247
Hampton, Jean, 207 n.31, 208–9 n.66
Hartsock, Nancy, 127
Hayek, Friedrich, 84 n.15
Hegel, G. W. F., 11, 56
Heidegger, Martin, 121, 231, 232, 240, 247
Hekman, Susan, 127, 145
Herzog, Don, 30
Hirschmann, Nancy, xiii, xv, 127–54
Hobbes, Thomas, xiv, 28, 29, 52 n.3, 112, 115, 118, 124 n.2, 130, 132, 137, 174, 180–205, 213–28, 228 n.10, 228 n.14, 228–29 n.17, 229 n.21, 229 n.38, 230 n.43, 242 n.15, 251, 266, 267
Hobhouse, L. T., 7, 56
Honig, Bonnie, ix–xvi, 127
Honore, A. M., 168
Hume, David, 33, 34

James, William, xi, 2, 9, 29, 35, 41, 44, 51, 56, 86, 87, 118, 119, 122, 123, 126 n.17, 266
Johnston, David, 195

Kafka, Franz, 252–54
Kant, Immanuel, 21, 56, 131, 212, 224
Kaser, Max, 168
Kateb, George, xiii, xiv, xv, 86–110
Kaufmann, Walter, 26
Kelsen, Hans, 161
Kierkegaard, Søren, 9
Koselleck, Reinhart, 234
Kraynack, Robert, 203
Kripke, Samuel, 53 n.9

Lawrence, D. H., 109 n.5
Levy-Bruhl, Henri, 155
Lincoln, Abraham, 238
Livy, 165
Locke, John, 56, 212, 213

MacCallum, Gerald, 177
Macedo, Stephen, 16, 122
Machiavelli, Niccolò, 27, 28, 200, 211 n.112
MacIntyre, Alasdair, 18
Mapel, David, ix–xvi
Marcian, 164
Mencken, H. L., 238
Mill, John Stuart, 24, 46, 56, 104, 118, 212
Montaigne, Michel, 33, 115, 118, 213, 267
Muhammed, 238

Naaman the Syrian, 219
Neal, Patrick, xi, xii, xiv, xv, 1–32, 237
Nehamas, Alexander, 109 n.19
Nietzsche, Friedrich, x, xi, xiii, 20, 21, 29, 30, 35, 51, 56, 86, 87, 88, 104–5, 109 n.19, 113–15, 118, 121, 125 n.11, 126 n.17, 213, 214, 236, 238, 239, 241, 245–50, 252, 254, 255, 261, 266, 267
Norretranders, Tor, 264 n.19
Norton, Anne, xi, xiv, xv, 231–43
Nozick, Robert, 3

Oakeshott, Michael, x, xi, xii, xiii, 17, 22, 31, 56–85, 113, 118, 124 n.2, 125 n.14, 126 n.17, 257, 258, 266
Okin, Susan, 145
Ortega y Gassett, José, 26–28, 56, 118, 146
Ostwald, Martin, 162

Pascal, Blaise, 33
Paul, St., 193
Pears, David, 43
Perloff, Marjorie, 53 n.7
Pettit, Philip, 155
Philo, 173
Pitkin, Hanna F., 162
Plato, 62, 69, 90, 206 n.9
Poirier, Richard, 109 n.15
Polybius, 165
Prigogine, Ilya, 263 n.5
Proust, Marcel, 45, 46, 49, 56

Rawls, John, xii, 3, 7, 8, 13, 33, 56, 121, 122, 131, 149, 181, 197, 206 n.8, 212, 266

Rooney, Ellen, 8
Rorty, Richard, 30, 33, 240, 247
Ross, Andrew, 242 n.16
Rousseau, Jean-Jacques, 56, 89, 90, 129, 135, 212, 216, 218, 219, 221, 223–27, 229 n.41, 230 n.42, 230 n.43, 239, 266
Ryan, Alan, 204, 211 n.26

Saint-Pierre, Abbé de, 224
Sandel, Michael, 3
Sartre, Jean-Paul, 10
Scanlon, Thomas, 7
Seligman, Martin E. P., 144
Sextus, 33
Shakespeare, William, 26, 27, 48
Skinner, Quentin, 155, 156, 177, 191, 192, 193, 204, 207 n.45, 213
Socrates, 87, 89, 90
Sorell, Tom, 209 n.73
Staten, Henry, 53 n.9
Steiner, Hillel, 153 n.31

Taylor, Charles, ix, 3, 102, 129, 135, 153 n.30

Ter Hark, Michel, 51, 53 n.5
Thoreau, Henry David, 89, 92, 94–97, 104, 107, 118
Tocqueville, Alexis de, 90, 115, 116, 118, 125 n.13
Truman, David, 33
Tuck, Richard, xiv, 212–30

Van Gogh, Vincent, 238

Waldron, Jeremy, xiv, 180–211
Walzer, Michael, 3
Weber, Max, 118
Whitman, Walt, x, 89, 92, 94, 95, 96, 98, 99, 100
William of Ockham, xi, 29, 266
Williams, Bernard, 210 n.91
Wittgenstein, Ludwig, x, xi, xii, 3, 10, 20, 34, 36–56, 59, 60, 66, 117, 130, 135, 146, 213, 245–47, 249, 266

Xenophon, 165

Zerilli, Linda, xi, xii, xv, 33–55

www.ingramcontent.com/pod-product-compliance
Lightning Source LLC
Jackson TN
JSHW070313120426
100741JS00007B/37